The Olin Institute at Transaction Publishers

The late John M. Olin, a prominent industrialist and philanthropist, was deeply concerned about his employees and employment relationships in general. In recognition of Mr. Olin's lifelong commitment to positive employee relations, the Foundation that bears his name established, in 1995, the John M. Olin Institute for Employment Practice and Policy at George Mason University.

In 1996, the Olin Institute expanded its research and information function by acquiring the book inventory and all thereto of the former Wharton industrial Research Unit, University of Pennsylvania. Included therein were the highly regarded Labor Relations and Public Policy Series books and monographs, some of which were reissued and others updated thanks to grants made by the John M. Olin Foundation. New books were added to the series under the direction of Professor Herbert R. Northrup, who had inaugurated and directed the publication program at the Wharton School, and who served as director of the Olin book program after his retirement from the University of Pennsylvania until his death in November of 2007. He was succeeded as director by Dr. Armand J. Thieblot, author of the book in hand.

This book, the 39th in the series, is the first book of the Olin Labor Relations and Public Policy Series to be published externally under the new publishing relationship between the Institute and Transaction Publishers. Our expectation is that others will follow. A few of the more recent books in the Olin Labor Relations and Public Policy Series are available on Amazon; others may be available from our archives by contacting me.

Dr. James T. Bennett,
Director, Olin Institute
Department of Economics
MSN 364
Fairfax, VA 22030-4444

THE CASE AGAINST THE DAVIS-BACON ACT

THE CASE AGAINST THE DAVIS-BACON ACT

54 REASONS FOR REPEAL

Armand J. Thieblot

Routledge
Taylor & Francis Group
New York London

First published 2013 by Transaction Publishers

Published 2017 by Routledge
711 Third Avenue, New York, NY 10017, USA
2 Park Square, Milton Park, Abingdon, Oxon OX14 4RN

First issued in hardback 2017

Routledge is an imprint of the Taylor & Francis Group, an informa business

Library of Congress Catalog Number: 2012027391

Library of Congress Cataloging-in-Publication Data

Thieblot, Armand J.
The case against the Davis-Bacon act : fifty-four reasons for repeal / by Armand J. Thieblot.
p. cm.
Includes bibliographical references and index.
ISBN 978-1-4128-4988-3
1. Wages--Construction workers--Law and legislation--United States. 2. United States. Davis-Bacon Act. 3. Public contracts--United States. I. Title.

KF3505.C65T448 2013
344.7301'21--dc23

2012027391

ISBN 13: 978-1-4128-4988-3 (pbk)
ISBN 13: 978-1-1385-3453-7 (hbk)

Dedication

Dedicated to the memory of Dr. Herbert R. Northrup,
pluperfect pain in the butt, but teacher, friend,
editor, publisher, and longtime mentor
in all matters labor relations.

Table of Contents

Foreword

The Davis-Bacon Act is one of the original pillars of government involvement in labor relations, predating even the Wagner Act and the Fair Labor Standards Act. Having first passed Congress during the Hoover administration in 1931—more than 80 years ago—it is now totally obsolete. The law, however, is actively supported by a powerful interest group—construction unions and their contractors—and attended by a substantial bureaucracy.

With help from sympathetic administrators in the U.S. Department of Labor, its supporters have drawn such bright lines around all matters Davis-Bacon that even in the face of massive amounts of evidence of malfeasance and sham associated with every aspect of its operations, it has avoided being brought to the bar of audit or public scrutiny.

Thieblot's book documents a non-trivial case against Davis-Bacon that is neither judgmental nor political, but questions whether any valid public interest is served by maintaining a federal prevailing wage law. His analysis is highly detailed, especially about the wage-setting process, and he lifts the curtain to expose what strings the Wizard—in this case the Employment Standards Administration of the U.S. Department of Labor—pulls to allow the overwhelming majority of determination wages to be set at union rates even though, overall, unions control fewer than one in five construction workers' jobs. He provides a documented list of compelling reasons why the Davis-Bacon Act should be repealed.

I gratefully acknowledge the generous support of the Sunmark Foundation for underwriting the production of this book.

James T. Bennett
Director
The John M. Olin Institute
July 2012

Preface

I first became acquainted with the Davis-Bacon Act sometime in 1972, when Dr. Herbert R. Northrup, who was head of the Industrial Research Unit of the Wharton School at the time and had been my mentor and dissertation advisor, asked me if I'd be willing to undertake a study of it. The law had already been in effect then for about 40 years, and some construction users' group (he never did disclose which one) was interested in an evaluation of whether the higher costs it fostered for private as well as public construction buyers were worth it in terms of its offsetting benefits; it was also interested in a review of what the act's original purposes were and whether they were being achieved. The group sensed its members were being punished by Davis-Bacon, but wondered if others saw a continuing societal need for it, or if it had simply become obsolete over the years and benefitted only the politically well connected.

I said I would undertake the study. Prior to that time, my knowledge of this particular piece of legislation was limited to what I had seen in labor-law textbooks—something to do with preserving "prevailing wages," whatever those were—but it seemed an interesting, if limited, topic. Only after I got into it did I discover how far-reaching its tentacles were and how it drove up not only all public construction costs where it applied—which was to all federal and many state and even local building projects costing more than some trifling amount—but even those in private construction where there was no government funding, and how it became the basis for project labor agreements, living wage requirements, job targeting, and the like.

I found out that Davis-Bacon set out to achieve a statistical outcome that not only could never be achieved, but could not even be defined, much less be implemented fairly. I found out how its implementation encouraged a malign symbiosis between politicians and government regulators on one hand and construction unions on the other that drove the costs of public construction up in a lopsided way restricting and depressing modernization of training, work assignment, and technological change in all aspects of the construction industry. In essence, I learned it was, indeed, beyond being obsolete and unnecessary: it was also expensive and destructive—uniquely useful to the unionized segment of the industry that was increasingly unable to make it on its own in a freely competitive market. I could not identify any societal benefits or efficiencies it actually conferred on the industry or the people who worked within it.

That was the early 1970s, and I released my first book critical of Davis-Bacon in 1975. Another 40 years have gone by during which I've researched and written several additional monographs on the topic and a number of journal articles, testified on Capitol Hill and to various oversight agencies and in a number of state legislative assemblies on the related state laws—all reaching approximately these same conclusions from ever-expanding research: that prevailing wage laws in all their various guises are burdensome, wasteful, and unnecessary.

Yet, the Davis-Bacon Act has survived and even prospered. Now it is more than 80 years old and operates in labor conditions that are even farther removed from those that existed when it was first passed or when I first wrote about it. Efforts towards outright repeal in the late 70s fell to the combined exigencies of an almost institutionalized apparatchik within the U.S. Department of Labor and of organized labor's dedication to maintaining it through political muscle. Major efforts at partial reform launched every few years to allow, for example, determination rates to be issued for the semi-skilled workers (helpers) who make up upwards of 10 percent of all nonunion construction workers—and therefore around 9 percent of all construction workers—have been acknowledged but studiously ignored. Reviews and audits of specific administrative procedures by the General Accounting Office (now Government Accountability Office—still GAO) or the Congressional Budget Office have routinely found massive amounts of error in surveys and determinations, but degenerated into quibbles about minor details while the elephants of structural fraud and corruption in the room were ignored.

I'm pretty sure the failure of forcing change on Davis-Bacon has nothing to do with any misunderstanding on my part or on the part of other critical observers of how Davis-Bacon actually works. It was bad law when it was passed 80 years ago, and it is still bad law today. In its implementation, there seems to be no limit beyond which politicians and government agencies will not go to support the ever-decreasing proportion of union construction workers and unionized contractors at the expense of the far larger number of their nonunion counterparts who wish it were gone.

Rather than becoming weaker over the years, as its obsolescence increased the Davis-Bacon Act has gradually strengthened and expanded, especially in its administrative and enforcement details. It has undergirded project labor agreements, "living wage" initiatives, job targeting schemes and other pro-union activities, and "jobs initiatives" programs such as weatherization of older houses to save fuel resources. It has extended itself in all the ways by which politicians reward unions for unions' rewarding politicians. Over the years since I began studying them, federal and state prevailing wage laws have cost billions of dollars—possibly hundreds of billions—in unnecessary waste in public construction alone, accelerating with every passing year and it has built an ever-higher floor under union wage demands throughout the industry.

I hope that with this book I am finally able to make the case clearly enough to get you, whomever you may be, to help bring the era of Davis-Bacon to an end. Doing so could lead to a substantial decrease in unemployment in the construction industry, a vast savings (on the order of $50 or $60 billion over ten years) in the cost to taxpayers of public construction projects, substantial savings in administrative and enforcement costs by the Department of Labor, and salutatory improvements in the training, career development, and technological advance of the construction industry. The only cost to accomplish all this is an end to federal indulgence of construction unions and their anachronistic ways and methods.

Admittedly, repealing Davis-Bacon would involve a political cost to some politicians who profit from the current exchange with unions, and these politicians may be loathe to fall on their swords for the public weal. But my fondest hope is that the others, those who do not profit from the current exchange with unions or who put duty above campaign finance, will become emboldened to require it of them. Labor unions remain rich and powerful, but their underpinnings have become corrupted and their messages and demands obsolete. Their web sites bristle with the rallying cries of industrial suppression and victimhood reflecting the economic and social realities of 1932, sometimes even those of the 19th Century or the industrial revolution.

These do not match well with the realities of the unbridled union excesses of today—in Wisconsin, in public employment and lavish pensions bankrupting whole states, in open political rent seeking, and in so many other aspects of everyday life to which we have become inured. Unions are intensely aware that a blow against Davis-Bacon is a blow against their government-protected monospony in construction labor for public works that is, in turn, a blow against the whole idea of union suzerainty, forced collective bargaining, and extortionate labor relations. The purpose of this book is to show others, who are not unions or indebted to them, the same thing.

Before proceeding to the case against Davis-Bacon, itself, I need to set out some housekeeping rules. First, this book is neither an entirely new study nor a simple recasting of my previous books and articles on Davis-Bacon. (A few relevant ones are listed in the appended bibliography and others are readily available on the web.) There is some re-hash here, but there are also updates and many new pieces, and the presentation format is entirely new. The book is divided into four major sections: The first section, Chapters I and II, deals briefly with the history, purposes, and administrative concepts of prevailing wage laws; the next, Chapters III and IV, provides an overview of the act's administration. The third section, Chapters V and VI, covers survey and determination process and goes into greater detail about administration of the act, especially with respect to the prevailingness of job titles or characterizations of work, the presumptive singularity of union wage rates by craft and class, and the creation and extension of determination rates; the final section, Chapter VII, summarizes direct and indirect costs, evaluates counterclaims on the economic impact of Davis-Bacon, considers compromises short of full repeal, and reaches its final conclusions. After these are seven appendices that serve mostly to relieve the main text of the mind-numbing detail necessary to illustrate some of the 54 main conclusions synopsized there.

In detailing these items, I assume the reader has a certain familiarity with the terminology of labor relations and I rely on the discretion of readers to understand that when I refer to—for example, "unions" doing this or that—that the personification should be given the characteristics derived from the context and interpreted as "the union movement" or "the leaders or directors of unions" or "union members," etc., as appropriate. I shall also usually refer to union organizations and to government agencies by their common acronyms or colloquial names rather than their full, official titles, unless confusion might result. People who can't interpret that USDL or DOL refers to the United States Department of Labor should go read something else.

In the body of the report I interrupt my own narrative with explanations of key terms or expositions of factual interpretations either in footnotes, if they are sufficiently succinct to not interfere with the essential flow of the narrative, or in referenced appendices if they require charts and graphs or are otherwise extensive. My intent is to produce a narrative that covers the fundamental questions in as straightforward a way as possible, while relying on the footnotes and inclusions to explain, justify, or support the narrative where necessary.[1] Otherwise, I have tried to eliminate as many detailed and repetitive citations as possible that appear in the typical footnotes of academic studies (including my own former ones). So many sources have become so readily available through Google or other portals to locate published materials on the internet that it seems both senseless and unnecessary to continue that level of elaboration.

This book is intended as neither a legal brief nor an academic exercise. It uses no mathematics more complex than algebra, no economic modeling. And although I hope its conclusions might be useful to lawyers seeking the repeal of Davis-Bacon, I'm afraid they will have to plough through and provide the necessary words of art and judicial precedents on their own.

[1] I also use the footnotes as a place to display my ironic or snarky comments, leaving the main text safe for humor-impaired and terminally earnest readers.

The 54 Reasons for Repeal

These 54 reasons to repeal the Davis-Bacon Act are found boxed in the appropriate places in the text. To find the details about any one of them, skip to the pages to find the correspondingly numbered box. (For numbers 18–30 and 36–42, further detail is available in Appendix Three and Appendix Five, respectively, at the second page number.)

No. 1. The original act was grounded on the false premise that new government demand would result in lower local wage rates. The opposite is true. Exogenous demand in any established market is either absorbed or it raises the clearing price of labor (wages). Always. (p. 6)

No. 2. In seeking to supplant market forces controlling wage rates in special circumstances or unusual times, the Davis-Bacon Act offers a permanent, imperfect solution to a temporary, self-correcting problem. This is almost a textbook definition of bad policy. (p. 9)

No. 3. The original act was naively static, assuming that low wage offers might draw alien workers used to lower wage rates into the market only when new demand occurred in that market. It also supposed that contractors denied the ability to compete on their most controllable factor of production (labor) would eschew gaming the system for advantage in other factors. Supposition of selective malfeasance is no basis for effective policy. (p. 10)

No. 4. The original act was passed either on the basis of anti-Negro animus or as an unnecessary solution to negligible or imaginary fears of low-wage itinerants. (p.12)

No. 5. The Davis-Bacon Act is a law grounded in inherent fraud. It promises what cannot possibly be delivered. (p. 14)

No. 6. The concept of prevailing rates is rubbish, and can't be translated into an objective statistic or made into a logical system. A law known to be impossible to objectify logically or to administer equitably is inherently flawed, if not outright fraudulent. (p. 19)

No. 7. In all but trivial cases, prevailing rates chosen by any plurality or modal rate or any measure of central-tendency make a middle rate the new minimum, eliminating the bottom part of any existing distribution of wages from use in the proposed government work. Rather than reflecting local wage rates, prevailing wage laws necessarily increase them, and therefore necessarily increase the cost of such work. (p. 20)

No. 8. The Davis-Bacon Act, as a minor substitute for a full bore minimum wage requirement became obsolete in 1938 when the Fair Labor Standards Act took over that duty in a more effective and more easily administered way. (p. 23)

No. 9. The wage selection process is unfairly biased toward a wage rate uniformity that exists exclusively in union work. (p. 34)

No. 10. The percentage of union rates published as prevailing in Davis-Bacon wage determinations is statistically impossible to have been achieved fairly. It could only have been accomplished through blatant and perhaps even fraudulent pro-union bias. This, of itself, should invalidate the law. (p. 36)

No. 11. Davis-Bacon determinations are too often inchoate with respect to any underlying local wage patterns. Senseless laws and regulations are worse than no laws and regulations, especially when they exist to serve the purposes of a special interest group, in this case construction unions. (p. 40)

No. 12. Davis-Bacon determinations are filled with union-supplied garbage. It has been included to accommodate various local unions and is exemplary of blatant pro-union bias that makes mockery of the fundamental concepts underlying prevailing wage laws. (p. 43)

No. 13. Davis-Bacon administration fraudulently pretends to a geographic specificity it does not follow, and in the process unjustly favors union rates and practices. (p. 46)

No. 14. Davis-Bacon administration fraudulently pretends to a survey frequency it does not possess, and in the process unjustly favors union rates and practices. (p. 51)

No. 15. Davis-Bacon Administration fraudulently pretends to not need surveys in “safe union territory,” and therefore unjustly favors union rates and practices. (p. 55)

No 16. Davis-Bacon’s arbitrary divisions among regimes of construction work (residential, building, etc.) unjustly favor union rates and practices. (p. 55)

No 17. The Department of Labor’s willingness to conduct special surveys of work or workers and issue determinations specifically for them unduly favors union wages and work practices. (p. 57)

No. 18. The Department of Labor’s victorious 20-year struggle to quash modest reforms setting wage rates for construction helpers, even in constrained circumstances and defined settings, shows undue bias towards union wages and work patterns. (p. 63; p. 170)

No. 19. The Department of Labor’s assertion that the viability of helper rates was adequately tested by the 78 surveys during the period of non-suspension is clear evidence of bias towards union rates and work methods. (p. 65; p. 178)

No. 20. The Department of Labor’s assertion that helper rates were difficult to compile is clear evidence of bias towards union rates and work methods. (p. 65; p. 181)

No. 21. The Department of Labor’s assertion that helper rates were difficult to identify for job content is clear evidence of bias towards union rates and work methods. (p. 67; p. 188)

No. 22. The Department of Labor’s assertion that helper rates were difficult to administer is clear evidence of bias towards union rates and work methods. (p. 67; p. 189)

No. 23. The Department of Labor’s assertion that helpers are not a sufficient construction class is clear evidence of bias towards union rates and work methods. (p. 69; p. 198)

No 24. The Department of Labor’s disproportionate rejection of helper rates in surveys is clear evidence of bias towards union rates and work methods. (p. 71; p. 201)

No 25. The Department of Labor's higher acceptance of semi-skilled rates in surveys where union orientation is not known, than of helper rates where it is known to be nonunion, is clear evidence of bias towards union rates and work methods. (p. 72; p. 205)

No 26. The Department of Labor's disproportionate acceptance of union helper-like laborer helper rates in surveys is clear evidence of bias towards union rates and work methods. (p. 72; p. 207)

No. 27. The Department of Labor's disproportionate acceptance of union tender rates in surveys is clear evidence of bias towards union rates and work methods. (p. 73; p. 210)

No. 28. The Department of Labor's assertion that helper designations in prevailing rate determinations would lead to contractor manipulation of job assignments is a red herring and a false basis for public policy. (p. 73; p. 212)

No. 29. The Department of Labor's assertion that helper designations in prevailing rate determinations would cause special enforcement problems is another red herring and a false underpinning of public policy. (p. 74; p. 214)

No. 30. The Department of Labor's assertion that helper designations in prevailing wage determinations would adversely affect apprenticeship programs demonstrates clear bias towards union rates and work methods. (p. 75; p. 214)

No. 31. The DOL's use of Dodge Reports as the primary data collection device is a flawed alternative to a random or properly structured sample of work previously done in a locality, and unfairly favors union rates and practices. (p. 79)

No. 32. The DOL's use of voluntary response to its elaborate data requests is a flawed alternative to a proper data collection method, and unfairly favors union rates and practices. (p. 81)

No. 33. The DOL's use of rates voluntarily submitted by non-employers is biased and flawed. It unfairly favors union rates and practices. (p. 82)

No 34. The rejection of wage submissions from small employers (5 or fewer workers) unfairly favors union rates and practices. (p. 83)

No 35. The acceptance of wage submissions from suspect sources providing duplicative information biases surveys towards an apparent uniformity that typically favors union rates and practices. (p. 84)

No. 36. DOL arbitrarily transmutes union rates found in surveys, treating all of them as identical to the penny, even if they differ by many dollars. This prejudices rate determinations towards union rates, and demonstrates clear bias towards union rates and practices. (p. 86; p. 222)

No. 37. Collecting manipulated survey data by union-supplied job title or consolidating it to DOL-supplied job titles is an example of obvious bias that unfairly favors union rates and practices. (p. 88; p. 225)

No 38. The combination of voluntary rates from various sources may result in duplication of submissions that unduly color the final results, and unfairly favor union rates and practices. (p. 90; p. 230)

No. 39. Accepting data from outside the established time frame of the survey, from other polities, or from jobs previously performed under prevailing wage mandates biases the results, and unfairly favors union rates and practices. (p. 91; p. 233)

No. 40. DOL arbitrarily selects which local union's rate prevails. This increases the arbitrariness of wage determination outcomes, and while demonstrating clear bias towards union rates and practices, helps render published determinations meaningless. (p. 91; p. 234)

No. 41. If DOL finds a union rate to be prevailing, the rate published in the determination may be considerably different from that found, and will reflect current rates published in some union contract. This increases the union orientation of wage determination outcomes, demonstrating clear bias towards union rates and practices. (P. 92; p. 235)

No. 42. If DOL publishes a union rate as prevailing in a determination, that rate is automatically updated to reflect the collective bargaining contract wage, automatically and in perpetuity. Determinations containing such information are called "updated," or "current." These automatic increases affect only nonunion contractors, since union contractors pay the union rate, regardless. Following this practice increases the union orientation of wage determination and demonstrates clear bias towards union rates and practices. (p. 93; p. 236)

No. 43. Allowing determinations to be issued without published rates for necessary trades is an example of union bias and is also an example of the arbitrariness and capriciousness of prevailing wages. (p. 99)

No. 44. Allowing determinations to be issued with rates adjusted to the territorial jurisdictions of various union locals is an example of union bias and is also an example of the arbitrariness and capriciousness of prevailing wages. (p. 100)

No. 45. Allowing determinations to be issued that add specialties in union trades that were not covered in surveys is an example of further union bias and is also an example of the arbitrariness and capriciousness of prevailing wages. (p. 103)

No. 46. Allowing determinations to be issued that publish absurdities, such as higher rates for lower related skills, is an example of the arbitrariness and capriciousness of prevailing wages. (p. 109)

No. 47. Allowing determinations to publish absurdly large differences in different localities within the determination areas differing only as to local union suzerainty, is an example of the arbitrariness and capriciousness of prevailing wages. (p. 111)

No. 48. Inexplicable anomalies pepper determinations. Each one is another example of the arbitrariness and capriciousness of prevailing wages. (p. 113)

No. 49. Davis-Bacon procedures foster anomalies that impede routine wage administration within the industry. It is better to have no law than to have a law that is arbitrary and senseless. (p. 116)

No. 50. Davis-Bacon procedures routinely allow implicit expansion of prevailing rates to unlisted and phantom union jobs but not to nonunion ones. (p. 117)

No. 51. The cost of Davis-Bacon is immense. But the cost question is less important than the fact that Davis-Bacon provides so few benefits to society. Only if a law achieves some necessary purpose that can't be achieved another, easier way can it claim that almost no level of cost is too great to sustain it. (p. 127)

No. 52. DOL will brook no change that diminishes the dominance of Davis-Bacon survey or determination processes by union rates and methods. The ills of Davis-Bacon cannot be cured by administrative reform. (p. 140)

No. 53. Davis-Bacon is outmoded, unnecessary, and selectively biased towards union rates and methods. It is also broken even under its own terms and it can't be fixed. It should be repealed. (p. 141)

No. 54. If one believes that the proper public policy should be to obtain the best government construction at the lowest price, the Davis-Bacon Act needs to be repealed. (p. 142)

Chapter I: Introduction

I have detailed the history of the prevailing wage movement and of the development of the Davis-Bacon act during the late 1920s in other places, perhaps most thoroughly in my 1986 book on prevailing wage laws,[1] but a brief summary is in order to get things started.

1. The Davis-Bacon Act before 1935

The very first prevailing wage laws were put into place by the states, led off by Kansas in 1891. By 1927, when the first of the discussions about prevailing rates began in Congress at the federal level, such laws already existed in eight states.[2] What they had in common, and would share with the original Davis-Bacon law, was the desire to protect the wage rates that existed in any given locality from the feared perturbations that might occur from government procurement practices based on awarding contracts to the lowest bidder—but not going so far as to require a specific minimum wage.[3] A mandated federal minimum wage was a third-rail issue even during the early New Deal through the time of the (failed) National Industrial Recovery Act, and it remained one until the Fair Labor Standards Act was

[1] A list of cited works by author, title, and date of publication is found in the bibliography at the end of this book. The first 43 pages of the relevant text, Thieblot (1986) *Prevailing Wage Legislation*, remain highly relevant with respect to a full understanding of the early development and initial deployment of the Davis-Bacon Act and the fundamental difficulty of providing a workable definition of "prevailing."

[2] Note that when these discussions began at the federal level in the late 1920s, it was during a period of prosperity and the administration of Herbert Hoover. This was before the New Deal and also before the institutional empowerment of labor unions.

[3] Their main initial function seems to have been to serve as 8-hour laws, requiring construction employees to be paid daily and in cash.

passed late in the depression, in 1938. A prevailing wage law was considered to be a first step towards this eschaton.

2. Economic Claims Supporting Construction Wage Protection

Especially for labor-intensive activities such as building construction (where labor is between one-quarter and one-half of the total cost of buildings) and where contracts are commonly awarded to the lowest bidder, the notion had long been forwarded by pro-union activists that contractors might "competitively underbid" one another with low labor rates in order to get the work, importing cheap itinerant labor from elsewhere thereby driving down local wages to "below the market rate" while still leaving themselves room for excessive profits.[4] Lawmakers have often accepted the political validity of certain aspects of this argument, particularly as to the matter of itinerant aliens willing to move to where work is available and work for less than the locals.

Ordinary supply and demand curves are a staple of economic modeling since being popularized a century ago by Alfred Marshall: the demand curve is downward sloping to the right (fewer widgets are demanded if their prices are higher) and the supply curve is upward sloping (more widgets are supplied at higher prices); where they cross is the clearing price, the market rate.[5] Changes in technology or in the number of complementary and substitute products or services or in other particulars add complications that can move the entire curves, not just the crossing point. Conditions of monopoly or monospsony also distort the result, and, of course, the whole apparatus is a gross oversimplification of the dynamics of a marketplace, in which several different price points might simultaneously constitute the bargain for

[4] Realistically, though it might be one or another of these, it can't be both: the scheming contractor who uses low wages to get the work will have gotten the work at a low bid, leaving little or no room for excess profits.

[5] Alfred Marshall, *Principles of Economics: An Introductory Volume* (1890 and many subsequent editions).

different individuals and other complications might also be determinative. (Is there a famine going on? Is war coming? Are more Hermes scarves demanded in spite of their idiotically high prices or because of their idiotically high prices? Was gold just discovered somewhere? Is corruption involved in forcing people to buy things they don't want or merely bad politics?[6] Did the OPEC cartel just turn off the flow of oil? Etc.)

These all distort the analysis of market-based supply and demand equilibriums and turn many graduate econ students into geometricians. But this much is reasonably sure: an offer unaccompanied by compulsion to buy at below the market price will not induce a sale.[7] (If it does, it has simply moved the market price lower.) The same is true of wage rates. An unscrupulous contractor may decide to base his bid on paying below-market wage rates, but he does so at considerable risk since he has no mechanism to compel the acceptance of substandard wages in anything but a purely monosopsonistic labor market. A below-market wage offer does not induce a greater supply of workers willing to work for the reduced rate unless those workers are forced into it and have no alternative employment opportunities.

---

[6] Examples or bad politics might include the forced purchase of health care insurance by young people or mandatory support by Catholic organizations for birth control or abortion services. Examples of corruption might include small business owners' requirement to buy "protection" from the same thugs who could smash their windows. In between are laws mandating oil companies to purchase biomass fuels in quantities that do not exist and then pay a fine for not buying them, or the NLRB's decision to allow Boeing to use its billion-dollar plant in South Carolina only after its union in Washington had been bought off. These all influence the market price for, respectively, health care, restaurant meals, gasoline, and jet planes, and it is somewhat difficult to differentiate them on the basis of either how they work or the results they produce.

[7] There is the famous Don Corleone exception, which, in essence, is the seemingly sophisticated arguments involving the power of monopsony. But notice that even Don Corleone's offer would have been declined were it not backed up by presence of Lucca Brasi.

Economists who assert the opposite tend to fasten on two nuances, which they claim overturn the basic analysis. The first nuance asserts that during economic hard times and other specialized situations (for example, during the Great Depression or in the rebuilding of New Orleans after the devastation of hurricane Katrina), the federal government acts as an actual or functional monopsonist. The second nuance asserts that new offers of work on large government projects at wage rates below local market rates will induce a supply imported from elsewhere, some place of even lower local wage rates.

A. GOVERNMENT CONTRACTORS AS EFFECTIVE MONOPSONISTS

If government were the only buyer of construction work, and therefore the only source of construction wages, the government (or contractors working on its behalf) could offer wages substantially below those that may have previously obtained in the local labor market and get applicants for work because it had "the only game in town."

But the government is never a true monopsonist of construction work, not even in times like the Great Depression. Those construction projects the federal government undertook under the WPA (Works Progress Administration) and CCC (Civilian Conservation Corps) were deliberately designed to not interfere with private construction contracting work. Government contracting of all sorts was a substantial percentage of available work by the late 1930s, but government was certainly not the only employer of laborers, just the only employer of them on its own "make-work" construction projects.[8]

[8] Government make-work had started under Howard Ickes in 1933, but the major government construction projects under the WPA of Henry Hopkins began in 1935, towards the end of the recovery period from the first (1929) depression. By 1938, when the second major dip of the depression hit, WPA had employed some 3.5 million workers, about 95 percent of whom worked in some form of construction. The Davis-Bacon Act had already reached substantially its current form by that time (see further discussion later in this chapter) and as a result it is interesting to see what wages

Skilled mechanics, as always, had other sources of employment in the private sector. In the case of the aftermath of hurricane Katrina, there was certainly no government monopsony, nor evidence thereof. What there was, was simply a panic cycle of readjustment to the disturbances caused by the storm, although some argued to the contrary.[9]

The 1995 storm devastated an area about ten times the size of the area devastated by Andrew a few years earlier. It created the instant

---

the government projects paid: Those employed on the tree-based projects of the CCC were paid $30 per month; salaries for other construction workers of the WPA were set at twice the level of welfare payments, well below union scale. The average salary of all 8.5 million employed by the WPA before it was disbanded in 1943 was $41.57 per month—approximately $10,000 a year in today's money, well below the poverty line. It might be noted that while all this was going on before the start of World War II, the overall unemployment rate remained above 15 percent and increased by another 25 percent during the second depression of 1938; and the GDP in 1939 was almost exactly the same as it had been in 1929. Clearly the problems of the Great Depression were not solved by the progressive movement or by Roosevelt or by make-work federal programs, but by the war and its needs for greater economic flexibility. It is also interesting to note that construction costs in Washington, D.C. under the WPA ran three-to-four times the cost of private work, according to sources at u-s-history.com. As a monopsonist, the federal government was a failure even during the time of its greatest influence.

[9] See, for example, Bennett Miller, "No Such Thing As a Free Lunch: Hurricane Katrina and the Davis-Bacon Act," *Review of Law and Social Justice* Vol. 16, 1 (2006) at 197 *ff.*, where the author concluded that the temporary suspension of the Davis-Bacon Act during a two-month period in the early cleanup after the hurricane did permanent damage to the wage base and societal structure of New Orleans. This was said to be because federal government acted as a functional monopsonist when dispensing over $100 billion of construction aid, the lure of which induced illegal immigrants to flood the construction workforce in search of alleged below-market wages, displacing the native black construction workers who had been there before. Much of the argumentation can probably be best summarized as tortured, but the section on basic economics is well done, if subsequently ignored by the author.

need for massive amounts of demolition, construction, and reconstruction, but the federal government was very far from being the only buyer, despite its spending of upwards of $100 billion. Housing projects, schools, post offices, hospitals, court houses, and other government-use buildings and roads needed rebuilding, but so too did stores, warehouses, factories, casinos, wharves, grain storage facilities, bars, private dwelling units, restaurants, and churches, among other things, and the work done for these was done privately, without direct federal involvement. In the immediate aftermath of the storm, much demolition and immediate work was done either by unpaid volunteers, owners with force-account work crews, or contractors who had to pay as much as ten times the market wage rate to secure workers of any sort, before the existing labor supply could adjust and expand to meet the new needs for laborers and mechanics. For the first few weeks, construction help was either free from volunteers and owners or very expensive.

> No. 1. The original act was grounded on the false premise that new government demand would result in lower local wage rates. The opposite is true. Exogenous demand in any established market is either absorbed or it raises the clearing price of labor (wages). Always.

B. GOVERNMENT CONTRACTORS AS IMPORTERS OF CHEAP LABOR

This brings up the second nuance. The way it is usually stated is that the availability of a large amount of work in an area—say, New Orleans after the storm—draws workers from other places (like Mexico) where native market wages are dramatically lower. These workers, being willing to work for less than the New Orleans locals, infiltrate the local market to snap up the low wage offers that presumably are still above their native wage rates, thus driving local market wages down. The supposition is that without wage protection, market rates drop when new demand occurs.[10]

This supposition overlooks the fact that in the standard Marshavian analysis of supply and demand curves, supply is dynamic rather than static. The perturbation of a large new demand initially causes the clearing price to rise, sometimes drastically, reflecting the scarcity of labor relative to the new demand. Then, the higher clearing price induces additional supply, translating both curves outward rather than moving along them to a new and indeterminate equilibrium.[11] Depending on the circumstances, the local labor market might be overwhelmed by the new influx, to the end that the clearing price

[10] Another of the several similar journal articles that appeared in 2006 to criticize the Bush suspension of the Davis-Bacon Act for two months during the fall after it, Haley Olam and Erin Stamper, "The Suspension of the Davis-Bacon Act and the Exploitation of Migrant Workers in the Wake of Hurricane Katrina," *Hofstra Labor & Employment Law Journal*, Vol. 24 (2006) at 145 *ff.*, reaches similar conclusions to the others about permanent damages to wage structures caused by the two-month suspension, and simultaneously resurrects and acknowledges the racist logic of the original Davis-Bacon act: "However, it is clear that the fear of cheap African-American labor, which gave rise to the act in 1931, has been replaced by [a putatively well-reasoned] fear of cheap *Hispanic* labor." (p. 159, emphasis in original, but my clarifying supposition.) The authors of this piece give the game away early on, however, when they note that the hurricane caused "cheap [Hispanic] laborers" to be attracted to New Orleans in the storm's aftermath: "Lured by the *promises of long hours and good wages,* thousands of workers left their families and homes in order to work in New Orleans . . . [for] construction wages [said to be] doubled to $16 an hour." (p. 145, emphasis added.) In other words, although they may have been cheap Hispanic laborers, they were drawn not by sub-standard wage rates, but by promises of sugarplums that may have been illusory or danced fraudulently before their eyes.

[11] The effect is not limited to labor. For a short period of time after the storm, the price of bottled water or ordinary foodstuffs in New Orleans was set by scalpers. But after a few days, the specially imported, high-priced water went unsold, and prices rather quickly stabilized at pre-storm market levels.

for labor actually drops to below the previous market rate, or it might be unable to supply the needs of the new demand, particularly for skilled and experienced workers, to the end that the clearing price for labor remains artificially high for the duration of the new demand.

In fact, both of these conditions, the high initial offer price for scarce labor and the lower offer price for excess labor, are self-correcting. Given a little time for supply and demand to adjust, there is no reason to believe that the post-event market price for labor in a market of increased demand will be any different from the pre-event market price. In the short term, there may be perturbations in the market rate for labor from an exogenous demand that outstrips the availability of local supply. And in much the same way that President Polk's announcement of gold strikes in California in 1848 triggered a mass migration of fortune hunters towards the hills of California, most of whom were disappointed when they got there, news of the shortages and opportunities in New Orleans blasting from every available news source for weeks on end triggered a mass migration of water sellers, emergency service workers, and construction workers to that area, seeking to cash in on the scarcity prices, some of whom may not have found such work actually available and who may have accepted less as an alternative to heading back home to the higher rates there. But note: the draw was not due to lower local wage offers, but to the promise of elevated ones created by the scarcity.

In short, market rates are always a matter of the dynamic nature of supply and demand. It is possible to hypothesize that having been lured by thoughts of high wages but faced with a reversion to ordinary ones immigrants might linger and accept offers to work for less. But it is hard to see why they would then linger in the low-rate area and not follow the displaced domestic others heading back to their homes where higher, "normal," market rates persisted. Mexican illegals willing to work for depressed market rates in New Orleans would undoubtedly be even more willing to work for the non-depressed market wages in Baton Rouge, or in St. Louis or Minneapolis or wherever. It is fatuous to assume that if market-level wage offers prior to the storm were insufficient to lure illegal aliens into the area they would suddenly become so after, when demand was higher and the rates allegedly lower.

No. 2. In seeking to supplant market forces controlling wage rates in special circumstances or unusual times, the Davis-Bacon Act offers a permanent, imperfect solution to a temporary, self-correcting problem. This is almost a textbook definition of bad policy.

C. GOVERNMENT CONTRACTORS AS MALFEASORS

In government contracting, awards are typically made to the lowest bidder. Proponents of wage protection like to point out that unscrupulous bidders will seek to skimp on labor costs in order to achieve the low bid unless wage floor protections are employed. But while labor costs are certainly important in contracting, it is also true that material costs and management and administration costs are important as well, and that control of competition on one factor of production (labor) may well induce those same unscrupulous contractors to seek advantage by slighting others (materials, administration). The latter produces a magnified impact on anyone employed on the project other than those specifically protected by the prevailing-rate floor, as well as and on suppliers and supply quality.[12] Other possibilities include gaming the project to force later addendums or to seek award by noncompetitive means.[13] Thus, the third of the reasons why the Davis-Bacon Act should be repealed:

[12] Scheduled labor, that is, the laborers and mechanics specifically covered by prevailing wages, is not the only labor on construction sites. According to the Bureau of Labor Statistics only about three-quarters (74 percent in 2002, the most recent available date) of "construction employees" are "construction workers." In addition, many employees of construction suppliers, service providers, or their delivery personnel are subject to the same cycles and forces as construction workers themselves, but are not afforded similar wage floor protection. Either similar protections should have been provided to these employees (at the time it could have been done with a minimum wage floor) or government should have stayed out of picking favored groups for bestowing its largess.

[13] Seeking awards by noncompetitive means might include bribery and graft but it also might include seeking to restrict awards to only bidders on

> No. 3. The original act was naively static, assuming that low wage offers might draw alien workers used to lower wage rates into the market only when new demand occurred in that market. It also supposed that contractors denied the ability to compete on their most controllable factor of production (labor) would eschew gaming the system for advantage in other factors. Supposition of selective malfeasance is no basis for effective policy.

3. Racial Animus, 1931

When Congressman James J. Bacon (R, New York) introduced the hearings on the proposed Davis-Bacon Act in 1931, he reiterated the original rationales, but added a new one. He testified that a new veterans' hospital was being constructed in his home district, and that although a number of local contractors had sought the work, they weren't able to compete effectively against an outside firm said to be importing itinerant laborers from the even-more-depressed South to "undercut the bids of the local firms."[14] The essence of this rationale has already been discussed in the last section. But in 1931, Congressman Miles C. Algood (D, Alabama), supplied further definition to the "itinerants" of that period by calling them "cheap colored labor," and noting with implied horror that "it is labor of that sort that is in competition with white labor throughout the country."[15] This sen-

---

some approved bidders list, or who were able to show "proper" training records, or who were certificated by some third-party authenticating group—all of which are things that can be and are, in turn, gamed.

[14] Note that even Cong. Bacon did not claim that local wage rates would be "driven down," only that the unemployed locals would remain unemployed. This is a subtly different argument, but equally foolish. From an economic standpoint, the condition of the itinerants was improved, but the condition of the locals was not changed, so the system achieved a net benefit without market interference, even as hypothesized.

[15] U.S. Cong., House, floor debate, Feb 28, 1931. 74 *Cong. Rec.* at 6510 (1931).

timent echoed the views of a lot of other people in those racially unenlightened times, but especially those of the craft unions supporting the bill, many of whom had color bars that would continue to be maintained for another generation or so.

These were late-added rationales to support the bill, but apparently they were successful in advancing it into law after earlier attempts in 1927, 1928, and 1930 had failed, so they deserve additional consideration. If the Jim Crow apparitions were determinative, this in itself would be sufficient reason to seek repeal of a law that has become so entirely obsolete with respect to the sensitivities of the current age. But if they were mere window dressing to the broader appeal of a law that would discourage itinerants as a generality (aliens, outsiders of any sort) from access to the local labor market, then the Davis-Bacon law was framed around a gross misunderstanding of the relationship between construction work and local labor markets. A big, new construction project can't be dropped on an area that didn't have such projects before without need for the contractors building it to import all of the specialized (and much of the unspecialized) labor required, at whatever cost it might take.[16]

In any event, the fear of itinerant contractors, whether or not they were dragging "cheap colored labor" with them, was overrated. A survey of public construction projects tabulated in 1930, near the time of the hearings, found that such itinerant workers as were employed on any of them worked mostly on just four projects undertaken in the

---

[16] The idea, that one might not be able to build a new hydroelectric dam in Nowhere County relying entirely upon locally available labor of hydroelectric dam builders, and that if there were such a locally available labor supply it could be enticed to work on the new project by the offer of debased wages below the local market rate, should not require much analytical support. Yet, that silly notion underlies all the prevailing wage laws. At least Congress was spared the Keynesian argument that would be risibly raised much later by Dr. Peter Philips and his associates at the University of Utah—that any additional cost to government buyers of construction that might be caused by higher prevailing wages would be more than made up for in increased tax collections from the workers who received them. Keynes's book would not be released until 1936.

then even more remote communities of Boise, Idaho; Fargo, North Dakota; Tucson, Arizona; and Juneau, Alaska. Excluding these projects (where the availability of local labor for a new project would have been severely limited and where any itinerants undoubtedly had to be paid elevated wages or per-diems to entice them to the sites), fewer than 10 percent of the workers on all other projects surveyed were non-locals, and there were none at all on projects undertaken in or near population centers.[17]

If exaggerated or imaginary fears of alien job seekers were deliberately raised to give cover to legislative action demanded by a pressure group (in this case, unions and their sympathizers), it would not be the first, nor the last, time in the history of the Republic that this occurred; but if true, it represents a form of fraud in the inducement, correctable only by repeal. Thus:

> No. 4. The original act was passed either on the basis of anti-Negro animus or as an unnecessary solution to negligible or imaginary fears of low-wage itinerants.

4. Probable Real Impetus for Davis-Bacon

In my opinion, the most likely true motivation for the Davis-Bacon Act was to preserve union wage rate premiums in local markets by increasing the cost of alternative labor without undertaking the drastic measure of requiring some specific minimum wage.[18] It was a compromise measure to hold the door open until pro-union pro-

[17] The numbers presented here were derived from a footnote in the Congressional Record of the 1931 hearings.

[18] One can never be sure of the "true" motivations lurking behind the published ones associated with this or any other piece of legislation, but based on extensive reading and analysis of this law in the context of the times, I think this is a reasonable supposition. Throughout this text, when I express opinions based on personal analysis and supposition rather than on statistics, settled economic theory, or other objective analysis, I'll either put them in footnotes or give clear indication in the text. The "union premium" mentioned here is a word of art that I'll define in a later section of the book.

minimum-wage sentiment could gather more strength. The law that ensued bears witness to the fact that this was not aggressive, groundbreaking legislation, but was intended as a stopgap measure.[19]

The fundamental characteristics of the Davis-Bacon Act as originally passed were these: first, it applied only to larger contracts undertaken directly by the federal government and required that the rate of wages paid by private contractors to all laborers and mechanics would not be less than the prevailing rate of wages for work of a similar nature in the city, town, village, or other civil division of the state in which the work was located; second, it did not contemplate predetermination or any external imposition of wage rates, leaving the definition of prevailing up to the contractors themselves, except that in the event of a dispute the contracting officer or the Secretary of Labor would be required to set a rate; and third, that the act could be suspended by the President in case of a national emergency.[20]

The legislation was short on details, and its vagueness posed an administrative problem from the start. Contractors objected that there

---

[19] As late as January 1931, Hoover's Comptroller General had expressed his opinion that a minimum or prevailing wage rate requirement on federal contracts was objectionable because it would remove an important cost element from competitive bidding and would tend to defeat the purpose of the federal procurement contract to acquire goods and services at the lowest competitive price. But apparently, the original Davis-Bacon act, which did not require predetermination of wages, seemed innocuous enough to President Hoover that he signed it into law over these objections.

[20] The original 1931 act in its entirely can be found in Appendix One. If nothing else differentiates changes that have occurred in the country since the time Davis-Bacon was first passed, consider that the entirety of this act is expressed in one longish paragraph, whereas the Obama Health Care act of 2010 requires some 2,700 pages to express its intent without even including the text of the thousands of embedded references that litter it. Construction then and health care now are each about 20 percent of the national economy, and although the Davis-Bacon Act extended only to the fraction of the federal government's interface with construction, the size difference of these two pieces of legislation is remarkable. And some say that at heart both are equally vague.

was no objective standard against which to measure wage rates. The concept of prevailing was also a subjective rather than a statistical one, so some definition was required to translate it into a measurable basis for action, but none was provided.

This brings up the most flagrant problem affecting the Davis-Bacon Act (as well as state "Little Davis-Bacon" laws, the Walsh-Healey Act, the Service Contract Act, and all other prevailing wage laws). The central concept upon which all are based is notional at best: most of the time, there is no such thing as an identifiable prevailing wage rate, nor any objective method that can identify, determine, or specify what one should be. A law that purports to find existing prevailing wages for construction work in a locality and reflect those back as specific wage requirements for like work in the future therefore promises what it cannot possibly deliver. It is a law grounded in inherent fraud.

> No. 5. The Davis-Bacon Act is a law grounded in inherent fraud. It promises what cannot possibly be delivered.

5. The Central Concept—Maintaining the Prevailing Wage

A wage requirement based on a concept that identifies existing prevailing wages in any given workplace (local or national doesn't matter) and mandates that identical wages be paid for future work is doomed to fail in any logical or objective sense because a prevailing wage can't be identified in any but the most trivial of circumstances. There is no statistically valid logic to support any particular wage amount as prevailing unless that outcome is intuitively obvious. "Prevailing" can only be recognized; it cannot be calculated. It works when an obvious preponderance of near-identical rates exists. In some other situations, an approximation may be made to force fit mechanically with the help of statistics, but there is no underlying logic to support it. And there are also times when a choice can't be made even with the best of intentions and deploying the best available mathematical tools.

Consider this contrived (though non-trivial) example: Envision two large piles of balls one pile red and the other green. Shown a sample drawn from those piles containing a mixture of 90 balls from the red pile and 10 from the green, most people could intuitively identify red as the predominant, or prevailing, color. But if the sample contained a mixture, say, of 54 balls from one pile and 46 from the other, a casual glance might not be sufficient to identify a prevailing color because the result is less obvious. At least some of the people might resort to counting the balls, but by doing so they would be making an implicit assumption that the prevailing color is the modal one—that is, the one that occurs most frequently.[21] But consider: if the mixture contained 50 balls of one color and 50 of another, no degree of perception or level of analysis would allow the determination to be made objectively as to what color prevailed. That is because none did.[22]

Furthermore, as mixtures become more complicated, the degree of difficulty in making determinations increases and the logic becomes more prolix. For example, if shown a mixture of 100 balls consisting of 90 of various shades of red and 10 of some identical shade of green, intuition would clearly select red, but modal analysis would, improperly to most minds, select green.[23]

A. NOT A STATISTICAL PARAMETER

A closely related problem is that the prevailing concept is not in itself a statistical parameter, nor is it measurable by a statistical parameter. It is not a measure of central tendency like the median, mean, or simple average. It is implicitly a single point rather than a range or

[21] Fair enough, but as I'll show in a moment, this is a contrived approximation, also.

[22] How Davis-Bacon handles rate determinations drawn from surveys where there are no data or an insufficiency of data for one or more necessary job titles will be taken up later. (You can probably already guess that it will produce one or more additional reasons to repeal the Act.)

[23] This is a pretty close approximation of modal differentiation between union (green) and nonunion (various red) prevailing rates, and its usual outcome incorrectly favoring the monotonic color.

area. The parameter it is closest to—though not the same as—is the mode.

The mode can be used as a measure of central tendency, but only when applied to normal, bell-shaped distributions. Otherwise, it can result in what amounts to essentially a random choice. In a list of numbers, the numeral that occurs most frequently is called the mode, even if it occurs only slightly more frequently than others. The concept of prevailing is similar, but intuitively would seem to require a stronger showing and a more obvious result. In many circumstances, neither produces useful insight into the distribution from which it was derived. Assume the following list of digits: 2, 2, 5, 8, 8. For this list, although the measures of central tendency can be calculated easily enough (the simple average, median, and mean all equal 5), there is no modal digit, and no logical, mathematical, or even intuitive way of determining which digit might be called the prevailing one (except that it certainly would not be 5).

Another contrived example illustrates the failings of prevailing as a statistical parameter (or as defined in terms of statistical parameters) for administering prevailing wage laws. Consider the following series of digits representing wage rates: 3, 3, 4, 4, 5, 5, 9, 9, 9. Although the details of various federal and state prevailing wage laws have not been introduced, it is instructive to preview how various laws might select a prevailing rate from this list.[24]

- The existing minimum wage rate in the distribution is 3. This is the rate that is presumably to be protected from the predations of government contractors. It would be selected by no known prevailing wage law.[25]

[24] This is jumping ahead a bit and assuming facts not yet in evidence, but the arguments that will be made here are not about inconsistencies in prevailing wage laws, but rather about the many ways that have been used to force the concept of prevailing into some objective framework.

[25] If prevailing rate laws actually were intended to ensure that government contracting would not "drive down" wages, then a law mandating that the minimum paid to any laborers or mechanics be sustained as the minimum

- The median is the middle rate when rates are arrayed in descending or ascending order, in this case 5. Absent other complications, this is the rate that would be taken as prevailing by the Service Contract Act, a federal prevailing wage law applying to contracted government services.
- The simple average is the sum of the different digits divided by the number of different digits, in this case 4.25. This is the rate that would be taken as prevailing by the state prevailing wage law of Kentucky and possibly others where the rate selection methodology to be used by officials is not identified or is simply called an "average."
- The mean (weighted average) is the sum of the different digits multiplied by the number of times each digits appears, divided by the total number of digits—in this case, 5.67. This would be the prevailing rate chosen by the Walsh-Healey Act (a prevailing wage law affecting manufacturing and supply firms) if the numbers in the list were representative of the minimum wages paid by different firms and the firms were all the same size. It would also be taken as prevailing by the Davis-Bacon Act under the current 50-percent rule (since 50 percent or more of the digits were not the same, the mean would be calculated and accepted) and by several of the states.
- The mode is the digit that appears most frequently. In this list, it is 9. It is the rate that in this case appears with a 30-percent plurality, so it is the rate that would have been taken as prevailing by the Davis-Bacon Act between 1935 and 1984 when the 30-percent rule was in effect. It is still in use on some state prevailing wage laws. In Maryland, the nec-

---

allowable on government work would be perfectly reasonable, and would avoid all of the hassle associated with the abstruse concept of prevailing. It would achieve the putative purpose of preserving local standards with minimum fuss and bother, but has never been taken seriously as an idea.

> essary plurality is 40 percent. Some other state laws rely on choosing the modal rate, regardless of its plurality.[26]

In the case above, various laws using differing interpretations of how to objectify the concept of prevailing would select (with equal lack of validity) 4.25, 5.00, 5.67, or 9 as the prevailing rate—half of these being rates that were actually paid to no individual in the survey.[27]

What is the actual prevailing rate? Intuitively, since two-thirds of the rates are 3s, 4s, or 5s, the actual prevailing rate might be "somewhere around 4," or perhaps "somewhere between 3 and 5." Curiously, almost all of the standard methods of reaching a prevailing wage law find an answer higher than this, and many would choose the highest number in the distribution, especially if that number represented a collective bargaining rate.

To the mounting list of reasons to repeal the Davis-Bacon Act, add the following, which is the most significant thus far:

---

[26] Where a pure modal rate is explicitly or implicitly sought, it can safely be presumed to presage union rates.

[27] The states have adopted many other ways of objectifying the prevailing rate. The 32 states that have prevailing wage laws set them in as many as 24 different ways, depending on how one counts minor variations. Massachusetts, Ohio, and New Jersey specify the prevailing rate to be the union wage, regardless of its predominance in the local labor markets, as would many other states after "ascertaining and considering" collectively bargained rates. Many other states wash their hands of the matter by declaring that the prevailing rate is whatever their labor administrators say it is. The study in hand is limited to analysis of the problems with the federal Davis-Bacon Act and is already complex enough without introducing the mindless minutia of the other federal prevailing laws and similar laws at the state and local levels, many of which differ in varying degrees from one another and from their federal counterparts. A compendium of the variances found in individual state prevailing wage laws as of 2009 (current at the time I viewed them), can be found on the ABC (Associated Builders and Contractors) web site under "Prevailing Wage Laws of the States."

> No. 6. The concept of prevailing rates is rubbish, and can't be translated into an objective statistic or made into a logical system. A law known to be impossible to objectify logically or to administer equitably is inherently flawed, if not outright fraudulent.

B. MORE PROBLEMS

Behind the concept of the prevailing wage is the idea that it would be a rate adopted based on an already existing distribution of rates in the locality that could be reflected and projected onto new government work without changing local wage terms. But when rates found by the secretary of labor or prevailing rate administrator by whatever formula or means are projected not as a new prevailing rate but as a new minimum that must be paid, rather than as a distribution, they necessarily distort the existing terms.

Except in the trivial case where all existing wages are identical or where the prevailing rate determined is lowest rate that existed in the distribution before, any determination rate necessarily has the effect of increasing the minimum of what can henceforth be paid, thereby raising the entire distribution of wage levels on government work, and therefore the cost of such work, above whatever market rates existed before would have produced. This is patently obvious in the case of prevailing rates chosen at the collectively bargained rate or by any central-tendency statistic, but it is even the case if the prevailing rate is obvious or chosen by intuition (the "somewhere around 4" rate).

When prevailing rates are applied, they are applied as minimums: contractors are free to pay more, but they cannot pay less than the determined wages. As a generality, if a central-tendency rate is used, about half of wage rates previously paid (the bottom half) are no longer available on the proposed work.[28] If the collectively bargained

[28] Of the federal prevailing wage laws, the one that comes closest to accomplishing the prevailing-wage eschaton of reflecting back the established local wage practice to preserve it against the depredations of exogenous

rate is chosen, then the prevailing wage law has the effect of setting the maximum from the old distribution as the minimum for the new one.

> No. 7. In all but trivial cases, prevailing rates chosen by any plurality or modal rate or any measure of central-tendency make a middle rate the new minimum, eliminating the bottom part of any existing distribution of wages from use in the proposed government work. Rather than reflecting local wage rates, prevailing wage laws necessarily increase them, and therefore necessarily increase the cost of such work.

6. THE DAVIS-BACON ACT AFTER 1935

As already stated, the first version of Davis-Bacon was not well received. In addition to the problems associated with vagueness, the new law also lacked policing and enforcement mechanisms, factors that made unions unhappy. Contractors objected to the possibility that the contracting agency or the secretary of labor might come along after a contract was awarded and require wage rates higher than the contractor had used to base his bids, thus opening up a new element of risk for contractors working for the government, so they were unhappy, too. And finally, contract administrators objected because they did not wish to be injected into wage disputes between contractors and their workers or unions.

The result was that almost immediately after passage of the act in 1931, new hearings were called for. Initially, these concentrated on enforcement problems and left the difficult, definitional problems

government demand driving it lower is the Walsh-Healey Act. Its operations are beyond our purview here, but are covered in my 1986 book. One reason why little attention has been paid to Walsh-Healey in the last 50 years may be that it achieves the stated objective with minimal administration and therefore doesn't cause much trouble. It doesn't do much more for protecting industrial wage rates from falling than my cat does protecting my house from elephants, but at least it does relatively little harm.

unresolved. In 1932, President Hoover issued an executive order calling for various enforcement provisions and also for the posting of wage rates (though not for their predetermination), and bickering continued. Then Congress passed major amendments, including predetermination, but President Hoover vetoed them because of the complications he saw with the predetermination process and the role of government in the labor market. His secretary of labor at the time, William Doak, commented that the proposals would be "obscure and complex and impractical of administration," and that their result "could only be dissatisfaction, endless controversy in enforcement, and great increase in expense to the taxpayer."[29]

In 1933, more hearings were held to prohibit contractors from requiring workers to kick back some portion of any wages elevated by prevailing rates. These resulted in the Copeland (Anti-Kickback) and False Statements Acts of 1934, newly requiring contractors to file weekly payroll reports and other certifications that continue to the current day.[30]

A. THE CURRENT DAVIS-BACON LAW

After the new administration took office in 1933 and failed to institute a national minimum wage by industry (as had been proposed by the National Industrial Recovery Act, found unconstitutional), it

[29] Herbert Hoover, "Memorandum Upon Senate Bill 3847" (Sen. Doc. 134), 1 July 1932, attached memorandum of Secretary of Labor. Doak was right.

[30] Copeland resulted in burdensome paperwork that has seldom been of use even in enforcement, and but few cases of contractor malfeasance have even been prosecuted under it. The Copeland Act resurfaced from obscurity after about 2000 and has played a major role in the judicial review of a union initiative called job targeting, which was the subject of my book, Thieblot (2008), *Job Targeting*. In a one-line summary, that book proposes that the price-inelastic vision of Davis-Bacon rates is what allows job targeting unions to underbid nonunion competitors by effectively paying less than prevailing rates, whereas their nonunion competitors, despite having actual lower costs, must pay them in full.

entertained a revisit to Davis-Bacon amendments that had been raised two years earlier. These had passed the previous congress, and had no trouble being passed again.[31] The amendments called for predetermination and posting of wage rates, the extension of the act to cover dams, levees, and various other public works projects in addition to buildings, and the inclusion of painting and decorating as construction jobs to be covered. It also had some new reporting and enforcement provisions. President Roosevelt signed them into law on August 30, 1935, not as amendments to the 1931 act, but as a substitute for it.

The new law still was somewhat vague about how the prevailing rate determination formula would be applied, and left the wage-setting process up to the individual government contracting agencies. This remained the case until 1971, when the Branch of Construction Wage Determinations of the Wage and Hour Division of the Employment Standards Administration was assigned responsibility for setting the prevailing wage county-by-county throughout the United States, thus consolidating the process in DOL. Fringe benefits had been added in 1964 and a few minor changes occurred subsequently, such as the change from the 30-percent rule to the current 50-percent rule. But the essence of the 1935 law is still the law of the land and remains in about the same form now, three generations later.[32]

---

[31] Since almost all characteristics of the bill vetoed in 1932 were repeated in the amendments made subsequently in 1935, Secretary Doak's comments could have applied to the new act with equal vigor and equal foresight.

[32] Davis-Bacon was brought to its present form by the amendments of 1935, but not to its present extent. The inclusion of Davis-Bacon requirements in public works construction in which the federal government is not a direct party but rather provides aid (in the form of grants, matching funds, guarantees, or the like) to federal agencies or for state or local projects has been a major extension. The 1935 act, for example, did not cover construction projects for the Public Roads Administration, the United States Housing Authority, the Rural Electrification Administration, or the Public Works Administration, contracts for all of which were classified as federal-aid contracts rather than contracts to which the United States was an actual party. As time went by, compliance with Davis-Bacon provisions was added to these acts and a great many more, which aggregate in dollar amount to more than

No. 8. The Davis-Bacon Act, as a minor substitute for a full bore minimum wage requirement became obsolete in 1938 when the Fair Labor Standards Act took over that duty in a more effective and more easily administered way.

Key Provisions

The key provisions of the new Davis-Bacon Act included: 1) predetermination and posting of wages; 2) modifications to include "pubic building or public works," rather than just public buildings, so as to cover levees, dams, and other heavy construction projects; 3) extension to cover painting and decorating as part of "construction, alteration, or repair"; 4) reduction of the contract threshold from $5,000 to $2,000, apparently because painting and decorating projects tended to be small; 5) a requirement that workers be paid weekly and in full; and 6) several enforcement provisions, including contract set-

---

the amount of direct federal purchases. The first extension was to the Housing Act in 1937; by 1960, the number of additional programs covered had grown to eight, including the Federal Highway Act of 1956; it grew to 62 by 1972 and 77 by 1977. Extensions have been made to areas not obviously connected with construction. It became part of the National Foundation on the Arts and Humanities act of 1965, the Heart Disease, Cancer and Stroke Amendments of 1965, the Education Amendments of 1972, the Domestic Volunteer Service Act of 1973 the Indian Self-Determination and Education Assistance Act (1974), the Developmentally Disabled Assistance and Bill of Rights Act (1975), the Stafford Disaster Relief and Emergency Assistance Act for relief cleanup from hurricane Katrina in 2005, the Weatherization Act of 2008, and many more. It extends to buildings that might be built without any federal funding in them at all if the buildings are to be leased to federal agencies in whole or part. It extends by adoption into about half of the state prevailing wage laws, and in general, has many tentacles. In 2009, the federal portion of pubic works construction was about $86 billion, but Davis-Bacon requirements also applied to $134 billion of additional programs.

asides or terminations, blacklisting, fines, and the right to recovery of back wages by employees.[33]

Administratively, the most troublesome of the modifications was the predetermination of wages. So long as the application of the law was vague, the consequence of not being able to identify or even to define "prevailing" was not serious. But if rates were to be predetermined and published before contract award, someone had to accept the responsibility for establishing a working definition of the statistically indeterminate concept that underlay them. The new law required that the concept be applied, but did not delineate its meaning, so the duty fell by default to the secretary of labor. Frances Perkins, who held that job at the time, accepted the challenge with apparent gusto, and she and her successors have made all of the detailed decisions that characterize how the Davis-Bacon law applies in practice.

[33] See Appendix One for the text of the relevant portions of the revised law.

Chapter II: Overview of the Construction Industry and Its Labor Relations

It had been my original plan to avoid all background and set-up information if possible, but there are certain fundamental aspects of the construction industry and the organization of work within it that simply must be addressed. Even abbreviated discussion of these points, however, requires enough detail that I have relegated it to Appendix Two. Presented here below are simple summaries, my conclusions of what I feel you should know about this market that impact on, or have implications for, Davis-Bacon. Each of these is explained more fully, though still as succinctly as possible, in the corresponding section of Appendix Two. If any of the summarized conclusions seem controversial, I suggest not skipping the fuller discussion of them in the Appendix, because appreciation of the impact of Davis-Bacon on the industry requires an understanding of these things, and not all of them are common knowledge. Because this entire discussion is descriptive, no additional reasons for repeal are included in this chapter.

1. Fungible Construction Output

Construction work is controlled by contracts and specifications, and is fungible with respect to its labor input. A building built by a union contractor is indistinguishable from one built by a nonunion contractor. The union status of the laborers and mechanics that built a given building is no more relevant than their political party affiliation or Masonic membership.

2. Industrial Structure: The Union Pattern

Construction unions are based on medieval guilds. In union construction, journeymen originally owned the secrets of their work, were all presumed to be equally skilled, were assisted only by apprentices and laborers, and were all equally paid. Vestiges of this system remain although modern union contracts bristle with wage variations and semi-skilled workers have become prevalent in many unions. There is no vertical advancement within unions other than from apprentice to journeyman. If a given union comprises individuals who are designated as craft-related laborers (e.g. electrical groundmen), helpers (e.g., mason tenders), or semi-skilled workers (e.g., carpenter—acoustical tile installer), such individuals are not expected (or allowed) to advance to higher levels or to full journeyman status. Union workers are hired by the job from union-run hiring halls, and owe primary allegiance to their union.

3. Industrial Structure: The Nonunion Pattern

Nonunion construction work patterns developed independently, and are based on a combination of entrepreneurship and ordinary industrial practice. Work is owned by the contractor (who may also be an active participant) and employees are paid in relation to their varying skills. Employees are able to rise in rank both from below and to above journeyman status. They are more often permanently employed and owe primary allegiance to their firm.

4. Craft Unions in the AFL

The unions that still dominate the AFL are craft unions that were active at the start of labor organizing in the US. These unions continue to reflect the skills that were needed in the building construction of about a century ago. More modern skills associated with developing technologies in the industry (e.g., gypsum wallboarding, low-voltage alarm and communication wiring) or with task specialization (e.g., welding, basement or pool excavating, handling pre-formed roof trusses, erecting metal buildings) tend to be poorly or confusingly represented in the classic trades and therefore in modern unions. With the exception of the laborers' union, AFL unions are organized horizontally rather than vertically, by craft. In many unions (e.g., ornamental iron work, roofing) the journeymen of the union still maintain control over all supporting work and materials handling in addition to the skilled components of the work.

5. Semi-Skilled Workers and Helpers

Unions do increasingly employ helpers, craft-specific laborers, and semi-skilled persons; but with the exception of elevator constructors and boilermakers, unions use different titles for helpers, mostly calling such persons tenders (e.g., mason tenders) or giving them compound titles (e.g., carpenter, acoustical tile; or painter, brush and roller). For the purposes of prevailing rate determination, unions want to keep the titles of their own craft-specific helpers and semi-skilled workers separate from the more generic helper designations used in nonunion construction, and do not want their own helpers to be seen as persons engaged in on-the-job training or as rising journeymen. Although construction workers having the title of helper now make up almost 10 percent of the total number of workers in the field, it remains the practice of Davis-Bacon administration to ignore their existence and to require helpers, especially nonunion ones, to be paid at journeymen's rates. There is additional discussion of helpers not only in Appendix Two, but also much more concerning the failed attempt to require the USDL to issue determination rates for helpers, in Chapter V and in Appendix Three.

6. Union and Nonunion Wage Rates, and the Union Wage Rate Differential

At all three levels of skill (journeymen, helpers and semi-skilled, and laborers), union wage differentials in 2011 approximated 100 percent, average union wages being about twice as high as corresponding nonunion ones. Average nonunion wage rates, including fringe benefits, in 2011 were: journeymen, $24.60 per hour; helpers and semi-skilled workers, $18.23 per hour; laborers, $18.59 per hour. The corresponding union average wage rates were: journeymen, $48.56 per hour; helpers and semi-skilled workers, $37.70 per hour; laborers, $39.14 per hour. The variation is considerable in union wage rates at every level. For example, journeymen's wages by craft or even within craft in recent determinations covering a single state ranged from $34.00 to $63.18 per hour, reflecting local labor market conditions.

7. THE TOTAL UNION PREMIUM

The total union premium consists of not only the premium associated with higher wages and fringe benefits but also the premium associated with higher terms-and-conditions costs of union work (e.g., specific time allocated to cleanup, make-ready, coffee breaks; crew consist requirements, contractor-paid union stewards, etc.). The total union premium including these items is approximately 125 percent of the equivalent nonunion labor cost. In private work, the total union premium is such that unions can no longer compete effectively in these markets except in special circumstances covered in the next section. It even impedes their effectiveness in winning competitions for public work covered by Davis-Bacon and similar prevailing wage requirements, where nonunion firms retain an advantage despite having to pay union wages rates. This is why unions continue to move towards union-based project labor agreements that adopt union terms and conditions exclusively, and towards corporate campaigns, salting, environmental permitting, job targeting, and other programs that arbitrarily increase the costs of nonunion competitors or place them at a competitive disadvantage.

8. TYPES OF CONSTRUCTION MARKETS

For prevailing wage purposes, construction markets are divided into residential, building, highway, and heavy sectors, although not with great consistency. Better divisions along these lines would have separate sectors for educational and institutional building, for stadiums, for earthmoving, for industrial structures, and the like, but this would require additional levels of surveying and rate determination that would extend the work needed to administer prevailing wage laws. For other purposes, the division of construction markets into free-market, government-controlled, and affinity sectors is useful. Only the first of these is price elastic and representative of efficient distribution of resources. The other two are coercion-based, inefficient sectors.

Chapter III: Wage Determination Overview

The next several chapters concern analysis of the processes of Davis-Bacon administration, including the mechanics of both survey administration and wage determinations, and will illustrate the details of how the act is currently administered. There are three fundamental steps to the wage determination process. First is the establishment or selection of what wage rates will be issued for which classes of construction workers on what type of construction work, where. Second is the preparation and administration of surveys that will be the basis for such prevailing rates as will be determined and issued. Third is the actual issuance of determination wage rates, their promulgation and upgrading.

Wage determinations are the heart of Davis-Bacon. Federal law requires that some prevailing rate and prevailing fringe benefit payment must be paid to any employee working under a prime or subcontractor on any federally undertaken or federally involved construction project whose total amount exceeds some trivial threshold, and the source of such required amounts is the published wage determinations applicable to the locality where the project will be built and to the particular level of the construction project (residential, building, etc.). The entire impact of Davis-Bacon lies in wage and fringe amounts in these determinations and in the identities of the persons (or rather, the identity of job titles for those persons) listed in them.

This chapter reintroduces the calls for Davis-Bacon repeal that were temporarily set aside in the last one. Many of the new calls in this and subsequent chapters are related by the generalized theme that the Davis-Bacon Act and its administration by the Department of Labor are both unjustly and perhaps even unconstitutionally biased toward union wages, work practices, job ownership claims, training methods, and all the rest at the expense of and to the detriment of the corresponding wages, methods, and practices of persons who are not affiliated with unions or constrained by union ties. They are therefore somewhat repetitive. Partially, the repetition is meant to inculcate the reader to the pervasiveness of the bias displayed in the process, but it is also meant to illustrate its far-reaching and inexorable extent.

As a housekeeping matter, note that unlike my earlier practice, the boxed calls for repeal here in these chapters are presented as introductory rather than summarizing events.

1. Experience with Wage Determinations

The actual administrative processes for survey wage collection, summarization, establishment of prevailing-ness, issuance, distribution, and updating of determinations are all key to the outputs produced and required on government construction contracts. Given the importance of these processes, it is somewhat surprising that analysis of them does not travel over particularly well-trod ground. Most of the citations in this book are to my own works, where additional details to those presented here can typically be found. They are not restricted to my own works because I have any wish to massage my egotistical leanings. Rather, it is because analysis of the inner working of Davis-Bacon has simply not been performed by many other observers—reflecting, I think, not any lack of importance of the topic, but rather the mind-numbing detail required to carry it out.

Many of illustrations I will use here are from wage surveys and determinations done in the state of Pennsylvania, for two reasons: First, I had been invited in the late 1990s to evaluate an attempt made by that state to conduct a full-scale wage survey of the entire state to form a base line for its state-level prevailing wage determinations which, by state law, were to be set by administrative collection of and comparison to wage rates actually paid in the polity.[1] Then later, I

[1] Although the Pennsylvania prevailing wage law calls on the administrators to "ascertain and consider" a variety of rates, including union rates among them, they in fact limit themselves to ascertaining and mandating union rates. An attempt was made in 1997 to conduct a state-wide, full, prevailing rate survey, but the Commonwealth Court of Pennsylvania threw out the results as not representative because, it held, they unfairly failed to include in their surveys the rates previously paid on prevailing-rate work under previous prevailing rate determinations—rates that are expressly prohibited from consideration under ordinary circumstances for any Davis-Bacon build-

was asked to review one of the (surprisingly rare) actual area wage surveys conducted at the federal level to set residential and building rates for the region of the state near and encompassing Pittsburgh.[2]

---

ing or residential survey. (Decision 3291 C.D. 1997, Filed January 11, 1999.) Rather than redo the survey yet again—it had already been redone four times in response to various earlier union objections—Pennsylvania reverted to its old pattern. Since then, it has been unresponsive to requests to consider detailed submissions by nonunion contractors' associations even in counties where union representation is acknowledged by all parties to be negligible. For state-level building determinations, the Pennsylvania DOL simply adopts or imports union rates in all circumstances, tracks contract updates and any changes in union jurisdiction or jurisdictional areas for the individual union locals, and publishes them.

[2] These were originally rates set for the same six-county area encompassing Pittsburgh for which the survey was performed—Allegheny, Beaver, Butler, Fayette, Washington, and Westmoreland counties. By 2003, these were issued in General Decision PA020013, 04/18/2003, the 7th iteration of the determination initially published 03/01/2002. This determination was superseded by General Decision PA20030013, whose 4th iteration was published 01/23/2004, covering the counties of Beaver, Butler, Fayette, Washington, and Westmoreland together, but Allegheny County separately, whose own determination bore General Decision number PA20030033, the 3rd iteration of which was also published 01/23/04. By 2011, the determinations had morphed into four separate determinations: one that grouped Beaver, Fayette, and Washington Counties (PA100013, 03/12/2010, 15th modification published 07/22/2011) into a single determination although there were a number of internal split-outs of rates by geographic area; a second that was for Allegheny County, the 11th modification of which was published on 07/22/2011; a third that covered Butler County exclusively with the 8th modification from the same date of origin; and a fourth that covered only Westmoreland County in its 10th modification published 07/22/2011. (Also on the books were a 7-county building determination, PA1000001, of which the 28th update modification was published on 8/12/2011, adding Greene County to the others and a separate residential determination for Greene County (PA100055) showing the same date of origin (03/12/2010), published in its 4th modification on 07/01/2011.) Although the survey and original determination in this example was conducted about a decade ago, I have recently reviewed all current determinations in Pennsylvania based on those

For these two investigations, I was provided with access to each step of the original survey documentation (except for the actual survey collection sheets, Form WD-10), some of which was difficult to acquire. I have done similar analysis in other parts of the country and nationwide for individual job titles and types of work. Among others, I have extensively reviewed wage determinations for Montgomery County, Maryland, in the mid-1990s; all of the surveys conducted nationwide for setting rates for helpers, laborers, semi-skilled workers, and trainees during the period of non-suspension of the application of prevailing rates to helpers (to be covered in their own chapter, here next); determinations for landscape laborers; current (2011) nationwide determinations for weatherization workers; determinations in the New England region for rates associated with job targeting in steel erection during the 2000s, and all of the actual surveys conducted by the Department of Labor during one particular year (1995), among others. Details differ, but the essential process seems to be unchanging. Many of the details will be documented in the next few chapters for the Davis-Bacon process in Pennsylvania, but similar levels of elaboration and detail in the output of wage determinations, similarly based on scant or even insufficient input and similarly handled after being initially issued, are found in all of them.

A second reason for reporting on wage determinations in Pennsylvania is that Pennsylvania is an acceptable surrogate for the country as a whole in many of its demographic elements. What I observed of the wage-setting process there is not atypical of what I observed elsewhere. Demographically, Pennsylvania is also typical of the coun-

---

surveys and ascertained that they are still the most recently performed. Depending on the needs of the context, I have sometimes updated wage rate details to information current as of the fall of 2011, but the wage data collected by the original survey have not changed, and so have not needed to be updated. I have no idea how this patchwork of expanding and contracting determinations evolved from the initial survey and determinations after 2003, but for whatever reason, they were all given a new (and therefore misleading) initiation date in March of 2010. No surveys were actually conducted in March of 2010.

try as a whole. For example, its overall union density in 2002 was 15.5 percent. Its construction density was higher, but still only 24.8 percent—a bit lower than its neighboring states to the north and east, a bit higher than those to the south and west, and a little higher than the nationwide averages for both categories.[3] There are 14 Standard Metropolitan Areas in Pennsylvania, for which union density estimates from the Current Population Survey exist for nine. The nine have union densities from a low of 4.5 percent in Lancaster, to a high of 14.4 percent in Erie.[4] These reflect the informal consensus that union influence is strongest (though nowhere is it statistically dominant) in the corners of the state, around Philadelphia, Pittsburgh, Erie, and Scranton,[5] and that in the remaining 50-or-so counties making up the vast center of the state, especially the watershed area of the Susquehanna River and the south-central Amish regions, there is only token union presence. All of these factors make Pennsylvania a reasonable representative for the national patterns, which have similar regional differences of about the same orders of magnitude, even if not in exactly the same places.

Before starting with the details of Pennsylvania determinations, however, a somewhat more generalized overview is called for, and that is the subject of the balance of this chapter.

---

[3] BLS estimates, per Center for Labor Education and Research, website.

[4] From Current Population Survey, 2002, per Barry Hirsh and David Macpherson website at Trinity University.

[5] It has been suggested to the author that construction union dominance of the lucrative public works projects in the corner cities, especially in the Philadelphia area, is based less on numerical superiority (the highest estimates available for any of these areas, those of the CPS, put union construction density at only 30.4 percent) than on real or threatened violence against nonunion firms that might try to undertake it, and on subversion of the prevailing wage enforcement system to subject them to multiple audits if they did. (Interview in the author's files, February 2004, confidentiality to be maintained.) The author cannot attest to the accuracy of the audit claim, but the violent proclivities of construction unions are known and documented. *See* Thieblot (1999), *Union Violence*.

2. Overview of Wage Determinations

A. Hypothesized Uniformity

No. 9. The wage selection process is unfairly biased toward a wage rate uniformity that exists exclusively in union work.

The wage selection process is plurality-based, so sameness of wage amounts in surveys is important. The process therefore contains a built-in and well-known bias towards union rates. Government regulations prohibit most ordinary employers from consorting with one another to fix wages or prices, making it unlikely that their individual employees would be paid identical amounts, even those perceived to have the same experience and skills. But the anti-trust regulations exempted unions and their collectively bargained rates from the taint of rates arrived at through conspiracy. Craft union contracts could specify not only that all journeymen members of a covered class would be paid the same rate as all others, regardless of skill or experience, but also that all would be paid the same by any signatory employer. This contracted uniformity gives union rates a much higher chance of being selected as prevailing in surveys of existing wage practice that cannot be matched in any market for freely competitive labor, whose employers are prohibited from getting together to establish a common wage offer. Nonunion contractors have always seen the prevailing rate reliance of "rates to the penny," accurately, as a way for government to give unfair preference to unions while appearing to be even-handed.

The net result is that Davis-Bacon has always, from its first implementation, gone about its business biased towards the uniformity of union rates. Since most of these administrative decisions were originally made at a time when the unions commanded the overwhelming majority of the labor supply for the types of construction work most likely to be bought by government, it may have made somewhat more logical sense; but as time has gone by, for the secretary of labor to continue to follow union practices and patterns in predisposing wage rates has become primarily a matter of political expediency, and is more and more difficult to sustain based on any underlying logic.

The Davis-Bacon Act was not passed in order to protect union rates from competitive pressure, but only to protect those rates that generally prevailed in the locality, whatever they happened to be. And whatever else can be said about construction wage rates that actually prevail in any given competitive labor market, the most common ones will not be those that are paid to the high-priced union workers who are the elite of the industry and who are fewer than one out of five working in the field. A simple average of existing wage rates rather than a modal rate or a weighted average would certainly protect local wage rates from any putative negative pressures brought about by new government work; but then union rates would no longer dominate the determinations, so perhaps that is the reason such a simple solution is not used.

Whatever the reason, DOL continues to rely on the notion that the prevailing wage in a community is the one, identical to the penny, which appears most frequently in wage surveys.[6] In a subsequent chapter on wage survey mechanics, I will show that the "rate to the penny" rule does not, in fact, obtain in the real world, where even union rates are seldom identical to the penny. But even if they were, a process of wage determination based on survey sameness would be evidence of bias towards unions. It is not the only example of such bias.

---

[6] The prevailing rate is actually not a pure modal rate, but a constrained modal rate—the rate most frequently found provided it is found for at least 50 percent of the submissions to a rate survey. But the fact that it must be the "rate to the penny" effectively eliminates a nonunion rate (other than the trivial case of the federal or state required minimum wage) from ever being selected. The best that nonunionists can hope for is a not-union rate created by the weighted average of union and nonunion rates when a union majority rate is not asserted.

B. STATISTICALLY IMPOSSIBLE OUTCOMES

No. 10. The percentage of union rates published as prevailing in Davis-Bacon wage determinations is statistically impossible to have been achieved fairly. It could only have been accomplished through blatant and perhaps even fraudulent pro-union bias. This, of itself, should invalidate the law.

A major reason for the adverse economic impact of prevailing rates is that union wages, demonstrably higher than nonunion ones by approximately a factor of two, are represented in prevailing wage determinations to a much higher degree than can be accounted for by the overall density of unionism in the industry in any fair representation. Recent figures show that unions nationwide control something less than 25 percent of the journeymen in the 17 major building trades and fewer than one in six laborers.[7] The only skilled trade to have an actual union majority nationwide, though not a very strong one (58.8 percent) is that of structural metal workers, itself a relatively small specialty. No other trade group exceeds 42 percent union. By state, construction union density ranges from a low of scarcely 2.3 percent in North Carolina to a high of 48.2 percent in Illinois—nowhere a majority. By state prevailing law regime, even the 12 states with the strongest state-level prevailing wage laws had average union densities

[7] Figures derived by Barry Hirsch from BLS, *Union Membership, Coverage, Density and Employment by Occupation,* various years. The construction industry as a whole, depending on how it is defined and on how union membership is counted, is sometimes estimated to have even lower union densities, about 18 percent overall. That this is 50–60 percent higher than the overall level of union representation in all private industries taken together is testament to the continuing power of the Davis-Bacon Act. *See,* Thieblot (1997), *Fraud*, pp. 6–9.

of around 30.5 percent, while those with average-strength laws were lower, those with weak laws lower still; the 18 without any state laws were down into single digits—about 8.5 percent.[8]

These numbers clearly show that opportunities for union rates to prevail in any trade, locality, or type of construction (other than possibly structural steel work) are rare to none as a matter of statistical dominance, since it is only in that one trade that unions should be able to muster a statistical majority of union-level rates in some metropolitan areas or heavily unionized parts of the country. Nevertheless, over 29 percent of all federal wage determinations now in effect throughout the country are said to be in "safe union territory," where the USDL has decided union dominance is so great that surveys are not even necessary. In these areas, "prevailing rates" for each and every category of laborer and mechanic listed in them are automatically set at the union wage. A further 23 percent of the nation's determinations were mixed, containing some but not all union rates. Thus, something over 40 percent of all federal wage determinations had some or all mandatory minimums set at the union scale. There is, statistically, no way that these determination outcomes reflect any existential reality.

Here is the case for Pennsylvania, where unions are also known to represent fewer than 25 percent of construction workers (and undoubtedly far fewer than that on the private projects that are supposed to form the bases of Davis-Bacon determinations). In Pennsylvania, there are currently published 32 residential, 26 building, and 7 heavy

---

[8] Union densities are from BLS estimates for the year 2002, by state; prevailing law regime (strength) is from Thieblot (1995), *State*. It is interesting to note, in passing, two strong correlations: (1) The stronger the prevailing law regime, the higher the union density in construction: no law states, 8.5 percent; weak law states, 12.2 percent; average law states, 19.0 percent; strong law states, 30.5 percent. (2) The stronger the prevailing wage law regime, the greater the differential between union density in construction and overall union density in all industries: no law states, +1.4 percentage points; weak law states, +1.6; average law states, +5.4; strong law states, +11.8. This reaffirms the contention that prevailing wage laws, rather than a local tradition of unionism or any regional propensity towards it, are responsible for the higher union densities found in construction in certain states.

and highway Davis-Bacon determinations; in these, the proportion of 100-percent union determinations is close to the national average—29 percent; for the entire country the exact number and proportion of union rates among all those individually published in determinations is unknown, but Pennsylvania should provide a decent guide and in Pennsylvania, 81 percent of all published individual federal-level prevailing rates are union. These determination statistics are shown in Table 1.

Table 1

Federal Prevailing Rate Determinations in Pennsylvania
September, 2011
Number and Percent of Union Rates Found in Determinations and Among Individual Rates Published in Determinations

	Residential	*Building*	*Heavy/ Highway*	*All*	*Percent Union*
All Determinations	31	26	7	64	
All-Union Determinations (Every rate in determination at union scale)	3	10	6	19	29%
No-Union Determinations (No rate in determination at union scale)	13	0	1	14	21%
Individual Rates Published in Determinations	493	1,017	534	2,044	
Individual Rates Published at Union Scale	211	925	530	1,666	81%

The statistical improbability of this outcome, and the fact that over 80 percent of all individual rates, in all areas, for all trades, for all categories of construction were determined to prevail at the union rate, cannot be overstated.[9] Note also that overall union densities of 20 percent do not forecast that 20 percent of individual determinations might be all union, much less that 20 percent of published determinations would be union in every category of workman. Indeed, any level of union density below 50 percent forecasts that *no* prevailing rates should be union, since union rates are supposed to prevail only if a pure majority union rate exists—it is never the result of averaging. In fact, the statistical situation is even more desperate than indicated there, because the great majority of union work is already done on public rather than private construction, and much of that is supposed to be excluded from the statistical base for new residential or building determinations. Actual union construction density would have to be two to three times greater than it now is—that is, something on the order of at least 60 or 70 percent—for its non-public-works proportion to achieve this result as a matter of mathematics.[10]

Further along, I will consider several examples of wage determinations surveys, among them the survey and determinations for residential work for a six-county area of southwestern Pennsylvania including Allegheny, Beaver, Butler, Fayette, Washington, and Westmoreland counties, three of which are officially designated as "rural" by the Center for Rural Pennsylvania.[11] In such circumstances—residential and largely rural—union densities are known to be substantially lower than the national or state averages, possibly in the

---

[9]All state-level prevailing wage rates in Pennsylvania, 100 percent of them, are set at the union level as well.

[10] See the extended discussion in Thieblot (1997), *Fraud.*

[11] On its website in 2003, The Center for Rural Pennsylvania, a Legislative Agency of the Pennsylvania General Assembly, designated Butler, Fayette, and Washington counties of Pennsylvania as "rural," citing U.S. Bureau of Census, "Census of the Year 2000," as its source. CRP calculated the average population density (persons per square mile) for all Pennsylvania counties and designated those with less than the statewide average of 274 persons per square mile as rural. The population densities of the six counties in the Pittsburgh-area determination were, in order: Allegheny, 1,755; Beaver, 418; Westmoreland, 361; Washington, 237; Butler, 221; Fayette, 188. The last three clearly met the definition for rural.

single digits. Thus, in this area for this kind of work, no more than isolated union rates, if any at all, should be expected to found in wage determinations. It should therefore be astonishing to note that residential determinations for these counties in late 2011, listing rates for 26 different job categories, had 23 of them (88 percent) set at the union rate.[12]

For all building construction in Pennsylvania in 2011, 1,017 rates were found in the rate determinations for separately identified job categories. Of these, 694 were set at union journeyman rates, 151 were set at union laborer rates, 80 were set at union helper and semi-skilled rates. Only 92 were set as not-union rates of any sort. Thus, in Pennsylvania, where 18.9 percent of construction workers are in unions, 91 percent of determination rates are set at union scale, allegedly as a matter of mathematical dominance, each being achieved through a majority of rate submissions in surveys. Conversely, although 81.1 percent of construction workers in the state are nonunion, only 9 percent of determination rates are set at not-union levels. As in earlier examples, this illustrates the extraordinarily high proportion of union rates in comparison with the small proportion of union representation known to exist that seem to be the standard in rate determinations allegedly set by survey of local wage practices. Such results are not statistically possible. How and why do they come about?[13]

[12] A hint at the impact of this on future public residential construction costs is found in the fact that the average for the union-dominated rates in those determinations was $31.49 per hour (counting fringes), whereas the average of the three not-union ones was $19.74 per hour, about 40 percent less.

[13] Further discussion of this mathematical miracle and some suggestions for answer to the query in the text can be found in Thieblot (2005), *The 20-Percent Majority*.

C. SENSELESS VARIATIONS IN DETERMINATIONS

No. 11. Davis-Bacon determinations are too often inchoate with respect to any underlying local wage patterns. Senseless laws and regulations are worse than no laws and regulations, especially when they exist to serve the purposes of a special interest group, in this case construction unions.

The senseless variations in wage rates for ordinary construction employees doing ordinary construction jobs is exemplary of how prevailing wage laws have conspired to create a separate universe far divorced from any underlying reality. Consider the variations in wage rates issued by the USDL and others in ordinary wage determination just in the ordinary state of Pennsylvania, just for the ordinary job of construction laborer. The laborer is the common denominator of construction work. Many of his jobs (cleaning, moving materials about, lifting, unloading, carrying lumber, operating taping machines, flagging, etc.) involve "grunt work," that is, physical labor using no specialized tools or skills. Such work is generally quite similar in nature from job site to job site, especially in the regimes of building and residential construction, but pretty much through all varieties of construction work.

In the early 2000's, the U.S. Department of Labor had 31 active residential determinations covering all of Pennsylvania's counties. These set 76 separate minimum rates for laborers ranging in amount from around $5 (sometimes even below the current federal minimum, though more recently all determination rates are upped to current minimum wage levels) up to $35, with a modal rate of about $14. The 26 building determinations, that also covered the state then, had another 294 laborer rates, with one, two, four, six, seven, or up to eleven sub-categories separately identified and sometimes elaborately split along complicated geographic lines established by various local unions. Rates in the building regime ranged only slightly higher than residential ones, from $9 to $36, but the modal rate was $24 per hour, substantially higher, because of larger proportion of union rates included in the breakouts.

Besides the two sets of federal determinations, there were also separate determinations issued by the state for nonfederal public works. These were issued individually for each building project (though not for residential projects, and it is not known how these were covered). I chose one example of a building project randomly from recent jobs in each county and evaluated the laborers' rate requirements. In this case, the number of separate laborer rates I found was 386. Some individual counties had ten or more categories of laborers listed per determination, as well as geographic splits.

All the rates determined by the state wage setters were union rates, and all were said to be current. Curiously, although conventional wisdom supposes that all union rates for any given craft are the same, the hourly rates found for some union laborers working on building projects was as low $21, while for others across the state with the same job title who were members of the same international union, it was as high as $38, almost twice as much.[14]

In total, for this most common and similar of all construction work categories, the concurrently specified prevailing rates in Pennsylvania differed from one another by more than a factor of six—from under $6 per hour to over $38 per hour. The job of laborers working on most residential and building construction may be about the same in fact, but was nowhere near the same in prevailing wage determinations, where its subcategories and rates of pay were found in 756 variations.[15] Just for laborers. Just in a single state.

---

[14] Curiously, although many of the paired state and federal building determinations follow union jurisdictional lines, and both are automatically updated, their amounts may differ from one another by a dollar or two.

[15] This does not count the individual jobs named within each rate grouping separately, which would be a much, much larger number (well into the thousands), but only the number of different rate categories. (E.g., Group 1a Laborers . . . Group 9 Common Laborers.) It also covers only residential and commercial construction, ignoring federal heavy and highway determinations covering Pennsylvania that would add their own levels of complexity. For unskilled laborers, the common denominator of the construction industry, there were 21 different (union) rates for heavy and highway construction in the 67 counties ranging from $20.15 in 4 northern counties to $35.15 in the 5 counties around Philadelphia. No two of the (union) unskilled laborer rates were the same to the penny.

D. GARBAGE FILLED DETERMINATIONS

No. 12. Davis-Bacon determinations are filled with union-supplied garbage. It has been included to accommodate various local unions and is exemplary of blatant pro-union bias that makes mockery of the fundamental concepts underlying prevailing wage laws.

It is not only the height and union-ness of wage rates, nor even their variation from one circumstance to another that is the true problem with Davis-Bacon rates. It is how these determinations are prepared and distributed. I'll have a great deal to say about this later, but wanted to give a brief demonstration here of how even ordinary determinations for ordinary residential jobs in ordinary suburban and rural areas have spun out of control and are filled with union-supplied garbage.

The example I've selected is from a Davis-Bacon residential determination for Monroe County, on the Eastern border of Pennsylvania, a bit north of Allentown. This county has a population only about one-quarter of Allegheny County's (the county that contains Pittsburgh), with around 6,000 workers in construction occupations at any level compared to Allegheny County's 32,142. Its population of only 228 persons per square mile classifies it as "rural." Despite these characteristics, in the mid-2000's, Monroe County had its own, independent, residential wage determination, not shared with any of its neighbors. The determination listed 35 categories of workers, covering around 225 named or implied sub-specialties, a palette that was about 20 times larger than Allegheny County's. One of those named subcategories was the Group 1 classification of operating engineers (also known as power equipment operators), whose description included in the determination I will now reproduce, suitably annotated:[16]

[16] Power Equipment Operator, Group 1, from Pennsylvania General Decision PA20030065, Residential Construction for Monroe County.

Power Equipment Operator, Class 1: Autograde (C.M.I. and similar); Backfiller, Backhoe – 360 degree Swing; Cabelway; Caisson Drill (similar to Hugh Williams) [*one hopes this to be a brand name, not a person*]; Central Mix Plant [*probably not on job site, and would represent an unauthorized extension of prevailing rates if off-site, so reason for including is unknown*]; Concrete Paving Mixer; Concrete Pump (self-propelled) [*a stationary concrete pump is a Group-2 job at $.26 less per hour*]; Cranes; Cranes (boom or mast 101 ft. or over up to & including 150 ft. inclusive of job + $.25; Boom or mast over 150 ft. up to and including 200ft. inclusive of job + $.50; Boom or mast over 200 ft. inclusive of job + $.75; Tower-Stationary – Climbing Tower Crane) [*Difficult to parse: if these are definitions of "cranes," as implied by the parentheses, they are far from comprehensive and leave many types out; if they are special types of cranes to be paid differently, the last-named categories should have been left out; "job" undoubtedly is a typo and should have been "jib"*]; Derrick [*hard to differentiate from a crane*]; Derrick Boat [*drivers? crew? operators of derricks on Derrick Boats? brand name?*]; Dozer (d-6 & over) [*a particular model of the Caterpillar line; unknown how to relate to other manufacturers' models of different combinations of dimensions, horsepower, or capacity*]; Dragline; Dredge; Dredge Hydraulic [*redundant?*]; Elevating Grader; Franki Pile Machine [*don't ask*]; Gradall (remote control or other-wise) [*a redundant note*]; Grader (power-fine grade) [*unknown reference, perhaps an uncapitalized brand name*]; Helicopter [*pilot? co-pilot? hoist operator on helicopter? only while hovering on site, or also away from work site?*]; Hillift (4 cy. and over); Hoist 2 Drums or more (in one unit) [*a single-drum hoist, except possibly in helicopters, is in Group 4 at $4.37 less per hour*]; Hydraulic Boom Truck (with pivotal cab) [*non-pivotable cab is Group 2, at $.26 less per hour*] single motor-Pitman or similar) [*can't tell if this is some different type of equipment or part of the Hydraulic Boom Truck explanation*]; Local [*?*]; Locomotive (std. Gauge) [*narrow gauge locomotives are in Group-2, but it seems improbable that either would appear on a residential building project*]; Metro-chip Harvester or similar [*?*]; Milling Machine (Roto Mill or similar) [*not known to be a device used in residential construction*]; Mix Mobile; Mucking Machine (tunnel) [*resi-*

dential!]; Pile Driver Machine [*that one hopes is related to the Franki Pile Machine, but if so, one or the other is redundant*]; Pipe Extrusion Machine; Prespliter Drill (self-contained) [*there does not seem to be an alternative such as a Postspliter Drill in the listings*]; Refrigeration Plant (soil Stabilization) Rough Terrain Crane [*hard to parse for meaning, as a rough terrain crane is already a crane, thus covered earlier; but the relationship of it to either a soil-stabilizing refrigeration plant or to either part of that is unknown*]; Scrapers; Shovel-Power; Slip from [*sic*] Paver (C.M.I. and similar); Trenching Machine; Tunnell [*sic*] Machine (Mark XXI Jarva or similar) 1 Whirley [*unable to parse, even with spelling correction*].

This is just one of the four groups of power equipment operators described, and is not the most complex such description in the determinations at hand. Similarly impenetrable descriptions perfuse the determinations for all levels of construction, but surely they are an abomination in residential determinations.

3. Anatomy of Wage Survey Process

The typical wage determination process starts with a survey of existing wages and conditions to find out what wages exist that must be protected by the proposed determination. Questions arise immediately. Davis-Bacon applies to the entire country, but its stipulated rates are supposed to reflect those in the locality to which its proposed determination relates: How is that locality defined for survey purposes? How often must surveys be repeated for them to remain current, and what defines currency in this context? How shall projects be selected for their existing wage rates to be considered in a survey? What workmen (or job titles) will be included in the survey? Who may submit wages to the survey, and how are these verified? Over what time period will survey rates be sought? What shall happen if no survey rates are submitted for some job title, or if insufficient data are available to make a statistically adequate determination for some necessary or important job title? How are "rates to the penny" to be interpreted for selection by modal or majority rate? Each of these will be answered in turn, and in each case the overwhelming extent of pro-union bias will be illustrated.

A. GEOGRAPHIC EXTENT OF WAGE SURVEYS

No. 13. Davis-Bacon administration fraudulently pretends to a geographic specificity it does not follow, and in the process unjustly favors union rates and practices.

Davis-Bacon administrative rules specify that prevailing wages will be determined for "city, town, village, or other civil division of the State in which the public buildings are located." Davis-Bacon administrators decided early on that "county" would be the appropriate geographic area for residential and building determinations, and determinations are currently published on what is seen as a county-by-county basis, although instances of "area" surveys covering more than a single county are not unknown (including our 6-county Pittsburgh-area residential survey). What is not so well known is that the surveys from which the determinations are derived are very seldom limited to within county boundaries. Although they are generally published separately and are independently updated for changes in local union contracts applicable in individual counties or parts thereof, they are based on initial surveys that may homologate data from a much broader geographic area.[17]

As of fall 2011, residential surveys in Pennsylvania can be identified as having been conducted at various times for groupings of counties numbering from 1 to 26, covering populations of widely disparate sizes.[18] To illustrate the complexity, consider the 28-county survey undertaken in two broad swaths in 1999. The survey area

[17] Some of this geographic imprecision has already been reviewed above. *See* discussion, fn. 2.

[18] Mega surveys occurred in 1991 (4 counties), 1993 (5 counties), 1995 (7 counties), 1999 (26 counties), and 2002 (6 counties). There were also two-county pairs combined in 1992, 1993, and in two more 1999 surveys. Combined populations in these mega-surveys ranged from around 200,000 to over 2 million, and individual counties with populations as small as 5,000 were combined in the same survey with others as large as 321,000. As of late 2011, no further surveys had been conducted after the 6-county, Pittsburgh-area survey of 2002.

spanned most of the northern counties of Pennsylvania, then through the north-center of the state to the eastern border. It included two non-contiguous counties from the southern and western edges of the state, and contained carve-outs for other small counties in the north-central area and for two "safe union territory" counties (Mercer and Monroe on the western and eastern borders, respectively). The resulting determination was published as though it were 7 different surveys covering from 1 to 7 counties. Determination R-3, covering Armstrong, Clarion, Crawford, Forest, Indiana, Jefferson, and Venango counties and determination R-9, covering Clarion, Clearfield, Clinton, Elk, McKean, Potter, and Warren counties both came from this survey, and all fourteen of these counties, along with Greene (R-16) and Lawrence (R-19) have identical nonunion rates for most listed trades; but the counties in R-3 and R-9 share 5 different union bricklayer rates, and those in R-9 also have a union backhoe rate. Greene, geographically separated from the others, has 2 more (different) bricklayer rates, and Lawrence also has union bricklayer rates, but in fewer divisions.[19]

It is fair to question why variable numbers of counties are grouped together for surveys (especially, as in the case of the six-county survey in the Pittsburgh area, when their separate construction populations indicate several could stand alone), but no explanation is available. The surveys do not follow the lines of standard metropolitan areas, or any other organizing principle (with the possible exception of domains of powerful union locals). The geographic extent of the surveys also suggests that the possibility may exist of gerrymanders of rural areas being dominated by urban ones.

The individual determination rates first published after the 1999 surveys in Pennsylvania have remained unchanged if they represented nonunion rates (except for being brought up to current federal minimum-wage amounts, if applicable), but the union rates included have

[19] The Greene County situation is particularly curious. It was included in the 1999 mega-survey, but its building (as opposed to residential) rates were lumped into the 2002 Pittsburgh-area survey area in 2004. It residential rates, however, continue to be published as a separate determination.

been updated with each successive contract iteration, and union jobs and job divisions have also been tracked and reflected in the determinations.[20]

There is much more of the same, but clearly, independent surveys are not made for each locality, whether defined by county or any other consistent geography. It also should be clear that in compilations of survey data from counties of widely disparate size, the local rates that may obtain in the smaller of them are subordinated to those in the larger population areas or are completely ignored, so that rates tend to be imported from larger population centers to smaller ones. Unions thrive only in the larger population centers, where they may spread unnecessarily and unjustifiably to the smaller ones.

As a specific illustration, Fayette County was included in the 2002 Pittsburgh-area survey. The total contribution of wage rates collected for this survey from Fayette projects was 5 separate reports of 4 union unskilled laborers working together on residential projects valued at between $2,275 and $6,315, and one report of 2 elevator constructors being the sole workers on a $46,000 senior housing project. These are obviously not rates derived from contractors' wage reports on previous projects built, but rather were rates submitted to the survey by union agents or other non-employers.[21] No contractors' reports were submitted for any projects in the county. As it happened, in the ensuing determination, a nonunion unskilled labor wage was

---

[20] It is apparent in some cases that the only reason for different determinations to be issued for individual counties or groups of counties is because of different local union ownership of the union-rate jobs. (As has already been seen, most of the rates in the 1999 mega-survey are not-union—that is, they are survey-averaged rates—but the 7-county rates of determination R-3 differ from the 7-different-county rates of determination R-9 only with respect to the rates to be paid to different union locals of bricklayers in each.)

[21] With respect to the 5 sets of 4 laborer rates, these would eventually be counted in the survey compilations as 20 employee wage reports—although they were clearly five reports of the same 4 workers. This practice by DOL of indiscriminate acceptance of flawed, or at least suspect, rates will be taken up in a later section and evaluated further in Appendix Five and illustrated in Appendix Seven.

imposed on Fayette County, which is reasonable, even if the nonunion laborers' wage in Fayette County as represented by the 5 sets of 4 wages was something different. But the wage determination for Fayette County also set wage requirements that had no obvious base in the county—specifically union wages for bricklayers, carpenters, and power equipment operators.

Although the only insight into Fayette County wage practices discovered by the survey was exemplified by a handful of laborers and a single elevator constructor, builders of residential, government-sponsored projects in that county must pay a minimum of the hourly rates specified (in late 2011 determination) of $32.82 to bricklayers in Jefferson and Washington townships but a differently composed $32.82 (different wage and fringe amounts summing to the same total) to bricklayers in the rest of the county; $21.75 to a particular set of carpenters identified as "Carpenters (Including Drywall Hanging and Vinyl Siding Installation)"; $31.40 to another set of carpenters identified as "Soft Floor Layers (Including Carpet Laying)"; $33.475 (three decimal places) to Power Equipment Operators operating "Cranes (Boom or mast over 200 feet) (Track, Crawler, or Pedestal type)"; $25.50 to "Painters; Brush, Roller (Excluding Spray)"; and various rates to 13 other, named journeymen and laborers or groups thereof.[22]

[22] These wage requirements may seem comprehensive, but they are not. Residential construction, at the simple end of building sophistication, uses predictable skills in predictable ways, so it is the level of construction least likely to require unusual labor inputs or great differences from project to project or county to county. Nevertheless, many of the routine skills and jobs necessary for almost any residential project are rarely, if ever, found in determinations. Determinations routinely leave out air conditioning installers, Tyvec, batt, blown, pipe, or duct insulators, security and communications system wirers, basement excavators, concrete form-setters, slip-form pourers, waterproofers, kitchen and cabinet installers, landscapers, bathroom, patio, or floor tile layers, Bobcat operators, stair setters, window installers, gutter and downspout installers, acoustical tile soundproofers and drop-ceiling mechanics, pool installers, entertainment or computer system wiring and cable routers, fireplace and flue setters, wallpaper hangers, closet system

These wage requirements may have reflected the wage practices of its neighboring counties in the combined survey (although many originate from the whole cloth of union contracts), but it is certain that they reflect nothing of actual wage practices in Fayette found in the survey. Perhaps there are too few construction projects undertaken in the county for there actually to be an identifiable prevailing rate for bricklayers or carpenters or power equipment operators in the county. But if that is the case, the DOL should either seek more input, or it should acknowledge defeat. The fact that the DOL, instead, makes rates up on their behalf or imports them from other counties or encourages that they be substituted from rates published for other sorts of workmen simply illustrates the travesty that the entire process has become.

As another example, each of the fifteen smallest counties in Pennsylvania has a construction population of less than 1,200 workers. Seven of these counties are officially rural, seven are neither rural nor part of standard metropolitan areas, and only one is part of an SMSA. In their residential determinations, these small, mostly rural counties confirm that their areas are wellsprings of nonunion rates: six had 100-percent nonunion determinations,[23] and on average only

---

designers, septic field installers, driveway pavers, well drillers, and fence erectors, among others. Almost none of these jobs, each of which also has its own specialists, are routinely identified or have wages routinely set for them in rate determinations. Also, although most private residential construction is done by higher-skilled lead-workers assisted by lower-skilled craft specialists or helpers, helpers are left out. Although they make up nearly 10 percent of all hourly construction workers, no rates are issued for anyone called "helper" in federal wage determinations unless they are traditional union helpers, and even some of those have had to be given new names. And if any helpers might be needed or used on an actual covered project to be built in the county, they would have to be paid at some rate specified for other types of workers, unless the contractor were willing to engage in a lengthy process to get other rates approved, a process said by those who have attempted it, to be expensive, time consuming, frustrating, and economically dangerous.

[23] Deduced from the fact that the determined fringe benefit amounts are consistent with no union rates having been included in their weighted aver-

21 percent of their combined determined rates were union, as compared with 44 percent union for the grand average of all counties.

Yet, when these counties, with their same local workforces, were packaged with different sets of other counties in building (as opposed to residential) determinations, their determinations looked quite different: the average percentage of union rates shot up from 21 percent to 93 percent, even higher than the grand average for all counties, which was 89 percent. Five of the six small counties that had 0 percent union in the residential surveys were determined to have 100 percent union rates in the building determinations, and the sixth had 92 percent union.[24]

Clearly, union rates were imposed upon, not found in, the small counties, and there is something fundamentally unfair about that.

B. AGE AND FREQUENCY OF WAGE SURVEYS

> No. 14. Davis-Bacon administration fraudulently pretends to a survey frequency it does not possess, and in the process unjustly favors union rates and practices.

---

ages. This indicates the complete absence of union presence in these counties.

[24] From the same surveys: The five counties (Sullivan, Montour, Union, Juniata, and Tioga) that all had 100 percent nonunion rates (no union rates present in averaging) in residential determinations are also found to have had 100 percent union rates (all set by majority rather than averaging) in building determinations. The second part of this is preposterous. These five rural counties had an average construction population of 734 persons of all types and grades. The total number of building jobs having determination rates in all five counties together was 166, an average of 38 per county—the equivalent of having a separate prevailing rate for each 20 randomly selected construction workers. Cameron County, the smallest in Pennsylvania, has a construction population of 95 workers. Nevertheless, 89 percent of the building rates in this county were set at the union scale. All told, there were 101 separately identified union prevailing rates set for those 95 workers in Cameron County, each allegedly based on what they had been paid in the past. (Perhaps some of the workers held more than one construction job.) Results like this show the absurdity of it all.

The USDL guideline manual for wage determinations states that "Each state is surveyed every three years," and that "All construction types are surveyed."[25] It lies. If it were true, then, since it is the long-standing interpretation of DOL[26] that "locality" means "county," every state would be surveyed by county every three years for each category of work—residential, building, heavy, and highway. There are about 3,000 counties in the United States, and if each were surveyed once every three years for four levels of construction, something over 4,000 surveys would be conducted each year. Every determination comprises from about 15 to 100 job categories (or more; an Alaska state determination lists 125 basic rates, plus up to 5 fringes each, covering about 550 separately identified construction job titles), and each of these would need a statistically adequate number of survey rates drawn from private construction performed within some recent time period. In essence, a full survey process would require contacting tens of thousands of firms each year, gathering perhaps 10 million wage rate details, each of which would have to be checked, validated, and processed into determinations.

Despite this challenge and the fact that establishing wage rates is arguably the most important function of DOL's Wage and Hour Division, that division spends only about 8 percent of its $200 million budget for surveys and rate determinations, whereas it spends approximately 80 percent of its budget for enforcement activities (directed almost entirely at nonunion firms). As a result of the size of the task and the limited funding devoted to it, the DOL is unable to make surveys with anywhere near the required frequency, and the number of full surveys conducted each year is estimated to number no more than 100 to 150. At this frequency, each county could expect a survey about once every 20 or 30 years for any type of construction.[27] In

[25] USDL, *Prevailing Wage Resource Book* (November 2002), Sect. 13, p. 1. (This manual is apparently still current as of late 2011.)

[26] I use USDL and DOL interchangeably as the fancy strikes me. Both, of course, are acronyms for the United States Department of Labor.

[27] Although I have not been able to verify this, I have been told that some parts of the country have not had an actual survey performed since 1935

actual fact, in 1995, the year of an inspector general's audit that will be discussed subsequently, a mere 70 survey determinations were made, about half the usual number, because that year the DOL's survey resources were tied up doing a careful job on the resurveying necessary to replace a single tainted determinations in Oklahoma.[28] But even in an ordinary year, the number of actual surveys is on the order of 100, and the number of fully independent surveys is considerably less.[29]

The mega-surveys in Pennsylvania were mentioned in the last section, where the areas covered were discussed. The dates when those and similar mega-surveys were conducted are also of interest: they were done in 1991, 1993, 1995, 1999, and (most recently) in 2002. Indeed, for any of the 67 counties of Pennsylvania, the most recent date of survey that could be identified as of late fall 2011, was 2002.[30] The mean age of all known surveys in Pennsylvania, both of

---

because they have always been considered "safe union territory." (I'll get back to that.)

[28] On this basis, with existing resources, it appears DOL could accomplish about 10 *careful* surveys a year, leaving them about 3,990 short.

[29] Of the 78 surveys performed during the time frame of non-suspension of helper rates for some 21 months of 1992–1993, it could be reasonably argued that the number of "real," viable surveys was 58 or fewer, depending on how one counts, (thus, an annualized rate of no more than 33 "real" surveys). This is because four surveys were "landscape only," apparently designed to settle jurisdictional disputes among competing unions for ownership of this work; three were "water and sewer only," which is only a subset of heavy construction; two were Tennessee building surveys that were counted as different although they were close duplicates of two other Tennessee surveys with which they shared over 95 percent of their individual findings; 12 of the 16 highway surveys were in a single state and used common data, 17 of the 34 building surveys were in only three states and used common data, and 10 of the 14 residential surveys were done in only two states, again using common data. In other words, many of these were not independent surveys, but only geographically independent subsets of single, larger surveys.

[30] The survey dates for Mercer and Monroe counties could not be ascertained, because both of these counties—improbably, because of their small-

individual counties and combined ones, was then just shy of 14 years.[31]

Determinations to be used in bidding on new work in Pennsylvania are issued on approximately a weekly basis, and may be found on the web in careful profusion. These are all called "updated" or "current" determinations, and carry current dates, as though each were a reaffirmation of something based on new or recent findings of existing conditions. In fact, except for union rates in them, they are current on average only to about 14 years ago when not only prevailing rates but also the jobs for which prevailing rates would be determined were set. Their union rates are carefully updated to whatever contract wages and fringes the unions have been able to get and also, as will be seen below, to any changes in union domains or organizational structure, but this hardly makes them actually current, or any better reflections of actual wage rates and work patterns in their areas.

Not only in Pennsylvania but also throughout the country, real wage surveys are a rarity. Instances can be readily found of decades or generations of time since one was last performed. The longer the time between actual surveys, the greater is the possibility of union rates still dominating the determinations.

---

ish size at opposite ends of the state, away from any particular population centers—have 100-percent union rates prescribed, and therefore no unchanging not-union rates with which to date the survey. But my first personal experience with their rates predates 2002, and I can assert without fear of contradiction that any real survey made at a later time would have failed to duplicate those all-union results. So any surveys actually performed in those counties are at least a decade old, and probably a generation or more. They are simply counted as "safe union territory" by DOL, and may have been so from time out of mind.

[31] Actually, 13.95 years.

4. Safe Union Territory

> No. 15. Davis-Bacon Administration fraudulently pretends to not need surveys in "safe union territory," and therefore unjustly favors union rates and practices.

As already discussed, there should be no such thing as "safe union territory," given the low levels to which average union density has fallen. The most charitable thing that can be said about the fact that as recently as 1995 DOL acknowledged that 29 percent of all federal Davis-Bacon wage determinations were from what it considered safe union territory—so safe that all job categories, 100 percent of them, listed therein had rates set at the union scale—is that unions may have dominated those areas at some time in the distant past, and that no one has bothered to check, since.

But because DOL does not recheck or survey in "safe union territory," the actuality of all-union-rate determinations persists, and because they are updated to reflect the latest contract information, they are called "current." The union proportion of actual working population has been falling precipitously over time, and clearly, the longer determinations are reissued without re-survey of market conditions (even biased or skewed re-surveys), the longer such determinations retain the fiction that union job ownership and union wages dominate or prevail in the marketplace. In reality, there is not (and should not be) any "safe" union territory, whether protected by government action or by its inaction.

5. Arbitrary Divisions among Work Regimes

> No 16. Davis-Bacon's arbitrary divisions among regimes of construction work (residential, building, etc.) unjustly favor union rates and practices.

The regimes into which construction work is divided by DOL for ratemaking purposes are usually rendered as four (residential, building, heavy, and highway). These divisions are arbitrary, are not consistently followed, and fail to reflect better alternatives. Heavy and highway surveys, for example, are usually combined into single statewide units although the nature of the work is greatly different in them. This works to unions' advantage because essentially all highway work is done for public buyers so there are no private-market wage rates to leaven those already set at prevailing rates. These, for a number of commonly named job titles such as carpenter or electrician, tend to dominate the heavy regime unless there happens to have been a large-scale heavy project built in the survey area in the survey time period.[32] For these reasons, heavy and highway determinations tend to be 100-percent union with even greater frequency than determinations in the other two regimes.

The most troublesome regime, however, is the building regime, because the nature of the projects encompassed by it are so different from one another in scale and complexity—individual projects running from a few thousand dollars for school repair work to hundreds of millions for a stadium structure or an urban high-rise office complex. When the size of projects is not differentiated in building surveys, it is axiomatic that individual large-scale projects will dominate because of the number of workers involved.

As an example, consider a building rate survey for Montgomery County, Maryland, some of whose details are shown in Appendix Four (*q.v.*). In this building survey, one that compiled data from several hundred projects, a single $275-million project alone accounted for 21 percent of the total number of wage rates submitted. It was unilaterally responsible for setting the determination rate for 7 job categories out of the 33 total that were eventually published—for 3 of

[32] Having rates based on individual large-scale heavy projects creates problems of its own, because heavy projects, being rare, can almost never be built using local resources for workmen, and therefore almost never reflect actual local wage-rate practices. It might be said that no harm is done in setting prevailing rates based on alien (traveler) wages since it is such workers who would likely be working on the next heavy project in the area, but it does rather defeat the premise of having to have determined rates to protect local wages.

them exclusively. It completely overwhelmed data from any other projects in the survey.[33]

DOL also seems willing, on some occasions, to carve out areas for special survey, sometimes with respect to specialty projects such as water and sewer projects (a subspecialty in the heavy regime), and sometimes with respect to specialty job titles such as landscape laborers or weatherization workers. These are the subject of the next section.

6. Specialty Work and Worker Surveys

No 17. The Department of Labor's willingness to conduct special surveys of work or workers and issue determinations specifically for them unduly favors union wages and work practices.

Although some of DOL's surveys seem unnecessarily broad in their inclusion of projects within the various construction work domains, others are unnecessarily narrow, and seem to be that way deliberately to aid union wages and practices.

In Pennsylvania, for example, within the larger domain of "heavy and highway" work are found surveys limited to dredging projects (covering 73 job titles from messman to deep-sea diver), Heavy Sewer/Water Treating Plant construction in the eastern half of the state (listing 125 all-union rates, among them 12 different rates—differing by 50 percent in amount—for electricians in 12 separate geographic areas following lines of control of different electricians' locals), but no different rates for transmission line construction, interior-wiring electricians, or other categories of electricians differentiated by skill or job demands.

A second such determination covers the same type of plants in the western half of the state (listing 152 all-union rates, including 14

[33] To make matters worse, this was identified as a building survey, but the $275-milion project was for a "resource recovery facility" that probably should have been categorized as a heavy project.

bricklayer rates—of which 3 also embraced marble setters and stonemasons, 3 included only the additional stonemasons, and 1 that added marble, terrazzo and tile setters—8 different electricians' rates, three operating engineer rates—one for 7 levels, one for 8 levels, and one for 11 levels of work differentiation (again following local union boundaries), 10 ironworker-related variations, 23 classes of laborer rates, etc., without survey foundation.

Three more determinations were for heavy and highway rates separated by geography that together contained 233 different rate mandates, among them 2 truck-driver rates set to 4 decimal places each ($30.0225 and $29.7725), plus elaborate paid vacation and holiday benefits for 9 holidays not ordinarily covered (Thanksgiving, Christmas, and New Years Day are not among the 9). All such special carve-outs of heavy and highway rates tend overwhelmingly to have all union rates.[34]

A second type of specialty survey seems designed to establish union ownership of certain made-up job specialties that otherwise might have been included as common laborers' work. The DOL conducted a number of special surveys in the 1990s, especially around the Chicago area to establish prevailing rates for a category of worker that did not exist before, having to do with landscape labor. In addition to differentiating this work from that of common laborers (and getting a new category of work covered by the system—rather like painting, decorating, and carpet-laying had been added in 1935, but without the legislative authority) these surveys also tended to establish geographic boundaries within which the landscape laborers orga-

[34] One exception to this that I observed was also in Pennsylvania. An extremely limited subset of heavy and highway rates for "TV/Grout Sewer/Water Pipelines" was established for four nonunion sewer-cleaning jobs. It is based on a 20-year-old survey that is probably a testament to some nonunion contractor's pull with some Pennsylvania politician of that era. (Once determinations are made, they tend to stay on the books for long periods of time. In this case, being nonunion, they are not updated, and therefore are no trouble to maintain, and the number of jobs involved is probably too small to concern unions or anyone else.)

nized separately by teamsters, carpenters, and laborers would be the acknowledged job owners.

A similar establishment of new Davis-Bacon rate setting was for the categories of laborers designated to do weatherization work, a priority enterprise of the newly elected Obama administration after 2008. These were three specialty laborers whose job titles were invented for the purpose of having rates established for them, as there is no evidence of such job titles having surfaced at any prior time, and very little demand for having specialty prevailing rates for such workers. But the stimulus funds allocated for weatherization carried with them the need for the work to be done under prevailing rates.

Nevertheless, a nationwide survey was conducted and determinations were published for three weatherization job titles in every county in the country in 2009 and perhaps again in 2010.[35] It is hard for me to envision how this was done, since the only survey process published by DOL requires a minimum of three wage rates submitted from at least two different employers (or projects) in each of the 3,007 counties, plus various independent municipalities, parishes, and other denominators at this level, for workers having been paid for performing jobs that did not exist as a recognized category before that survey was conducted.

However these rates were established, they were issued for every county-level polity in the country. I reviewed the results for two selected states—Alabama because it is reliably nonunion, and Pennsylvania because it is my mixed-rate surrogate for the entire United States for Davis-Bacon determinations. Weatherization determinations published for both 2009 and 2010 (as of late 2011 there was no update for that year) for Alabama, shows small variations from year to year. Since these are all nonunion rates, they must have been the result of putatively different surveys, because there is no mechanism by which DOL can adjust nonunion rates without establishing them

35 I have not been able to ascertain how much of DOL's total survey budget was devoted to this task, but my guess is that it used up at least the lion's share, postponing yet further the possibility of routine updating of county surveys for ordinary work.

again by another survey.[36] In 2010, the weatherization workers' rate (for which the closest approximation is common laborer) averaged around $10.50 for all counties, compared with $7.74 for the cognate class; the door and window replacement workers' rate averaged $19.67, compared with the Alabama carpenters' rate of $11.18, and the weather HVAC mechanic (sheet metal worker) rate averaged around $30.00, compared to its cognate's $12.16. Thus, all weatherization rates exceeded those of their cognates by something on the order of 70 to 75 percent.[37]

Pennsylvania, being a state with a more complex labor market, has a set of weatherization determinations that is also more complex, but that follows no discernible pattern. Nevertheless, both union and nonunion weatherization rates tend to be somewhat higher than for their likely cognates,[38] some of them remarkably so. Sullivan, Sus-

---

[36] There is one trivial exception. DOL has taken to updating ancient nonunion determinations whose published rates are below the current level of minimum wage to reflect the current minimum wage. This is both a trivial and an unnecessary change (the prevailing rate is a minimum, and if the statutory minimum is higher the statutory minimum takes precedence over the determination minimum in the same way that union contract rates take precedence in union construction over lower determination wages). The updating is probably performed to make the ancient surveys upon which they are so often based seem less outdated. This exception had no part in any of the updates or changes between the two survey years in the determinations I examined, if for no other reason than because the statutory minimum wage did not change in that time period.

[37] I did not seek access to the DOL WD-10 and WD-22a survey forms to see where the weatherization rates were derived from, but I think that would make an interesting exercise. All of these rates (for Alabama) are published as though based entirely on nonunion survey submissions, since no fringe benefit amounts are included, as would have been the case if the surveys were compounded from both union and nonunion rate entries. But no one would have been able to make such submissions, since the job title did not exist, before.

[38] The cognates chosen here were selected as being my best guess as to what corresponded to the three weatherization job titles, as no guidance was available for selecting otherwise. My guesses were: laborer for "Weatheriza-

quehanna, and Tioga counties, for example, found what are said to be not-union weatherization rates that were $12, $13, and $21 per hour higher than their respective cognates. Berks, Mifflin, Juniata, Snyder, Union, and Montour counties, all of which have minimum-wage laborer rates based on a 19-year-old survey, now have weatherization worker minimum rates almost 4 times as high—over $25 per hour.

In all counties, weatherization worker rates range from around $23 up to over $43 per hour; door and window weatherizers had rates ranging from around $22 up to $92 *(sic)* per hour, and weather HVAC workers from around $18 to over $62 per hour.[39] These are pretty fancy rates for jobs requiring, in general, minimal levels of skill. The $92 per hour rate in Philadelphia County puts the door and window replacement and weatherization workers in this county among the sainted top-1% of construction workers across the state, and probably the nation.

These extraordinary minimum wage amounts did not even come about because of direct union demand or from union contracts. (No union contracts I have reviewed as of late 2011 mention weatherization workers, or contemplate fringe benefits of over $50 per hour for any class of workers.) But they certainly reflect or protect high union wage practices, and do so with considerable apparent help from DOL.[40]

---

tion Workers," carpenter for "Doors and Windows Replacement and Weatherization Workers," and sheet metal worker for "HVAC/Furnace/Heating & Cooling Mechanic."

[39] Some of these amounts are stratospheric because of what can only be described as runaway fringe benefit amounts: $19.49, $56.60, and $38.86, respectively for the three classes in Philadelphia County, $10.93, $19.21, and $28.93 in rural Wyoming County. These are much higher fringe benefit amounts than exist in any union contracts in Pennsylvania, and their origin is a mystery. Their only possible source is some frenzied imagination from within the DOL.

[40] They may also ensure that no weatherization work, as such, actually gets done in places like Philadelphia, with its $34.92, $71.83, and $92.19 hourly rates for this low-class work.

Chapter IV: The Helper Experiment

Department of Labor treatment of helper, learner, and semi-skilled rates in surveys shows massive evidence of undue bias toward union rates and ways. Particularly in its handling of helper rates, the DOL's actions in both survey processing and wage determinations have been so egregiously pro-union that, in my opinion, they could only be corrected through nullification, that is, through repeal of the Davis-Bacon Act in its entirety. DOL had the opportunity to provide some level of accommodation to the nonunion alternative approach to job identification and pay and skill administration, but spurned it. Instead, it fought vigorously over a twenty-year period to preserve its biases towards union rates and practices. Undoubtedly it would do so again if offered any compromise short of repeal.

The entire discussion of what came to be known as the Helper Controversy is too lengthy to be included here, but I have put forth a fairly complete analysis in Appendix Three.[1] A number of specific reasons for repeal of Davis-Bacon arising from this controversy will be set out baldly below with a minimum of discussion, but they are repeated and amplified in the Appendix, which should be consulted for explanations or questions.

1. THE HELPER RATE CONTROVERSY

A. DOL MINDSET

> No. 18. The Department of Labor's victorious 20-year struggle to quash modest reforms setting wage rates for construction helpers, even in constrained circumstances and defined settings, shows undue bias towards union wages and work patterns.

[1] More complete discussion can be found in Northrup, Thieblot, and Baskin (2008), *Construction Union Tactics*, Ch. 7, and in Thieblot (1999), "Helper Regulations."

In 1982, Congress passed a modest reform to Davis-Bacon rate determination practices, calling for allowing rates to be set for the class of semi-skilled workers called helpers (who make up almost 10 percent of the total construction workforce), in defined circumstances with respect to their scope of work and in limited numbers with respect to the number of journeymen employed. Over the next 20 years, pro-labor courts, Congress, and the DOL struggled until DOL ended the matter by issuing a final rule denying the possibility, in 2002.

The new regulations had been proposed in 1982, but had been blocked from being implemented until the end of January 1992. Then, for the following 21 months, until November 1993, they were at least theoretically in effect. During this period, DOL conducted a small number of surveys (78). Many of these were deeply flawed with respect to helpers, but they did include at least the possibility of determining prevailing wages for them. Thereafter, the proposed new regulations were either re-suspended or unimplemented until DOL formally rejected them all at the end of 1996 and codified its decision in its Final Regulation on the matter, November 22, 2000.

The helper controversy was over, and the unions had won: no prevailing rates would henceforth be issued for nonunion helpers other than those that had an established union counterpart (*e.g.*, elevator constructor helpers). The flawed case presented by the DOL as to why the revised regulations should not have been implemented depended on several assertions. First was that helper rates had been adequately tested and found wanting in those surveys it conducted during the short period of time between suspensions of the proposed new regulations.

DOL also asserted that helper rates were difficult to compile, difficult to identify for job content, and difficult to administer. It further asserted that helpers were not found with sufficient frequency to merit determinations and that even if they had been, establishing rates for them would not have affected construction patterns or costs. And finally, it asserted that issuing rates for helpers would have opened the door to contractor manipulation of the system, required costly additional enforcement mechanisms, and detracted from the apprenticeship system. These items will be treated in turn. A number of other lessons learned from review of the wage surveys and determinations that occurred during the 21-month period of non-suspension are also evaluated. See the expanded discussion in Appendix Three for all of the following boxed headlines at their corresponding headlines there.

B. TEST PERIOD ADEQUACY.

> No. 19. The Department of Labor's assertion that the viability of helper rates was adequately tested by the 78 surveys during the period of non-suspension is clear evidence of bias towards union rates and work methods.

DOL claimed it performed 78 wage surveys during the period of non-suspension, and that these provided an adequate test of whether prevailing rates could be issued for helpers. The number of actual, independent, ordinary surveys performed then was considerably smaller (58 or fewer) but even at the claimed number of 78, this was about 90 times fewer than would be needed for a comprehensive test. Furthermore, it was not a test designed to find out anything new about helper use or rates: it was not a structured test related to the new regulations, and it did not seek out nonunion input concerning helper use. It was neither comprehensive nor proactive. (In contrast, the weatherization surveys performed after 2008 were both. Those were able to find or prescribe three levels of previously unknown weatherization worker rates for each of all 3,007 counties in the country despite the previous rarity and lack of differentiable job content for such jobs.)

DOL's effort during the period of non-suspension was an insufficient test of helper use or the consequences, if any, of finding prevailing rates for helpers. In pretending that it was, DOL was simply advancing an excuse for continuing to implement prevailing rates in ways more acceptable to unions, and for continuing to ignore developments in nonunion construction patterns and techniques.

C. COMPILING RATES FOR HELPERS AND SEMI-SKILLED CONSTRUCTION WORKERS

> No. 20. The Department of Labor's assertion that helper rates were difficult to compile is clear evidence of bias towards union rates and work methods.

DOL's claim of special difficulty in compiling survey rates for helpers can charitably be described as bogus. Not only have certain union helper rates—notably those for elevator constructor helpers—been routinely accepted in surveys and routinely found to be prevailing, but also helper rates of all sorts have been offered in surveys and sometimes accepted. There is nothing special in this, nothing magic. There is also nothing that differentiates helper rates submitted to surveys from rates for other jobs or categories of workers.

In the 78 surveys that took place during the period of non-suspension, rates were offered to the surveys for 47 different types of helper, tender (the union equivalent), or trainee construction workers. These were handled differently in many cases (see discussions below) but with no greater difficulty than any other of the 220 job title variations found among the residential and building surveys alone. (Heavy and highway surveys, which list hundreds of additional job titles mostly having to do with specific pieces of equipment operated, were excluded, but rates have been routinely found for selections of these, as well.)

Some of the job titles that DOL accepted into the surveys were Bidwell Operator, Broom Operator, Carpenters Including Carpenters Excluding Acoustic Ceiling Mechanics, Carpenter Insulation & Forms Also, Concrete Flatwork, Electric – Low Voltage Also, Elevator Constructor 70%, Insulator Batt & Blown, and Laborer Landscaping Only. If there is any possible logic that separates accepting rates into surveys for Shingler Helper from those for Shingler, or Sheet Metal Duct & Set Unit from Sheet Metal Duct & Set Unit Helper, it is well disguised.

Clearly, the DOL's claim of special difficulty in surveying for helper rates is no more than a ruse to deny that such jobs exist in profusion in construction, but if rates were set for them they would be set at nonunion levels because, with a few exceptions (elevator helpers, again) they relate to nonunion work or are found there in far greater profusion. Such rates set with reference to merit shop (nonunion) wages might allow nonunion contractors to continue to enjoy paying approximately the same wage rates to these categories of workers on publically financed jobs that they paid the same workers on private jobs. DOL apparently finds that idea repugnant.

D. DETERMINING JOB CONTENT OF HELPERS AND SEMI-SKILLED CONSTRUCTION WORKERS

> No. 21. The Department of Labor's assertion that helper rates were difficult to identify for job content is clear evidence of bias towards union rates and work methods.

What is the job content associated with the job title of Carpenter's Helper? Undoubtedly it varies considerably from situation to situation, is different in different levels of construction, and depends on the demands of the particular carpenters that the helpers assist. But similar variation is associated with all jobs in construction, because each construction project is unique and requires different inputs even from commonly named workers. What is the job content, to choose a random example from those included in the surveys noted above, of an Electric – Low Voltage Also electrician, or of a Carpenter Including Carpenters Excluding Acoustic Ceiling Mechanic? Both of these were not only included among those submitted to the surveys but they were found to be prevailing in at least one determination. If DOL can accept whatever job content variation is encompassed by these last two and find the job rates to be prevailing, surely it should have no greater difficulty in accepting the job content variation that might be found among Drywall Finisher Helpers or Garage Door Helpers.

Furthermore, it is definitively not the job of the DOL to determine and adjudicate the worthiness of job title designations or to vet the content of construction jobs. Their job is not even to determine what the local practices are—simply what rates of pay are to be protected. But DOL has apparently decided instead that its job is to determine and protect only the local union practices.

E. ISSUING WAGE RATES FOR HELPERS AND SEMI-SKILLED CONSTRUCTION WORKERS

> No. 22. The Department of Labor's assertion that helper rates were difficult to administer is clear evidence of bias towards union rates and work methods.

Just as DOL has no mandate to establish job content beyond identifying what prevails in a locality, it has no mandate to establish "ownership" of various pieces of construction work by one trade or another, or to impose union systems of job delimitation on nonunion contractors. Therefore post-determination administration should be no more difficult for helpers than for anyone else. In the determinations associated with the 78 surveys made during the period of non-suspension, a total of 343 different job descriptions were found to be prevailing and to have rates issued for them. A few of these were for helpers but most were not. The only post-determination administration required is ensuring that the persons performing those jobs are paid the rates prescribed for them. That some persons might be doing work that in other circumstances might be performed by other persons with different job titles and paid a different amount is a distinct possibility, but hardly unique to helpers.

Consider, for example, these two job titles found to be prevailing at the union rate: 1) Concrete Laborers (power buggy concrete saws, pumpcrete nozleman vibratorman); and 2) Concrete Laborer (curb and gutter, chute handler, grouting, curing, screeding). The holders of these two sets of job titles receive very slightly different prevailing rate coverage in their determination. Should it be up to the DOL to evaluate if a laborer in one or the other of these categories should rather have been assigned instead to be a Concrete Chipper, a Concrete Core Cutter, a Concrete Curer, a Concrete Finisher Tender, a Concrete Forms Cleaning and Handing, a Concrete Grinder and Sander, a Concrete Laborer (belt, pipe and/or hoseman), a Concrete Mixer, a Concrete Puddler, a Concrete Sawyer (hand guided), a Concrete Sealer, a Concrete Shute Handler—all of which exist in the determinations—or simply a Concrete Laborer, a Cement Mason Tender, a Mason Tender or even a Laborer or a Cement Mason, all of which titles also exist? These and similar possibilities abound, yet DOL exhibits no concern over administration of the fine differentiations of wage rates for sometimes as many as 11 different categories of laborers in a single determination to see if the persons receiving the rates are performing those particular jobs or if the jobs they are doing could also be done under some different job title paid at a different rate. To not cavil at these job contents but to worry over job content of nonunion helpers is evidence of how far DOL will go to protect and administer union practices, but only union practices.

F. SIZE OF THE HELPER CLASS OVERLOOKED BY PREVAILING RATE DETERMINATIONS

No. 23. The Department of Labor's assertion that helpers are not a sufficient construction class is clear evidence of bias towards union rates and work methods.

Unlike some of the job titles found in surveys and determinations (*e.g.*, Steam Point or Water Jet Operator, Tool Dispatcher or Checker, or "Work pertaining to or in connection with Repair of Stove, Blast Furnace, Basic Oxygen Process Furnace, Steeple & Stack, Annealing Process Furnace, Kiln, Soaking Pit, Coke Battery on Industrial Work"), the nonunion helper job title in construction is not rare. But whereas rare or uncommon union titles were all found in almost all prevailing wage determinations during the period of non-suspension, the titles of Bricklayer's Helper, Carpenter Helper, Cement Mason Helper, Drywall Finisher Helper, Electrician Helper, and Plumber Helper (among others) were not.

By BLS estimates in the Current Population Survey of 1995, about the time of the helper controversy, there were 3.1 million wage-earning journeymen, laborers, and apprentices in the construction industry, and 940,000 helpers. Thus, helpers constituted 23 percent of the total wage earners in the industry—a not-insignificant number. The fact that DOL found helpers of any sort to be a prevailing category in fewer than 3 percent of the determinations it issued during the period of non-suspension is therefore in and of itself an indictment of how DOL conducted the surveys and made the wage determinations during this period.

The next section examines the record of DOL's handling of surveys and determinations during the period of non-suspension and provides the most-likely explanation as to why the DOL was unable to establish prevailing rates for helpers.

2. SUMMARY OF DOL'S HANDLING OF HELPER AND HELPER-LIKE RATES

The result of what proportion of helper and helper-like job titles were found follows a consistent pattern. Of the generally nonunion helpers named as such, only 20 of their rates were found prevailing in at least one determination, a success ratio of 37 percent; semi-skilled workers who might have been doing helper work but whose union status was not known had 44 percent of their rate submissions found prevailing; helper-like laborers whose affiliation with unions was unknown but who were most likely union members had 51 percent of their rate submissions found to be prevailing; and finally, the almost exclusively union helper-equivalent tenders enjoyed a success ratio of 73 percent of their rate submissions.

These variations cannot be explained by any consistent application of statistical decision-making, and it is difficult to avoid the conclusion that they came about through deliberate or unintended bias on the part of DOL administrators towards union wages and work patterns.

This ends the section of lessons from DOL's handling of the helper crisis per se, the details of which are laid out in Appendix Three. In the next section, I shall now take up the broader questions surrounding the mechanics of wage surveys, to be followed by the mechanics of creating determinations, and the process of distributing and updating them.

3. DOL'S QUESTIONABLE IMPLEMENTATION OF HELPER USE IN SURVEYS DURING THE PERIOD OF NON-SUSPENSION

Evidence from the surveys done during this period of non-suspension raises the question of whether DOL wage specialists may have been applying different and more stringent standards in selecting categories of helpers to have prevailing rates set for them than in selecting other categories of construction workers doing work of similar nature and skill requirement but having different job titles (namely, union ones rather than nonunion ones).

An evaluation of how DOL reacted to and handled survey data on various job titles is enlightening. Persons called helpers had demonstrably different (lower) success ratios in having their job titles recognized and prevailing wages issued for them. Persons doing similar kinds of helper-like semi-skilled work and persons doing similar kinds of helper-like laborer work, both carrying titles more closely associated with union than nonunion characterizations, met with different (higher) levels of success. And so did union tenders in comparison to nonunion helpers (also higher).

Furthermore, helpers as such, semi-skilled operators performing helper-like functions, laborers performing helper-like functions, and tenders performing the same functions as laborers all appeared to be treated differently in the surveys, depending on their perceived union status. The WD-22a forms recorded the number of individual workers' rates submitted in response to the survey request and the number of different construction projects they were drawn from. Although DOL had no hard-and-fast rules for how many rates from how many projects would be enough to form the basis for a prevailing rate,[2] one might expect a direct relationship between larger numbers of rates and projects producing a higher probability of a prevailing rate being found. But this was not found to be true for any of the four categories.

A. SUCCESS RATIOS BY JOB TITLE: HELPERS NAMED AS SUCH

> No 24. The Department of Labor's disproportionate rejection of helper rates in surveys is clear evidence of bias towards union rates and work methods.

The helper category, as such, had 320 survey rates submitted for 55 job titles (inclusive of the two elevator helper titles that are traditionally union) in the 78 surveys during the period of non-suspension. Each one of the separate helper job titles had between 1 and 69 rates submitted. Sometimes, based on those numbers of rates, a prevailing rate was determined, and sometimes one was rejected.

Excusive of the union elevator helper category, 53 instances occurred where the rate was found to be prevailing (regardless of how many survey submissions there were even if there was only one), whereas 148 rates were rejected despite at least 3 survey rates being

[2] The usual minimum is three rates from at least two employers, but the minimum seems to be flexibly applied.

submitted. Thus, for helpers, the success ratio was only slightly higher than 26 percent. Some were rejected despite being supported by 20, 30, 40, or even up to 84 rate submissions, without explanation. From this it is fair to conclude that nonunion helper rates were disproportionately rejected, even when well supported by the data.

B. SUCCESS RATIOS BY JOB TITLE: SEMI-SKILLED WORKERS

> No 25. The Department of Labor's higher acceptance of semi-skilled rates in surveys where union orientation is not known, than of helper rates where it is known to be nonunion, is clear evidence of bias towards union rates and work methods.

The category of semi-skilled helper-like journeymen or specialty craftsmen had 116 survey rates submitted for 32 job titles, most of which can't be readily identified as deriving from union or from nonunion naming practices. In accepting or rejecting these rates as prevailing, DOL was considerably more open to accepting them than it was to accepting rates associated with helper titles that are known to be more frequently used in nonunion work. The success ratio of (mostly nonunion) helper titles was 26 percent; the success ratio of (mostly unknown affiliation) semi-skilled titles was much higher, 44 percent.

C. SUCCESS RATIOS BY JOB TITLE: HELPER-LIKE LABORERS

> No 26. The Department of Labor's disproportionate acceptance of union helper-like laborer helper rates in surveys is clear evidence of bias towards union rates and work methods.

A similar pattern emerges for categories of workers who might be called "hidden helpers." These are categories used mostly by union contractors for specialized laborers who, like tenders, have as the principal duties the support of either trade journeymen or more skilled laborers, but who are not always called laborers. In nonunion work, it is much more likely that these individuals would be called either helpers to the related trade journeymen or simply laborers, although some of the rates submitted for this group may have been for nonunion workmen. This group of what amount to mostly union helper-like laborers has a much higher success ratio than either the nonunion helpers or the mixed semi-skilled workers—about 50 percent.

D. SUCCESS RATIOS BY JOB TITLE: UNION HELPERS CALLED TENDERS

> No. 27. The Department of Labor's disproportionate acceptance of union tender rates in surveys is clear evidence of bias towards union rates and work methods.

The series is completed by examining what happened to the acceptance or rejection of rates for the category of workers who were called tenders. A tender (e.g., a carpenter tender) in union work is the exact equivalent of a helper in nonunion work, and just as few helpers named as such are used in union construction, few tenders named as such are used in nonunion construction.

Rates submitted to the surveys during the period of non-suspension for this category were not as prevalent as rates for the other categories already examined, but they achieved a very high level of success: of the 33 titles submitted and supported by at least 3 submissions, 24 were accepted as prevailing and only 9 were rejected. The success ratio of these (union) tenders named as such was therefore 73 percent—more than 2-1/2 times higher on the same criteria than the success for (nonunion) helpers named as such.

E. UNINTENDED CONSEQUENCES OF ISSUING RATES FOR HELPERS WITH RESPECT TO EMPLOYER MANIPULATION OF JOB ASSIGNMENTS

> No. 28. The Department of Labor's assertion that helper designations in prevailing rate determinations would lead to contractor manipulation of job assignments is a red herring and a false basis for public policy.

Prevailing wage administration is no harder when helper rates are in effect than when they are not. If unscrupulous contractors, given the availability of helper rates, might misuse them by paying for work that otherwise might be done by laborers or journeymen at higher rates, there is no identifiable prevailing wage issue, provided that paying such wages on private work in the area is also the prevailing practice. The same is true with respect to contractor use of persons with various other job titles.

DOL had expressed concern that unscrupulous contractors, given the availability of helper rates, might misuse them, presumably by paying workers whose work might also be done by laborers at rates other than laborers' or by paying workers doing semi-skilled trade work at rates other than the journeymen's rates for that trade. But DOL only expresses this concern with respect to helpers. DOL may not want to spend its time evaluating the job content of helper work, admittedly difficult to do, but there is nothing in Davis-Bacon administration that compels it to do so, nor anything that makes doing it for helpers any different from doing it for the other jobs found in surveys and determinations. In fact, DOL has no mandate to establish job content at all, beyond identifying what prevails in a locality. Nor does it have any mandate to establish "ownership" of various pieces of construction work by one trade over another, or to impose union systems of job delimitation on nonunion contractors. Therefore post-determination administration should be left to the concerned parties, and be no different for helpers than anyone else.

F. POSSIBLE UNINTENDED CONSEQUENCES OF ISSUING RATES FOR HELPERS WITH RESPECT TO ENFORCEMENT PROBLEMS

> No. 29. The Department of Labor's assertion that helper designations in prevailing rate determinations would cause special enforcement problems is another red herring and a false underpinning of public policy.

The enforcement issue is closely related to the contractor malfeasance one and yields to the same counterpoint. The DOL assertion is false, with no basis in fact. DOL has no duty to enforce the use of one category of workman over another or even a lawful right to do so. Its mission is to ensure payment of wage rates specified in determinations, so if the determinations list a rate for carpenter's helper at a certain sum, its enforcement duties stop at making sure that sum is dispensed by employers to carpenter's helpers, in exactly the same way as it would if the determinations listed a rate for "elevator mechanic, probational 70%."

It is true that some variations of the originally proposed helper regulation had maximum ratios of helpers to journeymen, added in deference to union rules limiting the number of apprentices to journeymen in many trades, but it was only after these proposals were removed that DOL voiced its objections based on enforcement difficulties. The original proposal would, indeed, have been difficult to administer, but also none of DOL's business.

G. IMPACT OF HELPER RATES ON APPRENTICES

> No. 30. The Department of Labor's assertion that helper designations in prevailing wage determinations would adversely affect apprenticeship programs demonstrates clear bias towards union rates and work methods.

During the helper controversy, DOL expressed concern that were they to approve rates for nonunion helpers, the apprenticeship system, the traditional formal training system of the industry, might be harmed in some way. The mechanism by which this might occur was not elaborated, and why DOL felt it was a proper concern for prevailing wage rates was not explained, but the fear was misplaced in any event. Revised helper rules might have allowed more semi-skilled, informal, on-the-job training to take place in both union and nonunion construction, and therefore might have encouraged rather than discouraged upward mobility.

In union work, laborers and even semi-skilled tenders and helper-like journeymen have dead-end jobs and are not permitted to aspire to full trade journeyman status. But helpers in nonunion work who use the tools of the trade under supervision of a journeyman can aspire to elevating themselves in the same way that persons in almost all other skilled fields elevate themselves—by accumulating enough on-the-job training and wisdom to advance. Rather than bemoan the potential negative impact on apprenticeship programs, unions should have welcomed the possible new ways to increase the number of journeymen.

The premise that helpers (or tenders, or other semi-skilled workers, regardless of their job titles) may never rise to journeyman levels is demonstrably false, even in union work. Although estimates vary somewhat, it is generally agreed that no more than one-third to one-half of the journeymen in the bigger construction trades (carpentry, electrical work, plumbing) achieved their status by completing formal apprenticeship programs, and the proportions rising that way in many of the smaller trades (ironwork, glazing) is even smaller. Those who achieved journeyman status by other means did so through military experience, on-the-job training, or self-instruction. Thus at least a measurable proportion of helpers and semi-skilled workers can be expected to move up, and the existence of helper categories facilitates this.

As it stands today, and stood in the early 1990s when the helper controversy was active, there are insufficient apprentices in the structured system to satisfy the future needs for journeymen even in the union segment where approved apprenticeship programs are more readily available, and certainly not enough to satisfy identifiable need for the industry as a whole. Formal apprenticeships are an anachronism of the guild system, and although they continue to exist not only in construction but also in many other industries, they are of vestigial interest everywhere but in construction. In construction, their continued reliance impedes industry advancement by giving too many participants too much of a vested interest in old technologies.[3]

4. Summary of the Helper Controversy

DOL's failure to find helper rates prevailing during the period of non-suspension had more to do with what type of surveys it conducted, where it conducted them, and how it interpreted the results

[3] *See* Northrup, Thieblot, and Baskin (2008), *Construction Union Tactics*, Ch. 7, for a complete discussion of the complex apprenticeship problem.

than with how many persons actually worked in the construction area as helpers. The few surveys that were done in nonunion areas, like western Virginia, Florida, Texas, parts of Maryland, or Tennessee, found a great deal (proportionately) of helper use. Not surprisingly, highly union areas, like New York, New Jersey, Massachusetts, or Wisconsin, found little.

If DOL had actually been interested in finding out the degree to which helper categories were (and still are) used in nonunion construction so as to form a better estimate of how they might impact Davis-Bacon determinations in the future, it had four options: 1) It could have continued to conduct surveys until the entire country was covered. Since the entire country has never been surveyed for Davis-Bacon purposes in its 70-year history, however, that probably was never a viable option. 2) It could have conducted the surveys it does do in a more balanced fashion, including more sun-belt and fewer rust-belt areas, especially since the sun belt is where most construction activity takes place. 3) It could have done specially focused surveys in depth (with follow-up phone calls, etc.) in selected areas in the same way it did surveys for landscape concerns. 4) It could have interpreted helper job titles and helper rates in the same way it interpreted titles and rates for tenders and various gradations of laborers and semi-skilled workmen that it administers on behalf of unions.

But DOL did none of those things. Instead, it made every possible choice and took every possible option that favored union wages and practices and obfuscated its choices with a series of bogus arguments to justify what it did. So today, despite an ever-growing coterie of helpers (and helper-equivalents in union work), its prevailing wage administrators continue to pretend that Davis-Bacon reflects local practice by ignoring them.

Chapter V: Mechanics of Wage Surveys

The wage survey is the first step in the establishment of new wage determinations for any given area. Its purpose is to identify existing wage and employment patterns on various levels of private work in local (county) areas that the Davis-Bacon law is designed to protect. Presumably, such surveys are done frequently enough for determinations to remain current and use contractors' payroll records or other verifiable sources of information for rates actually paid to each employee or class of employees employed. How should such surveys be carried out, and how frequently should they be done?

The Department of Labor does not follow a competent survey design to either establish the universe of similar construction projects and their contractors (perhaps from building permits), the universe of local contractors and their projects (perhaps from yellow pages), or the universe of construction employees (perhaps from workers' compensation filings). Nor does it attempt to use structured or random sampling techniques.

Instead, DOL conducts surveys in a haphazard manner that consists partially of reaching out to contact contractors on selected earlier jobs in the locality of the survey to solicit their voluntary response to its data request, and partially of accepting voluntary submission of wage rates from any interested participant, including non-employers. All of these elements—how the reach-out is performed, how responses are solicited, and how voluntary data submissions are handled—are deeply flawed in ways that should not be countenanced, especially in surveys whose outcomes may be used for many years into the future, possibly even for generations, without review.

1. Survey Mechanics

A. Rate Gathering

No. 31. The DOL's use of Dodge Reports as the primary data collection device is a flawed alternative to a random or properly structured sample of work previously done in a locality, and unfairly favors union rates and practices.

What the DOL uses in reaching out to solicit wage payment information is a listing of projects followed by a private data-gathering organization and published as the Dodge Reports. Dodge does many things well, but of greatest relevance here is that it provides a networking service that lists construction projects by construction domain (residential, public, transportation, etc.), by the county where the construction took place or was initiated, by the winning bid or contract cost, and by the dates of expected completion, among other things; it is a huge database and a wonderful historical reference report. What its data have in common is that they pertain to large projects subject to competitive bidding—projects typically worth hundreds-of-thousands or millions of dollars or more.

The use of these large-scale projects as the basis for prevailing wage surveys ignores the small jobs where a large number of workers, perhaps even a majority of nonunion ones, may be employed in the local labor market area.[1] The wage rates that Davis-Bacon is supposed to protect, however, are those paid to all laborers and mechanics in the locality, who form a much larger cohort. Davis-Bacon does not overlook small projects. It covers even tiny contracts over $2,000. Therefore, the selection of prevailing rates from only large projects while ignoring small ones fails to be drawn from the same universe of projects to which its rates will be applied. In the process, it discriminates against the nonunion domain that continues to have much more representation in smaller projects than the union sector does.

[1] As already discussed in a previous section, project surveys are identified only by construction domain (residential, building, etc.), and no differentiation is made with respect to the scale of a project within the boundaries of that differentiation. Thus one $10-million housing complex performed once in a county might well set the wage rates for future $50,000 residential projects for many years into the future.

B. RELYING ON VOLUNTARY RESPONSES

No. 32. The DOL's use of voluntary response to its elaborate data requests is a flawed alternative to a proper data collection method, and unfairly favors union rates and practices.

In its survey process, DOL solicits information by mail about wage rates and fringe benefit information from contractors identified from the Dodge Reports, but it cannot compel response. (Nor should it be able to.) Contractors who are not interested in competing for Davis-Bacon work have no incentive at all to provide wage information and some motivation not to participate.[2] These contractors are overwhelmingly in the nonunion sector. Union contractors, on the other hand, have every incentive to participate in surveys that provide them a means to decrease their union premium by raising their nonunion competitors' costs.

Wage specialists do little if any outreach. The jobs for which wage information would be most readily available is that for earlier Davis-Bacon projects, because of the weekly wage reports required on such projects, but these projects are specifically excluded from being considered except when they might be needed to cover data insufficiencies. Therefore, such outreach as is performed must be done the hard way, by contacting individual contractors' administrators to cajole them into submitting wage data.

The net result is that most survey wage data is voluntarily submitted by employers. It is overwhelmingly submitted by just two classes: nonunion employers who might want to break into government contracting or have some other specific motivation to participate, and union contractors who want to impose their high wage rates

[2] Motivations to not participate include such items as the possible risk of sanctions arising from even innocent but erroneous rate submissions, and the possibility of the firm coming to the notice of union organizers, among others.

on nonunion competitors so as to remain competitive in future bidding.[3] As the second group is far larger than the first, additional bias is created towards union rates (and away from the market rates of smaller, nonunion contractors). It also means that even in large states or counties with many active contractors and building projects, the rate determination process will be based on very few actual wage returns in a survey. The DOL has therefore adopted the policy of accepting wage data directly from union and nonunion contractors associations, union business agents, and perhaps other non-employers to increase the size of the survey base.

C. *WAGE DATA ACCEPTANCES FROM NON-EMPLOYERS*

No. 33. The DOL's use of rates voluntarily submitted by non-employers is biased and flawed. It unfairly favors union rates and practices.

The motivational problem for non-employers is no less intense than it is for employers. Nonunion contractors associations such as Associated Builders and Contractors are undoubtedly motivated to solicit and submit wage data of behalf of nonunion contractors in surveys (and sometimes they lobby vigorously to have surveys performed in areas where their members are active—as was the case in the six-county Pennsylvania survey soon to be discussed) but only their members who might be interested in working on Davis-Bacon projects will be motivated to submit wage data. Submitting data involves some risk if erroneous submissions might be made, it takes a lot of accounting time and effort to accomplish, and it would be of no direct benefit to most nonunion contractors—those uninterested in working on government projects.

On the union side, both union contractor associations and unions, themselves are very highly motivated as are their members, if for no

[3] In some parts of the country that are heavily nonunion, such as the deep South, nonunion contractors who already do prevailing wage work might also be motivated to submit wage rates in order to preserve their nonunion status. In most such areas, however, surveys are rare events.

other reason than that Davis-Bacon and other public work makes up such a large proportion of what they do. (Union contractors' work in the present day is almost exclusively limited to publicly supported projects and the much smaller number of projects in what was called the affinity sector, described above in Chapter I.) The net result, again, is bias towards the submission (and therefore the eventual acceptance) of union rates in surveys; it also results in surveys that are based on only partial information about actual local labor markets.

D. REJECTION OF SUBMISSIONS FROM SMALL FIRMS

> No 34. The rejection of wage submissions from small employers (5 or fewer workers) unfairly favors union rates and practices.

DOL's official position on minimum contractor size to be surveyed for rates is that no rates will be accepted from contractors who have fewer than 5 employees. This leaves out an increasingly large portion of the industry, especially in the residential sector. If seeking wage submissions for large employers biases the results towards union rates and practices, disregarding them from small employers biases them against nonunion rates and practices.

Independent contractors are common in all forms of construction for detail work where an increasing number of entrepreneurs specialize in some construction sub-specialty or other, especially in residential work. Crews of wall-boarders, concrete stampers, smoke-alarm fitters, etc. go from job to job doing small, specialized tasks using customized techniques and efficient equipment. Only a few of these are independent entrepreneurs: most have a few associates, as well as laborers or helpers to back them up. All this increasingly large coterie of construction workers is excluded from the prevailing wage survey process. The smallest firms are also those most likely to be nonunion, so surveys excluding them are biased away from nonunion wages and practices.[4]

---

[4] There is much evidence in the raw survey data reported on forms WD-22a that a similar prohibition of small workforces (as distinct from small

E. ACCEPTANCE OF SUBMISSIONS FROM SUSPECT SOURCES

No 35. The acceptance of wage submissions from suspect sources providing duplicative information biases surveys towards an apparent uniformity that typically favors union rates and practices.

DOL accepts wage data from many suspect sources. An example is shown in Appendix Four. This is a list of suspect project data accepted in a Montgomery County, Maryland survey conducted in 1994.[5] Data accepted included that from, among other suspect sources: a $30,000 project said to have employed 50 electricians and 5 other workers in its peak week; a project said to have employed both 68 structural ironworkers and 68 ornamental ironworkers at identical rates, tallied separately; three successively numbered projects each employing the same work crew of about 20 carpenters, 2 laborers, 3 carpet layers, and 4 resilient floor layers all tallied separately for each project; and a $275 million project that dominated the survey and established the determination rates for several different categories of workmen.[6]

---

employers) does not exist. Many individual projects in surveys show total employment in what is supposed to be the project peak week of very few workmen, sometimes only a single worker. These undoubtedly are based on data supplied by non-employers or possibly by employers sending out small crews to work on a succession of projects. These cases also distort the final wage determinations, but in different ways that will start to be discussed in the next section.

[5] This was previously reported in Thieblot (1997), *Fraud*. The wage rates were much less then, but otherwise, despite the 1990s date, there are no significant differences. The other information is similar to that I have seen in many other compilations of Davis-Bacon survey reports, before or since.

[6] These were not the only suspect submissions. At the opposite end of the spectrum was a $900,000 project whose only listed worker for the peak week was a single laborer. But these were representative of the ones that tended to set wage rates.

These projects represented submissions whose acceptance loaded the count of "identical wages to the penny" for various job categories in possibly erroneous or duplicative ways, but that were unquestioned by the DOL wage specialists. I have found similar examples in every survey compilation I have examined.

2. DOL's Manipulative Mechanics in Surveys, Illustrated by the 2002 Pittsburgh-area Residential Construction Survey

I would like now to begin consideration of details of the previously introduced 6-county residential and building surveys in the Pittsburgh area of Pennsylvania in 2002 and use them to illustrate the degree to which DOL is apparently willing to manipulate wage data, survey submissions, survey compilations, and rate selection from surveys in an apparent effort to aid or favor union rates and practices. As I did previously with respect to the lessons arising from the helper controversy, I shall present here the baldly stated lessons and reason for repeal set off in boxes and supported by brief synopses. I also provide more complete documentation for each point in this section at the correspondingly number boxes in Appendix Five, and encourage readers with doubts or questions to go to that appendix first to see if they are assuaged or answered. There are no substantive differences in the way the residential and the building surveys were conducted or handled, so except where noted, the illustrations will be drawn from the residential survey.

It is difficult not to be impressed by how far DOL will go to accommodate complexities unique to union organizations, such as inter-union jurisdictional disputes, local and regional differences in job-naming conventions, pay grades, fringe benefit differences, and the like. It is also difficult not to be impressed by how little the output of the wage determination process resembles the input wage data.

The first step in the transformation that will be discussed below has to do with how DOL identifies rates found in a wage survey that are "identical to the penny." There are actually several steps that occur even before this—having to do with how the surveys are conducted and who is allowed to submit wage rates to a survey and such matters as whether the same rate paid to the same person on a succession of short jobs counts as one rate submission or many—that are questionable in application, but for the purposes here it will be enough to see how the data are transformed even after they are collected.

A. THE MONOTONIC UNION RATE ASSUMPTION

No. 36. DOL arbitrarily transmutes union rates found in surveys, treating all of them as identical to the penny, even if they differ by many dollars. This prejudices rate determinations towards union rates, and demonstrates clear bias towards union rates and practices.

Conventional wisdom about collectively bargained rates is that they are monotonic (as in, "*the* union rate"). This may once have been generally true, but if so, it was long ago. Union rates in the present day are not only not identical one with another, they are often not even close. But for whatever reason, DOL's wage specialists routinely excuse union rates from actually having to be the same in order to be counted as identical.

One way this is done is by conflating widely differing union rates submitted to wage surveys, tallying them as though they were identical regardless of their actual differences. Both unions and the DOL are sensitive to the fact that if union rate differences in surveys were treated the same as others, the likelihood of union-majority rate determinations would be greatly lessened, and in the final wage determination average rates, not union ones, would obtain more often. Rate consolidation is done exclusively for union data, and it is done routinely. It is also done in the absence of any enabling Davis-Bacon administrative regulations and in clear violation of the spirit of prevailing wage laws. But it is only the first of what will turn out to be many levels of arbitrary data consolidation and transmutation that will be explained subsequently.

How this first transmutation works is easily seen in the Pittsburgh-area survey where the fact that the determination established a union-majority rate instead of an average (not-union) rate for certain trades depended entirely on it. For the trade of drywall finishing in that survey, for example, DOL received a total 74 wage-rate submissions, and its wage specialists asserted that 42 of them, a clear majority, were union rates, so the union rate became the prevailing rate. Fair enough.

But in this instance, no more than 16 of the 74 rates submitted were actually submitted at the same dollar amount. The 32 nonunion rates were all widely different, as might be expected, ranging from under $12 per hour to around $19 per hour. More surprising, however, the 42 union rates had almost as much variation, ranging from around $21 per hour to around $30 per hour. Furthermore, although all of the union workers on any given project received the same hourly wage amount, the amount was different on each of the five union projects submitted. Among union rates for drywall finishers, there were 7 at $21.08, 12 at $21.11, 4 at $28.90, 3 at $28.96, and 16 at $29.64.

Only by counting all of these varying union rates as identical to each other would the selection heuristic (majority paid the same rate to the penny) allow "union rate" to be called the majority, but that is what was done. It could not be argued that the differences were trivial ones that could be ironed out to achieve the outcome, because neither the 19 union rates around $21 per hour nor the 23 rates around $29 per hour were enough to form an independent majority. The outcome could only have been reached by counting $21 an hour to be the same rate to the penny as $29 an hour—a very long stretch.

The conflation of union rates for this craft is far from unique. Other union rates in the same survey were compounded in similar ways. Counted as identical to the penny were: five different union rates for carpenters; six different union rates for cement masons; eight different union rates for electricians; nine different union rates for bricklayers; and ten different union rates for painters. Within the same craft, rates $14 apart were counted as identical, as were rates differing from one another by more than 40 percent.

Much of the difference here probably has to do with the fact that different locals of union workmen have different contracts, and more than one local may be involved in work in any one county or area, partly because of where the lines of geographic demarcation of local unions fall and partly because unions use travelers, that is, workmen imported from other locals when the local demand exceeds local supply. (There may also be recording or transcription errors. The survey summary forms are filled with omissions and improbable juxtapositions.) But counting these disparate rates as identical for survey and determination purposes clearly violates both the letter and spirit of the Davis-Bacon Act. Administration reform would not change this because current administration rules already prohibit it. Only repeal of the underlying law would cure it.

B. ARBITRARY UNION-CENTRIC JOB TITLE ACCEPTANCE

> No. 37. Collecting manipulated survey data by union-supplied job title or consolidating it to DOL-supplied job titles is an example of obvious bias that unfairly favors union rates and practices.

Union contracts have become more and more cumbersome and identify many fine distinctions in job title, work assignment, and pay within each broader category of workmen. Furthermore, the distinctions are different between different locals of the same union. Just within the state of Pennsylvania, laborer unions' contracts may differentiate unskilled laborers into anywhere from one to six groups for residential work, and one to 11 groups for building work.

In the case of the 6-county survey, the survey summary forms WD-22a associate all laborer wage rates with a particular category called "Laborers, Unskilled." Although two different wage rate for union laborers appeared in the survey, in any given submission all of the laborers covered appear to have been paid identical amounts (24 at $23.41 and 18 at $23.22). There is no variation in job title and no variation in rates within the job title depending on the exact work performed, as demanded by the union contract.

Therefore, there are only two possibilities, both involving wage fraud: either the union agents reported fictitious wages and job titles so that they would appear to have a large number of workers paid the same rate to the penny, or the DOL consolidated the wage rates and titles on behalf of the unions. (A later transmutation by DOL would further consolidate union laborers' wage rates by recording the two already fictional submitted wages, $23.41 and $23.22, as identical to the penny, thereby inflating the sameness and possible prevailing-ness of union rates.)

Similar fraudulent recordings occur in every wage survey I have reviewed that contains union wage rates for trades that are commonly divided by unions into groups or categories for wage purposes, including especially laborers, teamsters, and operating engineers, but also to a lesser degree electricians, plumbers, cement masons, painters, and sheet metal workers, among others. The union contracts for all these trades specify different wage rates for different skills, specialties, and job contents that almost never appear with their corresponding wage differences in the surveys.

The opposite effect, disaggregating and repackaging common job titles and rates, is illustrated by the contract of the Greater Pennsylvania Regional Council of the United Brotherhood of Carpenters and Joiners of America with its union employers that was in effect at the time of the Pittsburgh area residential survey. This contract provided a single rate for journeymen carpenters doing not only routine carpentry work but also forms building, concrete pouring inspection, countertop handing and installation, ceiling installation, and other tasks, all described together as carpenter/lathers; it also established separate rates for floor-laying carpenters, millwrights, and piledrivermen. What it did not provide was a rate for carpenters described as "carpenters, inc drywall & siding." Nevertheless, this is the only carpenter rate found in the WD-22a's of the survey.

If all carpenter rates submitted by either union or nonunion sources were submitted as "Carpenters Including Drywall & Siding,"—and similarly all painters as "Painters, Brush & Roller," all cement masons as "Cement Mason/Finishers," all crane operators as "Cranes" (regardless of capacity), etc.—and all were paid the same listed rates, then such reports must be fraudulent, because they do not reflect either reality or the pay requirements of their contracts. And if unions did submit their wage reports accurately, with all of their variations in title and pay that exists in the contracts, then the consolidation was fraudulently performed by the DOL. Either case makes the entire prevailing wage identification practice a sham, and judging from the helper situation, there seems to be no possibility of responsible correction. The only alternative is to junk the present system and start over, or better yet, forget about it.

C. INADEQUATE SCREENING OF DUPLICATIVE DATA

No 38. The combination of voluntary rates from various sources may result in duplication of submissions that unduly color the final results, and unfairly favor union rates and practices.

DOL wage specialists collect survey data on the forms called WD-22a. These forms are physically compiled from raw data, and are then re-compiled onto the wage summary sheets from which the determinations are prepared. They list the project name and value, the job categories of the subject wage rates, the number of persons working on the project "in the peak week," and their wage rate and fringe benefits paid. A review of what these look like in detail is neither pretty, nor indicative of any attempt at accuracy.

The WD-22a's collected for the Pennsylvania residential surveys provide a case in point about problems with voluntary rate submissions. There is no way of knowing how many solicitations for wage data went out or how many were returned by employers as opposed to non-employers for those surveys, because such data are not shown and are not easily accessible. What is known, however, is that whatever the source, only wage rates from about 380 different projects from across all six counties were found in the survey. These projects were clearly not random or chosen from a structured plan.

Furthermore, many of the project reports contained obvious anomalies, such as far too many or too few workmen in relation to the value of the projects, or evidence of multiple reporting of the same workmen's wages on successive, small jobs. Indeed, many of the projects represented gave evidence of being merely a succession of different houses on the same streets, or even different residential units in the same complex that were probably covered by single building permits. In addition, too few showed acceptable amounts of craft diversity for them to have been submitted in response to a project data request.

Nor is this the only problem. Fifty-nine of the 71 total rates in the survey for bricklayers were reported to be on projects where the only workers were bricklayers. More than half of the rates collected by the survey for ornamental ironworkers, plumbers, sheet metal workers, crane operators, elevator constructors, carpenters "including drywall and siding," and soft floor layers were also rates from single-craft projects.

D. FLEXIBLE SURVEY BOUNDARIES

> No. 39. Accepting data from outside the established time frame of the survey, from other polities, or from jobs previously performed under prevailing wage mandates biases the results, and unfairly favors union rates and practices.

It should not be necessary to go beyond established survey geographic or time parameters or to accepting previous, self-perpetuating Davis-Bacon rates in new survey inclusions. DOL does it only because it so often finds itself with too few survey submissions to support even a rudimentary list of job titles in a wage determination, even by its most relaxed standards for how many survey rates from how many different sources are sufficient to justify a new rate issuance. But by doing so, it violates its precept of finding and preserving "whatever rates actually prevailed" in the locality of new work. They come from outside the locality, or they were not normal, free-market rates.

The number of late-dated rates for bricklayers, drywall finishers, plasterers, and carpenters is large enough to have produced different determination rates than would have obtained without them. For example, 86 percent of the plasterers' rates and 62 percent of the drywall finishers' rates were submitted from dates outside the established survey range. In all cases, these added rates were union rates.

E. ARBITRARY UNION RATE SELECTION

> No. 40. DOL arbitrarily selects which local union's rate prevails. This increases the arbitrariness of wage determination outcomes, and while demonstrating clear bias towards union rates and practices, helps render published determinations meaningless.

A second transmutation occurs once a plurality has been established by conflation of the various union rates it finds in surveys. Having decided that the (combined) union rate prevails, DOL's wage specialists must then select a single union rate that will be called "prevailing." It would seem better if this rate bore some relationship to one or more of rates actually submitted, but there are no known guidelines. The rate finally selected might be significantly higher or lower than some or even all of those in the survey (or any statistic drawn from their distribution). One wage specialist might decide to record all the rates as though they were the highest, arguing that these might best represent the most recent union contract, but another specialist might decide to record them all as though they were at some other rate that he or she felt might, for whatever reason, be more representative, regardless of its plurality within the survey. If there is a conflict of union locals that had submitted different rates, perhaps the wage specialist simply selects the one he or she know best or likes the most. There are simply no guide rules.

When union rates are selected as prevailing, they are always listed in the wage summary sheets as having a rate of "$.000." In the case of the drywall finishers, the amount said to prevail two years after the first issuance, in 2004, was $22.44, so the original determination must have been more clearly aligned with the lower group of rates than with the higher one despite the fact that the lower group of rates numbered only 19, while the higher group numbered 23. So the selected rate was apparently aligned with a minority within the union section, much less within the entire survey. Prevailing rates set for a number of other trades in this determination also seem to have been based on minority, lower, or earlier-dated entries among the union survey submissions.

F. ARBITRARY UNION RATE PUBLICATION

> No. 41. If DOL finds a union rate to be prevailing, the rate published in the determination may be considerably different from that found, and will reflect current rates published in some union contract. This increases the union orientation of wage determination outcomes, demonstrating clear bias towards union rates and practices.

The 4th iteration of the original six-county residential determination was published in 2004, newly shorn of Allegheny County, which had been given its own, separate determination with no rate designated for drywall finishers. This now-5 county determination showed the union rate of $22.04 for drywall finishers, a rate aligned with a lower group of union rates within the survey where there were also a larger number of union rates in the $28 range. Over time, however, it would not matter that the initially established union rate was based on the lower number, because once established, like all union determination rates, it rose over time with each successive union contract, until at an unknown (to me) time between 2004 and 2011, the rate was reallocated to a different union local and jumped back into the higher rate ranges. By 2011, when the original 6-county determination had been split again, now into 4 pieces with new rates for drywall finishers reallocated based on findings in the original survey and perhaps some additional ones added with respect to Allegheny County. In 2011, Allegheny County was determined to have a nonunion drywall finisher's rate of $18.48, the combination of Beaver, Fayette, and Washington counties, also now had a nonunion rate of a couple of dollars more, and the separate Westmoreland County determination now had no rate specified for this trade. But Butler County retained the original union prevailing rate, but it no longer was an upgrade from the $20.11 6-county determination. Drywall finishers in Butler County now had a rate risen to $35.66, almost exactly double the nonunion rate, but also about 30 percent above the previous union rate.

G. ARBITRARY UNION RATE UPDATING

> No. 42. If DOL publishes a union rate as prevailing in a determination, that rate is automatically updated to reflect the collective bargaining contract wage, automatically and in perpetuity. Determinations containing such information are called "updated," or "current." These automatic increases affect only nonunion contractors, since union contractors pay the union rate, regardless. Following this practice increases the union orientation of wage determination and demonstrates clear bias towards union rates and practices.

By this point, any resemblance between the rates published in the determinations and those originally submitted to the survey was due either to happenstance or to a connection made by the thread of a wage specialists' perceptions of union preference. It also should be clear that, once a union determination rate is specified, the amount does not remain static. All union rates published in wage determinations are updated to the current collective bargaining contract covering it for each new contract iteration, in perpetuity or until a new survey is conducted. All 26 prevailing wage determination for building work in Pennsylvania and most of those set for residential work, 5 of the 6 heavy and highway determinations, and all determinations set by the state for building work under the Pennsylvania prevailing wage law, show evidence of this sort of such escalation because all of these have at least some union rates that are routinely updated by means of current contract provisions.

This practice is sanctioned by Davis-Bacon administrative procedures (though why this should be so is lost to history), and to carry it out the DOL maintains a large file of union contracts from which it routinely transcribes union rates, job distinctions, employment-related impositions upon contractor employers (such as vacation days, hazard pay, and wage differentials by class or equipment operated). This does not, however, make it less unfair or less false to the spirit of prevailing wage determination, which was based on the idea of continuing and protecting whatever individual wage rates had been paid in the past, not on insuring that the latest union rates would be the current minimums imposed on union and nonunion contractors alike.

The frequent updating of union rates in determinations allows DOL (or state agencies) the pretense that the determinations in which the most recent union rates are published are made current thereby, masking the need for new surveys that might test their underlying validity. As discussed below, one result is that genuine updates based on surveys are rare, and most determinations are hopelessly outdated.

It is worth repeating that only nonunion contractors are affected by the impact of automatic updating of union wages in the determinations. Both union contractors and their employees are governed by union contracts that take precedence over any lower prevailing rate. Up-to-the-minute rates also don't affect union members' employability by nonunion contractors, as union members are not allowed to work for them. There is perhaps some small competitive benefit to nonunion contractors if union rates are not automatically updated, but this benefit is nowhere so large as would be the benefit that might obtain to them if surveys actually had to be redone to be considered current.

As a reminder, I note that additional details and further discussion are available in Appendix Five for all of the points raised in this section at corresponding reason numbers. Some are supported by additional illustrations drawn from the determinations, and may be of interest to certain readers. Also included in Appendix Five is the full illustration of rate collection, rate consolidation, survey determination variable publication, and routine upgrading associated with the obscure trade of drywall finishing in residential construction in the Pittsburgh area of Pennsylvania. I have compressed it down as much as I could, but it still takes a couple of tables and something over ten pages to lay out—more than I was willing to include here in the main text. But I do encourage those who admire intricacies to visit those last pages of Appendix Five.

Chapter VI: Anatomy of a Wage Determination

Chapter V, with additional details provided in Appendix Five, told the complex story of the many data modifications involved in setting the rate for a minor craft in the simplest type of construction work in a six-county section of Southwestern Pennsylvania, but additional levels of data transformations from the same original survey materials beyond the simple upgrading of determinations to new union contract rates remain to be discussed. The emphasis now shifts to multiplying rates rather than consolidating them.

So that I can continue to relate determination outcomes to specific survey data input, I have chosen to illustrate the points to be made with the current residential wage determination for Beaver, Fayette, and Washington counties of Pennsylvania, three of the six counties originally surveyed in 2002. Most any other determination for any construction domain in any area of the country outside of the deep, nonunion South would show evidence of similar adjustments before and after publication. Practically every individual wage requirement in the determination has its own story to tell, so I shall go through them seriatim. Each provides another reason why the Davis-Bacon Act is administered against its own original intentions, and why repeal is the only reasonable corrective.

1. Illustration from a Current Determination

A. The Pretense of Currency

In boxed, highlighted exhibits, the current residential wage determination for Beaver, Fayette, and Washington counties are presented below. I have not bothered to use titles to identify the separate pieces separately. With the exception of this first presentation that includes both the preamble and the relevant parts of the coda, the contents of the determination are shown in order, and completely, and each part will be used to illustrate a generalized point about determinations.[1] This first piece of the determination illustrates a point made earlier, so it simply amplifies one of the reasons for repeal rather than adding to the list.

```
General Decision Number: PA120013 02/10/2012
PA13

Superseded General Decision Number: PA20100013

State: Pennsylvania

Construction Type: Residential

Counties: Beaver, Fayette and Washington Coun-
ties in Pennsylvania.

RESIDENTIAL CONSTRUCTION PROJECTS (consisting of
single family homes and apartments up to and in-
cluding 4 stories)

Modification Number     Publication Date
          0               01/06/2012
          1               02/10/2012
```

This first piece of the determination shows that it is the first modification after the original publication date January 6, 2012. This implies that this is a pretty fresh determination, and that something happened on the January date to cause the original publication. But nothing is apparent on the record, and in the main the not-union rates continue to reflect the survey performed in 2002. The previous iteration of this determination that I happened to review in July of 2011

[1] I actually performed this analysis on determinations that I had printed out in late July 2011, but by the time I came to write up the results, that copy was all scribbled over, so I pulled the new one, seen here. It is the same in structure, and only differs in having some higher wage rates.

was called the 15th modification of a determination with an original publication date of March 12, 2010. The only differences between the two are differences in amounts of union contract wages, so there seems to be absolutely nothing to distinguish or modernize this iteration of the determination from any other.

B. INTRODUCTION AND THE CAPRICIOUSNESS OF NO RATE ISSUED

> No. 43. Allowing determinations to be issued without published rates for necessary trades is an example of union bias and is also an example of the arbitrariness and capriciousness of prevailing wages.

The coda to the determination contains some boilerplate, including the messages boxed, below.

```
Unlisted classifications needed for work not in-
cluded within the scope of the classifications
listed may be added after award only as provided
in the labor standards contract clauses (29CFR
5.5 (a) (1) (ii)).
                    . . .
Union prevailing wage rates will be updated to
reflect any changes in the collective bargaining
agreements governing the rate.
                    . . .
Survey wage rates will remain in effect and will
not change until a new survey is conducted.
```

The first item asserts one of the silliest aspects of prevailing wage administration, namely that if no prevailing wage can be found to exist for some category of laborer or mechanic, that category of worker will have to be paid some other laborer or mechanic's prevailing wage.[2] Although this particular determination contains a fairly comprehensive listing of the standard residential building trades, the companion determination (drawn from the same 2002 survey) for Butler County has no rates listed for carpenters, none for roofers, none for HVAC duct work, and none for power equipment operators other than backhoe and loader operators. The companion determination for Westmoreland County has no rates for plumbers or roofers, none for HVAC duct installers, no plasterers, none for drywall finishers. A residential construction project cannot be completed without using these un-determined trades, and not having them subjects nonunion contractors (union contractors always have to pay their contract rates, so it is of no matter to them) to unnecessary costs if they seek supplementary rates and to expensive risks in guessing wrong if they choose not to—their only alterative recourse.

The related Greene County determination has what must be a nonunion majority rate (no fringe benefits at all) of $11.50 for power equipment operators operating rollers but a union rate more than four times as high—and to three decimal place, $46.795—for power equipment operators operating backhoes. No other power equipment operators are mentioned, and there is no generic Power Equipment Operator (PEO) rate specified. How would a contractor know what wage rate include in his contract estimates for power equipment operators operating scrapers, or compactors, or cranes, or skid-steers? This point is important enough to warrant its own reason for repeal.

[2]As noted, there is an elaborate and time consuming procedure for establishing a special rate for unlisted classifications, but it requires paying some prevailing rate from the start and the risk of back wages if the initial guess was wrong, so it is not often followed.

C. CATERING TO DIFFERENT LOCALS OF THE SAME UNION

> No. 44. Allowing determinations to be issued with rates adjusted to the territorial jurisdictions of various union locals is an example of union bias and is also an example of the arbitrariness and capriciousness of prevailing wages.

The second part of the determination covers bricklayers:

```
 BRPA0009-023 06/02/2011

BEAVER COUNTY
                          Rates       Fringes

BRICKLAYER.............$ 27.95        16.00
----------------------------------------------
 BRPA0009-024 06/01/2011

WASHINGTON (Cross Creek, Hanover, Jefferson, Mt
Pleasant, Nottingham, Peters, Robinson, Smith,
Union Twps) COUNTY

                          Rates       Fringes
BRICKLAYER.............$ 29.77        16.03
----------------------------------------------
 BRPA0009-030 06/01/2011

FAYETTE (Jefferson &amp; Washington Twps) County
                          Rates       Fringes
BRICKLAYER.............$ 29.45        15.69
----------------------------------------------
 BRPA0009-031 06/01/2011

FAYETTE (Except Jefferson &amp; Washington Twps)
County
                          Rates       Fringes
BRICKLAYER.............$ 29.46        15.69
----------------------------------------------
```

Although this is supposed to be a single determination covering three counties, with respect to bricklayers it divides the counties into pieces that match the boundaries of jurisdiction of bricklayers' local unions number 23, 24, 30, and 31 who among them have four slightly different rates. Which of these, if any, represents the wage rate for bricklayers discovered in the original 2002 survey? There is no way of knowing because of how those union survey rates were consolidated. But after consolidation, one of those union rates was announced to prevail. In the published determination, there is not one union rate, but three (or four, depending on how one counts) different by the magic of the DOL pen. And curiously, despite all the apparent precision—involving which union gets to control wages in exactly what parts of which counties—in this determination no bricklayer rate is specified for Washington County except in the 9 named townships.

Many examples of even more elaborate local union delineations abound throughout prevailing wage determinations. Here is an example for the area in which one particular determination wage must be paid to electricians affiliated with one of the five electricians' locals in a single county, Bucks County, following the boundaries of local union control:

```
ELEC0098-002 05/02/2011

BUCKS COUNTY:  Starting at the Delaware River and follow-
ing the west limits of the Borough of Bristol, along the
continuation of U.S. Highway 13 and under the Pennsylva-
nia Railroad Bridge to Route 09113, north 09113 to Route
152, north along Route 152 to the Humeville Road, east on
Humeville Road to Route 333,north on Route 344 to the
junction of Spurs 281 and 252,continue north on Spur 252
to Route 09028, west on 09028 to Route 152, north on 152
to TR 232, north on TR 532 to TR 113,north on TR 113 to
TR 232 at Anchor Inn, northeast on TR 232 and continue
northeast along Route 659 to Route 09060, west on 09060
to Route 402, north on 402 to the Borough line at the
southwest corner of the Borough of New Hope. The Borough
of New Hope is excluded. Starting at the Delaware River
and proceeding southwest along the Plumstead-Solebury and
the Plumstead-Buckingham Township lines to Route 09064,
northwest on 09064 to U.S. Highway 611 south on 611 to
the spur of Route 270, northwest along the spur to Route
397, Southwest on 397 to Route 350, southeast on 350 to
```

```
Route 395, southwest on 395 to Route 09060, southeast on
09069 to Route 09041 southwest on 09041 to the Montgomery
County line.
----------------------------------------------------------
```

This is one of five patches of ground into which the county is carved, each belonging to a different local. The differences in rates associated with them are consequential, as the rates range from $51.46 to about 50 percent more, $78.82, for the same job titles in the same trade in the same IBEW union in the same county. Prospective electrical contractors should be well advised to carefully parse exactly where in the county their project will be built before estimating, or chance losing their shirts.

D. CATERING TO UNION JOB SPECIALTIES NOT IN SURVEYS

> No. 45. Allowing determinations to be issued that add specialties in union trades that were not covered in surveys is an example of further union bias and is also an example of the arbitrariness and capriciousness of prevailing wages.

The third part of the determination covers carpenters and electricians:

```
 CARP0142-003 06/01/2011
                                   Rates   Fringes
CARPENTER (Including Drywall
Hanging, Vinyl Siding
Installation, and Asphalt
Roofing)...................... $ 17.80    8.93
----------------------------------------------------
 CARP1759-008 06/01/2011
                                   Rates   Fringes

FLOOR LAYER:  Carpet..........$ 28.77   12.90
----------------------------------------------------

* ELEC0005-012 12/23/2011
FAYETTE AND WASHINGTON COUNTIES
                                   Rates   Fringes

ELECTRICIAN...................$ 21.73   11.80
----------------------------------------------------
```

```
* ELEC0712-006 12/26/2011

BEAVER COUNTY
                                   Rates  Fringes

ELECTRICIAN...................$ 16.63  13.19
----------------------------------------------
```

The determination with respect to electricians is fairly straightforward, the only complication being that two different electrical locals are involved, but their boundaries follow county lines, and their different rate requirements are only about $4.00 apart. The carpenters' determination follow largely along survey lines, where DOL consolidated all carpenter wage submissions except from those doing carpet laying into two categories, one called "Carpenter (Including Drywall Hanging and Vinyl Siding Installation)," and the other some variation on "Floor Layer" involving carpet installation. One job title entirely missing from the survey, however, was added to this determination without any underpinning, that of "Carpenter (Including Asphalt Roofing.)" So for these three counties, there are two defined carpenters' rates, one for "Carpenters (Including . . . [the 3 defined subcategories], at $25.98 and a second for carpet installers at much higher rate, $39.92. Other carpenter jobs covered by the master contract for western Pennsylvania, including forms building, ceiling installation, pile driving, supervising concrete pouring, and many others, are not mentioned. Although they are certainly covered by the major title, it remains curious that carpet installing is not, but that siding application and asphalt roofing are.

To further complicate matters, the related residential determinations find the same titles in Allegheny, but with different rates, $25.98 for both the broader category and carpet layers—two different locals of Carpenters' 1759 controlling. Another local covers Westmoreland with the same rate but for persons simply called "Carpenters" and with no identification or separate call-out of Soft Floor Layers. Butler has no carpenter rate defined. The corresponding building determination for all these counties, which derives from the same master contract but which does not separate out locals, has a rate for the broadest category, there called "Carpenter/Lather," of $45.51 and a second rate for Soft Floor Layers of a bit less, $40.53, but still only a little higher than for the same title on residential jobs in Beaver, Fayette, and Washington. The building determination also establishes separate rates for millwrights and piledrivermen, also subsets of carpenters.

The carpenter determinations illustrated above are pikers, however, compared with the coverage in the determinations of operating engineers (or, power equipment operators, PEOs). This is a continuation of the same basic point as above, but in spades.

In the original (2002) residential survey, rates were submitted for operators of particular pieces of equipment, rather than the general category of PEO or operating engineer. Through various iterations of data collection and subsequent reevaluation, with respect to the current county split in determinations there seemed to be enough survey rates to justify a prevailing determination in Allegheny for Bobcats and backhoes at a nonunion rate, for backhoes and possibly loaders in Butler, for scrapers, bulldozers, and possibly loaders in Westmoreland, and for cranes in Beaver, Fayette, and Washington.

In the current residential determinations, Allegheny corresponds pretty well: it is found with Bobcats ignored but with a nonunion backhoe rate. The Butler determination also corresponds pretty well with the survey data, having a union rates for backhoes and loaders. Westmoreland does not track well, however, showing no determination rates for scrapers (the single piece of equipment with the largest number of survey submissions), bulldozers, or loaders, but with union rates for backhoes based apparently on three survey submissions, only two of them union. But the most amazing determination transformation is that for Beaver, Fayette, and Washington. Based on a total survey submission of 4 union crane rates from one project and one each from two others—a total of 6 rate submissions from all three counties, all for cranes—rates were set for operating engineers as in the following selection from the counties' determination:

```
* ENGI0066-020 07/01/2011

                          Rates   Fringes
Power equipment operators:
     CLASS 1..........$ 31.045   15.75
     CLASS 2..........$ 27.36    15.75
     CLASS 3..........$ 25.64    15.75
```

POWER EQUIPMENT OPERATORS CLASSIFICATIONS

CLASS I

Asphalt Paver, Asphalt Roller, Asphalt Plant Operator, Athey Loader, Auger (Truck or Tractor Mounted), Auto Grader (C.M.I. and similar), Backhoe (180' and 360' swing), Back-Filling Machine, Batch Plant, Bulldozer, Cable Layer, Cableway, Caisson Drill, Central Mix Plant, Compactor with Blade, Concrete Pump (all types), Over-Head Crane, Crane (Crawler or Truck Mounted)*, Tower Crane (Stationary or Climbing Type), Rough Terrain Crane**, Wagon Crane, Crushing and/or Screening Plant, Derrick Traveler, Derrick (all types)(when assistance is needed it will be an oiler or apprentice), Derrick Boats, Dragline, Drill (Davey or similar), Dredge, Drill (Well and Core)(Truck or Skid Mounted), Elevator, Excavating Equipment (all other), Fork Lift (Lull or similar), Franki Pile Machine (or similar), Guard Post Driver, Gradall (all types), Grader, Elevating Grader, Equipment Greaser, Helicopter, Helicopter Hoist Operators, Front End Loader, Hoist, Hydraulic Boom Truck, Jumbo Operator, Kocal, Koehring Scooper, Locomotive, Metro Chip Harvester (or similar), Mix Mobile, Mixer - Paver, Mucking Machine, Multiple Bowl Machines, Pile Driver (Sonic or similar), Scrapers, Shovels (powered), Slip Form Paver (C.M.I. and similar), Spreader (Concrete, Asphalt, or Stone), Tire Repairman (when assigned to a jobsite), Tower Mobile, Tractors (all types), Trencher, Tug Boat, Vermeer Saw, Welder (repairman), Whirley

* Cranes with Boom or Mast length (including jib) 100 ft or over shall be paid an additional $.50 per hour for each 50-foot increment of additional boom and/or jib length)

** Rough Terrain Cranes with Boom or Mast length (including jib) 101 ft or over shall be paid an Additional $.50 per hour for each 50-foot increment of additional boom and/or jib length)

Note: An additional $1.25 per hour (not counting boom pay) shall be paid for any crane (excluding overhead cranes) rated 100 ton or over.

CLASS II

Ballast Regulator, Boat (material or personnel)(powered), Boiler, Boring Machine, Compressor (combined with Air Tugger, Air Pump, Gunite Machine, or Sand Blaster), Concrete Belt Placer, Concrete Saw, Conveyor, Carry Crane, Crushing/Screening Plants, Curb Builder (self-propelled), Forklifts (ridden or self-propelled), Form Line Machine, Generator (over 5KW), Grout Pump, Heaters, Hoist (monorail, roof, one drum-regardless of power used), Huck Machine (or similar), Hydraulic Jack (single or multiple)(power driven), Ladavator, Mortar Mixer, Mulching Machine, Pavement Breaker (self-propelled or ridden), Pin Puller (powered), Pipe Cleaning Machine, Pipe Dream, Power Broom (except push type), Pulverizer, Pumps (regardless of power used), Roller/Compactor (Dirt), Refrigeration Plant, Ross Carrier (or similar), Seeding Machine, Skid Steer Loader (or similar), Slab Lifting Machine (hydraulic), Soil Stabilizer (pump type), Spray Cure Machine (power driven), Side Delivery Shoulder Spreader (attachment), Steam Jenny (or similar), Stone Crusher, Stone Spreader (self-propelled), Siphon (steam or air), Tie Tamper (multiple heads), Tractor (when used for landscaping, snaking, or hauling), Truck (Winch)(when hoisting and placing), Tube Finisher (C.M.I. and similar), Tugger, Water Blaster, Welding Machine, Well Point System

CLASS III

Brakeman, Deck Hand, Helicopter Signalman, Oiler*, Elevator (Alterations & Remodeling Commercial Buildings),

* Oilers on Truck Cranes: less than 50 ton shall receive $.10 over the Class III base rate; 50 ton up to 100 ton rated capacity shall be paid an additional $.25 per hour over the Class III base rate; 100 ton and over shall be paid an additional $1.00 per hour over the Class III base rate.

General Note: Hazardous Material Sites Level C & D receive $1.00 per hour premium for all classifications and Levels A & B receive $2.50 premium for all classifications

----

In this fairly standard recitation of the narrowly defined variations of operating engineers, an inordinate amount of detail is provided about cranes. "Rough terrain cranes" with booms of 150-foot length are to be paid \$.50 more per hour, but their extra pay is differentiated from "cranes" in that cranes with booms of that specific length are to be paid \$1.00 more per hour, unless either one is rated at 100 tons or over, in which case the operator is to receive \$1.25 more per hour but not receive the \$.50.[3] Notice, too, that although cranes were the only equipment submitted to the original survey, meaning that no rates at all were submitted from any of the three counties for scrapers, compactors, backhoes, rollers, Bobcats, fork lifts, bulldozers, or loaders, this operating engineer assertion of job control gives the operators of each and every one of these pieces of equipment a prevailing rate minimum of \$46.795. And, of course, it requires similar rates to be paid to a good many people or things that do not seem to be directly related to power equipment operating, such as tug boats, other kinds of boats (excluding sailboats and possibly livestock-carrying boats), elevators, helicopter signalmen, locomotives, and

[3] I think. You can try your own hand at parsing it. It's all there in the determination.

oilers (basically helpers) who get more required premium pay for oiling bigger pieces of equipment. And, of course, there is also premium pay for working on hazardous materials sites (in those residential neighborhoods).[4]

E. PUBLISHING ABSURDITIES AS PREVAILING RATES: RATES INVERSE OF SKILL

> No. 46. Allowing determinations to be issued that publish absurdities, such as higher rates for lower related skills, is an example of the arbitrariness and capriciousness of prevailing wages.

The next part of the determination covers ornamental ironworkers and cement masons. The cement mason rate provides the example relevant to reason number 46, but before turning to it, the ornamental ironworker rate reinforces another point made earlier about the importation of union wage rates to areas where they have no foundation.

```
IRON0003-005 06/01/2011
                            Rates      Fringes

IRONWORKER, ORNAMENTAL...$ 30.38         24.20
-------------------------------------------

PLAS0526-010 06/01/2010
                            Rates      Fringes

CEMENT MASON............$ 21.94         10.39
-------------------------------------------
```

The ornamental ironworker rate seen here seems to have been fairly enough derived as a union rate from the original survey, based

[4] I know it is probably some sort of special pipe cleaning machine, but I do love the idea that the PEO determination sets its second-highest rates for "Pipe Dreams."

as it was on rate submissions for 19 individuals (although one might quibble at the 3 to 5 workers in this trade reported then to have been engaged simultaneously on tiny projects in the $3,000 to $20,000 range). But there were 19 reports from 5 projects, and 16 of those were even at the same union rate, so a prevailing rate at the union level was justified.

But all 19 were reported working on projects in Allegheny County, none from any of the other five. So for the companion determination to this one published in 2011 for Allegheny County, a union ironworkers' rate of $54.58 per hour was justified, even if it showed a rate that has almost doubled in the ten years since the survey was performed—a huge increase compared with other construction wage increases over the period. On the other hand, there is no justification at all that I can find for a determination requiring union ornamental ironworkers' rates in the Beaver, Fayette, and Washington joint determination. (No rates are specified as prevailing in the related Butler or Westmoreland determinations.)

The second trade noted in the above determination was cement masons. Note that this trade has a rate controlled by the plasterers' union, within which cement masons are a subset. In the original survey, however, cement masons were treated as a separate wage group from plasterers in the same way that carpet layers were treated as a separate wage group from the carpenters' union to which they belonged. The skill differences and the wage differences here between cement masons and plasterers are not huge, but the subset of cement masons has a union prevailing rate in the determination of $32.33 whereas the senior group of plasterers has a not-union rate of $22.98. So through the magic of prevailing rates, the lower-skilled subset must be paid about 50 percent more than the higher-skilled one.

Here are some additional examples, all drawn from Pennsylvania residential determinations in 2011: In Carbon County, caulkers, a subset of bricklayers, have a union rate of $44.75 whereas bricklayers have a not-union rate roughly half as much, $23.18. Lehigh and Northampton have these same rates for caulkers and bricklayers, and additionally have sprinkler fitter rates determined at more than twice as high as the plumbers to whom they are clearly related ($52.10 to $20.03.) By comparison, in Philadelphia County the situation is reversed: caulkers are determined to have rates only about half as high as plumbers ($31.46 to $68.01). Note that plumbers doing the same job in two different counties not that far separated from one another are to be paid 3 times as much for their labors in one compared with the other.[5] A related situation occurs in the highlighted determination within the single county of Washington.

An Erie County building determination provides an almost unbelievable example: the rate set for mason tenders, a helper category named in one of the 3 sub-groups of laborers, is $24.70 per hour; the rate for cement masons, whom the tenders would assist, is $12.96 per hour. One should be entitled to assume that since one or the other of these clearly fails to reflect actual local practice in the cement mason trade, the determination must necessarily be considered a failure. But such inversions are common, and are unflinchingly accepted by Davis-Bacon administrators.

F. PUBLISHING ABSURDITIES AS PREVAILING RATES: HUGE RATE DIFFERENCES EXIST DEPENDING ONLY ON WHICH UNION CONTROLS WITHIN THE SAME DETERMINATION OR EVEN THE SAME COUNTY

> No. 47. Allowing determinations to publish absurdly large differences in different localities within the determination areas differing only as to local union suzerainty, is an example of the arbitrariness and capriciousness of prevailing wages.

The following section from the determination shows the rates for plumbers:

```
 PLUM0027-004 06/01/2011

WASHINGTON COUNTY (Area West of a North-South
line drawn from East of McMurray to West of
```

[5] After a while one would think that any objective observer would have to give up and call the entire prevailing rate enterprise folly.

```
Fredericktown)
                                   Rates          Fringes

PLUMBER.................$ 35.85          17.57
--------------------------------------------

 PLUM0047-008 05/01/2011

BEAVER County
                                   Rates          Fringes

PLUMBER.................$ 20.08           9.14
--------------------------------------------

PLUM0354-007 08/01/2011

FAYETTE and WASHINGTON (Area East of a North-
South line drawn from East of McMurray to West of
Fredericktown) COUNTIES

                                   Rates          Fringes

PLUMBER.................$ 18.27          12.74
--------------------------------------------
```

Within the single county of Washington, depending on where one is with respect to a dividing line between two towns, what one would have to pay plumbers would be either $31.01 per hour or $53.42. Clearly both of these could not represent any actual rate prevailing in the county as a whole. One might assume that this result was one that followed the pattern already seen: similarly disparate union rates submitted to the original survey, called identical to the penny, union rate determined to prevail, set as $.000, published as separate rates for separate parts of the determination area covered by different union locals. In this case, the actuality is even worse. A grand total of two union rates were submitted to the original survey, both from Beaver County, and both at $38.96. In the current determination, Beaver has the lower union rate of some different local, Fayette is higher, and Washington is split between higher and much higher. None of these rates, with or without the elaborate geographic split, is justified.

G. PUBLISHING DETERMINATIONS WITH INEXPLICABLE ANOMALIES

> No. 48. Inexplicable anomalies pepper determinations. Each one is another example of the arbitrariness and capriciousness of prevailing wages.

The final piece of the Beaver, Fayette, and Washington residential determination, covering union rates for sheet metal workers and various not-union rates for six trades, including, inexplicably, sheet metal workers (again), is shown below.

```
 SHEE0012-007 01/01/2007
                              Rates        Fringes

Sheet Metal (Excluding HVAC
Duct)...................$ 16.61          8.46
----------------------------------------------
*  SUPA2002-002 11/25/2002
                              Rates        Fringes

DRYWALL FINISHER/TAPER..$ 16.35          5.39

Laborer, Unskilled......$ 13.88          3.26

PAINTER:  Brush and Roller
Only....................$ 16.36          4.79

PLASTERER...............$ 18.04          4.94

ROOFER (Excluding Asphalt
Roofing)................$ 18.94          5.62

Sheet metal worker......$ 16.00          3.08
----------------------------------------------

WELDERS - Receive rate prescribed for craft per-
forming operation to which welding is incidental.
```

The double inclusion of sheet metal worker rates in this determination is probably a typo, but it is totally inexplicable as to how it came about. Also listed here are five other rates set at nonunion or not-union levels, three of which, for drywall finishers, painters, and roofers (excluding asphalt roofing that, improbably, belongs to carpenters), had previously been set at union levels in earlier versions of the determination.[6] There are actually enough survey submissions to the original 2002 survey for a union rate to have been determined for all three trades for the three-county set (though not enough to determine any rate one way or the other in Fayette alone). So this must be put down as a second anomaly from the same determination.

Rather than burden this record with an additional several pages of similar anomalies drawn from other current residential determinations in Pennsylvania, I have relegated them to Appendix Six. Just for the flavor of it, I include one of them here, from building determination PA 38, which has these rates specifically for oilers (helpers) of power equipment: "OILERS/ On Tr.Cr. 100-ton and over.$ 23.65On Tr.Cr. 50-ton up to bu/ On Tr.Cr. 50-ton up to/ but not including 100-ton. .$ 22.90 13.91 [all *sic*]" and this note: "Oilers on Truck Cranes: les than 50 ton shall receive $.10 over the Oiler's base rate; 50 ton up to 100 ton rated capacity shall be paid an additional $.25 per hour over the Class III base rate; 100 ton and over shall be paid on additional $1.00 per hour over the Class III base rate." [Unfortunately, neither an oiler's base rate, a Class III base rate, or a defined Class III exists in the determination.]

There are a couple of dozen similar examples in Appendix Six, all drawn from a handful of building determinations in Pennsylvania, but of course the anomalies that seem to afflict all of Davis-Bacon determinations do not stop there. Pennsylvania also has 7 heavy and highway determinations that are presumably based on statewide surveys. In 2011, together these 7 determinations specified 534 prevailing rates, 530 of them at union levels and 4 at not-union levels. This

[6] I would like to be able to ascribe this to DOL beginning to get the message, but after a quick glance at the operating engineer situation in the same determination, I think that may be something for the Pipe Dream machine.

is considered to be a different construction regime, with the work and workers readily differentiable from commercial or building construction, and certainly from residential construction, so it is somewhat of a surprise to find that the heavy and highway determination for the five counties around Philadelphia has very little in it covering highway-centric skills in asphalt or concrete work, earthmoving, grading, striping, bridge erection, etc. that are not already present in ordinary PEO descriptions for even residential work.

More than half of the 14-page determination is devoted to sorting out the geographic sovereignty of various electrical and ironworker locals, 8 in the first case and 7 in the second, but gives much less coverage to the sort of electrical work that might be more specific to heavy construction projects (line construction), and that somewhat confusingly. (An elaborately differentiated part of Chester County has a different set of line construction rates from the others: it covers "Groundman, Truck Driver, and Winch Operato [*sic*]" at a pay rate of $35.58 and fringe benefits of 51%+.25, and "Groundman, Truck Driver, and Winch Operator" at a pay rate of $34.00 and the same fringe benefits, without any differentiation; and it covers "Lineman, Cable Splicer, Heavy Equipment Operator" at a rate of about $10 more. In the rest of the determination area, "Groundhand" is set at a different rate from "Groundman," 2 different rates are set for "Truck driver" and 2 other different rates are set for "Winch truck operator," but nothing for heavy equipment operators. It is also somewhat confusing that the lineman's rate of around $65 is lower than the ordinary electrician's rate in 3 of its 8 variations, and that the line construction helper (groundman or groundhand) rate of about $60 in parts of Chester County is about equal to or higher than that of 5 of the 8 journeyman electrician's rates.[7]

[7] A final note in passing: DOL should be happy that its Philadelphia area heavy and highway determination (PA 6), already 14 pages long mostly because of the 8 electrical locals and 7 ironworker locals in the 5 counties, did not have an equivalent number of power equipment operator, laborer, or teamster union locals, since some of those now divide their workers into as many as 13 elaborately identified classes, each recitation of which can take several pages.

2. Davis-Bacon Fosters Anomalies

No. 49. Davis-Bacon procedures foster anomalies that impede routine wage administration within the industry. It is better to have no law than to have a law that is arbitrary and senseless.

The variations in wage rates for ordinary construction workers elaborated in the federal determinations just for the state of Pennsylvania demonstrates how prevailing rates foster anomalies. To the degree that DOL allows rates to be published differently than they are collected, it encourages wide differences in rates for even common construction jobs where some local union or another may have achieved a local monopoly, and preserves them for the ages.

Consider that in one small subset of sewer project rates in one of four construction domains in their single-state subset of nationwide determinations, 54 different *categories* of operating engineers were rewarded with different prevailing rates, all of them union, all of them paired with thousands of variations in job title and machinery used. These may or may not be related to the 42 additional categories of rates found for other heavy project determinations, or to the 211 additional categories of rates for operating engineers found in the building and residential determinations.

Although it might be argued that operating engineers are a special situation, since they use a lot of different equipment—some large, some small, requiring different levels of skill—such an argument fails in the face of laborers, the lowest common denominator of construction work. In the various federal determinations establishing prevailing rates for persons who have the word of "laborer" in their job title, 314 separate, distinct, and different rates are found in current Pennsylvania determinations alone. They range in pay requirement from the minimum wage ($7.25 per hour, no fringes) up to $50.28 or more, with stops along the way for rates of $38.45 for "waterboy," $37.55 for a "clean up helps to maintain" laborer, and $36.80 for "flag person" in some areas. Most of this variation is among union rates that start in the $20-range and go up from there.

Could the huge variations be caused by where the laborers live or work? It is highly doubtful. Overall, current Pennsylvania laborer determinations show approximately 500 percent variation between the lowest and highest rates, and among just union laborers, about 200 percent. By contrast, the "PAS Merit 2011 Book" that publishes the nonunion wage rates that nonunion contractors employ in estimating contract costs on private work, identifies the average nationwide rates in commercial, industrial, institutional, residential, building, heavy, highway, and municipal employment for laborers as varying by less than 10 percent in wages and about 12 percent in fringe benefits. Regionally the category (there is only one) of "Laborers, General" ranges in straight wages in the book from $16.45 in the Southeast to $19.63 in New Jersey and New York, a maximum variation across 10 different sections of the country of little more than 19 percent.

So union laborers, whose rates are hypothesized to be identical to the penny, have rates that actually vary by at least $30 per hour, from under $20 to over $50—including rates for totally and completely unskilled work (water boy, flag person) in the mid ranges—while the highly disparate nonunion general laborers actually have rates that hover closely around $19, with little regional variation and little variation by laborer's tasks. The differences between these two patterns would be of no consequence were it not required of nonunion contractors (whose employees on private construction of similar projects in Pennsylvania seem content with their wages, and whose jobs are sought out, bragged about, and held up in comparison to other employments) to conform to the union rates and ways found in prevailing rates.

3. Implicit Expansions to Unlisted Rates

No. 50. Davis-Bacon procedures routinely allow implicit expansion of prevailing rates to unlisted and phantom union jobs but not to nonunion ones.

There are two forms of implicit rate expansion: first, extension of prevailing union rates to jobs not listed on wage determinations and, second, extension of lesser or diminished rates to phantom union jobs. Both of these grow from the fact that regardless of what job titles may or may not appear on rate determinations, contractors must pay everyone working on a job at *some* prevailing rate.

With respect to the first, as already discussed earlier, if a prevailing rate fails to be issued for some needed job (for example, for laborers, steamfitters, painters, drywall finishers, cement masons, plasterers, tile setters, bulldozer operators, Bobcat drivers, or others on the residential projects in Allegheny County), a contractor having to staff that job has two choices: he must either employ workers in some related published category (that is, employ carpenters as "laborers," perhaps) to work outside their trade while he seeks a special rate and written authorization to pay it from DOL—a procedure that might take more time than the life of the project—or he might hire whoever he can get and pay them at the local union rate. The former involves some risk unless the "closest rate" category is a union rate, both because of possible disagreement by DOL (which would invoke back wages and other problems) and also because of possible union-inspired enforcement risks. Paying the current union rate may not be required by the DOL, but it minimizes enforcement risks. In either case there is a strong proclivity towards union rates and ways, though this is one of the murkiest areas of prevailing rate administration.

With respect to the second, phantom jobs, these are helper-like jobs that don't show up in the determinations but that may also be used if "traditional." The import of these is not to extend prevailing rates to additional classes or categories, but to shield certain helper-like union jobs from having to be paid journeymen's prevailing rates. Examples include elevator helpers or "70-percent probationary elevator constructors" for elevator mechanics; pipelayers for plumbers; electrical groundsmen for electricians; pipe insulators for steamfitters; and several similar assistant or helper-like categories associated with traditional union work practices in certain areas. Information on whether such individuals are employed in public works in Pennsylvania without benefit of covering prevailing wage rates is not available, but they are known to have been employed in this way in other places. No traditional nonunion phantom jobs are known to have been permitted.

Chapter VII: Costs, Counterclaims, Compromises, and Conclusions

This chapter will cover a lot of ground, but succinctly. Unlike the analysis of the details of survey and determination that I (we, if you have been reading along) have slogged through, studies of the extra costs added by Davis-Bacon and other prevailing wage laws have been undertaken by a number of other analysts, as have studies offering counterclaims to the benefits of repeal and various reasons for retaining prevailing wage laws. I shall review both of those, but only briefly. The fundamental arguments on both sides have been made repeatedly and without much change for at least as long as I have been studying prevailing wage laws. There have also been several proposals to attempt to correct some of the faults of Davis-Bacon through administrative reform while leaving the system in place, some by government oversight agencies, and I and others have suggested modifications to the system short of repeal. Some of those deserve consideration, and I will provide it before moving on to my final conclusions about Davis-Bacon, which, if you have been paying attention, should not come as a surprise.

1. Costs of Davis-Bacon

In February of 1995, I prepared and delivered the following statement for the U.S. Senate Committee on Labor and Human Resources on the costs of Davis-Bacon.[1]

> The benefits of Davis-Bacon, such as they are, are not without cost. The exact amount is not only unknown, but unknowable, since much of

[1] "To Save Money and Create Jobs The Davis-Bacon Act Should Be Repealed," Statement by A.J. Thieblot testifying before the U.S. Senate Committee on Labor and Human Resources, *Hearings on S.141, Davis-Bacon Repeal Act*, February 15, 1995.

> it can be calculated only hypothetically. ("How much would that building have cost if it did not cost as much as it did?") Nevertheless, many estimates and ballpark figures are readily available, and they are staggering. Those that I have developed in the past find typical prevailing rate-to-open shop wage differentials to result in possible savings of around 6 percent of total construction costs. So if Davis-Bacon applies to $50 billion of public construction annually, its direct costs to be on the order of $2 billion to $3 billion per year.

The "$50 billion of public construction, annually," in the above statement was intended to represent the sum of both federal construction and the portion of state and local construction that Davis-Bacon controls (through state adoption of federal rates) or influences—about one-quarter of all state and local public construction spending.

To update this analysis to present-day costs, note that the total value of construction put in place in 2011 was more than double that of 1995, and that the proportion of it that was public was somewhat greater, especially after overall construction spending peaked in 2006 but public construction continued to rise. By U.S. Department of Commerce estimates, in January of 2012 federal construction was going on at about a $27-billion pace, and state and local construction at a $260-billion pace. If one-quarter of state and local construction spending was still controlled or influenced by Davis-Bacon (and by my estimate it was), the total amount of public construction currently affected would be roughly $90 billion; so the impact of Davis-Bacon on construction costs in today's dollars, as a first-order and conservative estimate, is perhaps something like $5 billion to $6 billion per year.

Continuing:

> This is consistent with the results found by other researchers looking at different prevailing rate comparisons. A Canadian study (Globerman, 12/93) reported that British Columbia's prevailing wage law added 6% to 7% to the total price of provincial construction projects. An open-shop study (Northrup, 1984) reported a For-

> tune 500 company found savings of 7% on the total costs of $3.4 billion of construction projects built open shop rather than union (a somewhat different comparison since Davis-Bacon rates are not always union rates). [*N.b.*: In Pennsylvania, as discussed above, although all may not be union rates, 81 percent are.] Studies performed in Florida, Iowa, Kentucky, Louisiana, Maryland, Minnesota, and New Hampshire in conjunction with repeal or attempted repeal of state prevailing wage laws in those states found average anticipated construction savings of 9.4% from eliminating them.

I'll return to my 1995 testimony a little later, but I wanted to include also a few cost estimates provided by other, more recent observers and analysts. Most of these have been variations of the "wage-differential x labor proportion of total cost x amount of public construction" variety that, although valid, require a number of limiting assumptions that are difficult to pin down and are almost impossible to compare directly with one another. Several of the others are attempts to compare more directly measurable differences, such as school construction budgets or projected savings (or increased costs) associated with eliminating, reinstating, or modifying prevailing wage coverage for selected building projects, mostly schools. This has happened or has been under enough active consideration in Florida, Michigan, Kentucky, Ohio, Indiana, Oklahoma, Minnesota, Maryland, California, West Virginia, and New York to warrant studies and data collection to support the legislative agendas in those states.

With a few exceptions, noted below, these more-focused analyses have found proportionally greater impacts (or anticipated impacts) than my own:

- (New York, 1993): Prevailing wages caused costs to be 27 percent higher on a particular project evaluated.[2]
- (Pennsylvania, 1994): "Pennsylvanians are paying nearly 30 percent more for labor on public construction projects

[2] "New York State Prevailing Wage Laws: An Investigatory Analysis," (1993) unpublished, New York, State Commission of Investigation.

performed by contractors than the same contractors are charging for private projects." "The extra cost of wage determinations, just in construction costs, not compliance or enforcement, was estimated at 9.6 percent of the total cost of the government projects."[3]

- (Ohio, 1997): "A study of several states that have repealed prevailing wage laws find an average savings of at least 15 percent." "Ohio Senate testimony showed that Kentucky saved 11 percent, before reenacting prevailing wage under union pressure." "Indiana saved 15 percent after repeal in 1995." "Total savings in Ohio were estimated at 20 percent."[4]
- (Minnesota, 1997): "Prevailing wage requirements boost total construction costs by a range of 4% to 10%."[5]
- (Michigan, 1999): "Prevailing wage laws increase labor costs by 40 percent, driving up total construction costs by about 10 percent." Actual school examples during period of suspension of state prevailing wage law: one project, 13 percent savings; second project, 16 percent savings; 20 additional projects, savings "well above 10%.[6]
- (Kentucky, 2002): A 24% increase in wage costs for all worker on prevailing wage projects in 1999 and 2000 compared to the total wages they would have been paid if

[3] Eleanor D. Craig, "The Impact of Pennsylvania's Prevailing Wage Law on Public Construction Costs," (1994), The Commonwealth Foundation for Public Policy Alternatives.

[4] "Documentation in Support of Excepting Primary and Secondary Schools from Prevailing Wage," (1997) unpublished, assembled for various state school board and business associations.

[5] "The Fiscal Implications of Prevailing Wage Law on Minnesota School Districts," (1997) unpublished, Minnesota Taxpayers Association.

[6] "Michigan's Prevailing Wage Law and Its Effects on Government Spending and Construction Employment," (1999), a Mackinac Center Report (Dr. Richard Vedder).

they were paid the same wage as they had previously earned on private projects.[7]

- (Kentucky, 2002): Wages of same individuals about 20% higher on prevailing-rate projects than they had received or were receiving on privately sponsored projects.[8]
- (Ohio, 2002): Savings when schools were exempted from prevailing wages in 1997-2001, 10.7%.[9]
- (Maryland, 2004): In 2001, the Maryland prevailing wage law changed, bringing more school construction projects under it. When it did, total construction costs for those projects increased 5% to 10%.[10]
- (Minnesota, 2005): Estimated savings of 7.4% to 10% of total projects costs in 2002 if the state used median wage rates instead of then-current state prevailing wage rates.[11]
- (California, 2005): "A new state law that would extend California's prevailing wage law to all state-subsidized housing construction would increase the cost of new con-

[7] "An Analysis of Kentucky's Prevailing Wage Laws and Procedures," (2001) unpublished, Legislative Research Commission.

[8] "The Effects of Prevailing Wage Laws: A Comparison of Individual Workers' Wages Earned On and Off Prevailing Wage Construction Projects," (2002), manuscript, Mike Clark, Chief Economist, Kentucky Legislative Research Commission.

[9] "The Effects of the Exemption of School Construction Projects from Ohio's Prevailing Wage Law," (2002), "S.B. 102 Report, Staff Research Report No. 149," Legislative Service Commission.

[10] "Analysis of the Impact of State Prevailing Wage Rates, Public School Construction Projects, State of Maryland, Fiscal Year 2001–Fiscal Year 2003," (2004) unpublished, Dr. Yale Stenzler.

[11] "Prevailing Wage Rates in Minnesota: An Examination of Alternative Calculation Methods and Their Effects on Public Construction Wages," (2005) unpublished, Minnesota Taxpayers Association.

struction by between 9 and 37 percent."[12]

- (Michigan, 2007): Prevailing wage adds 10% to 15% to the cost of construction.[13]
- (Weatherization projects, 2010): "Officials at the Department of Energy's weatherization assistance program said the requirements [to pay special prevailing rates for weatherization work] 'Will have a large impact in urban areas. . . . Because the wage rates are higher than they were expecting to pay they will have to reduce the number of homes weatherized.' DOE officials said prevailing wage rates for construction workers on wind and hydropower technologies program projects sometimes are 20 percent higher than wages paid for similar work."[14]
- (Federally funded construction, 2008): This study measured the difference not between open-market and prevailing rates, but between existing prevailing rates and what they would have been had they been derived by accepting construction wage statistics derived by the Bureau of Labor Statistics for its National Compensation Survey. "DBA [Davis-Bacon Act] prevailing wages are on average statistically higher than the wages reported by the BLS. Therefore, we are able to conclude that DBA prevailing wages drive up overall federal spending on construction (through inflating labor costs) and consequently place a heavy burden on taxpayers. In order to estimate how much DBA prevailing wages are driving up federal construction costs, we calculated a weighted average wage of the 80

[12] Sarah Dunn, John M Quigley, ad Larry A. Rosenthal, "The Effects of Prevailing Wage Requirements on the Cost of Low-Income Housing," *Industrial and Labor Relations Review* 59, no. 1 (October 2005).

[13] "The Effects of Michigan's Prevailing Wage Law," (2007), Paul Kersey, Mackinac Center for Public Policy.

[14] "Officials' Views Vary on Impacts of Davis-Bacon Act Prevailing Wage Provision," *BNA*, GAO-10-421, February 24, 2010.

> MSAs [metropolitan statistical areas] across the nine occupation groups using employment in each occupation as the weight. We found the weighted average wage for BLS to be $20.13 per hour, and $24.56 per hour for DBA, or DBA wages are 22% higher than BLS. . . . Applying this percentage to the public construction costs for 2007, results in about $95 billion applied to projects with DBA prevailing wages. This costs taxpayers $8.6 billion per year. In all, the DBA wage determinations add 9.91% onto each applicable construction project." Specific projects in New York and California were projected to have increased total costs of up to 25.1 percent.[15]

This list could be much larger, but little information would be added. There is general agreement that prevailing rates add to construction costs, and something of a consensus that it may be on the order of 10 percent, overall, and that leaves me comfortable with my own, more conservative estimate.[16] Experts can, and do, argue over

---

[15] Sarah Glassman, Michael Head, David Tuerck, and Paul Bachman, "The Federal Davis-Bacon Act: The Prevailing Mismeasure of Wages," (2008), Beacon-Hill Institute at Suffolk University

[16] There are pro-labor contrarian views, spearheaded by Dr. Peter Philips and his associates from the University of Utah. Nooshin Mahalia lists over a dozen in "Prevailing wages and government contracting costs: A review of the research," (2008) unpublished, Economic Policy Institute. These include studies and papers by Peter Philips, Mark Prus, Hamid Azari-Rad, Cihan Bilginsoy, Dale Belman, Paula Voos, Michael Kelsay, Randall Wray, Kelly Pinkham, Garth Magnum, Norm Waitzman, and Anne Yeagle, among others. The premier study of this sort was that released by Philips *et al* in 1995: "Losing Ground: Lessons From the Repeal of Nine Little Davis-Bacon Acts," (1995), University of Utah. Before becoming too carried away by the sophistication of the arguments presented in these highly academic papers, (such as regression analyses demonstrating that the government makes back more in tax collections than it spends in additional construction costs when wages are raised by prevailing rates), or that construction costs are not changed when a component acknowledged to be 20% or more of total skyrockets in price, I recommend a cursory review, at least, of my counterpaper, Thieblot (1995), *Failure of Arguments Support Prevailing Wage.* Not

how accurate any of these numbers or projections are and how much prevailing rates and Davis-Bacon in particular or general situations affect total costs, but precision is irrelevant. One can readily see two things: prevailing rates drive construction wage rates higher by significant, arbitrary amounts; and the cost of public construction is substantially higher than it would be if that were not the case.[17]

There are other costs besides those directly attributable to higher wage rates:

> There are other costs as well—costs of maintaining the federal establishment to collect, process, and disseminate the thousands of prevailing rates needed each year, enforcement costs, and administrative costs on the part of contractors to comply with the record-keeping requirement. But the biggest costs of all are almost impossible to measure, and those are of two kinds: First are the costs associated with upward pressure on wage rates throughout the construction industry caused by the prevailing rate, almost always at or above the market average, being required as a minimum, thus continually neglecting about the bottom half of wage scales. Second are the costs to the construction industry associated with being locked into the craft demarcations and training practices that happened to be in effect a half-century ago. For example, although a recent Delaware study (Delaware DOL, 1992) found more construction workers across that state who said they were construction helpers than who styled themselves as the aggregate of a drywall installers, concrete and terrazzo finishers, insulation workers, roofers,

---

only do I find many of their arguments unpersuasive, I find a measureable proportion of them intellectually dishonest. (Sorry, but I do.)

[17] It might also be noted that none of the reasons for repeal of Davis-Bacon that I have highlighted so far depends on the precision with which increased costs attributable to the act can be estimated.

> ceiling tile installers, tapers, lathers, plasterers and stucco masons, carpet installers, floor layers, glaziers, stone masons, tile setters, pipelaying fitters, and pipelayers, *combined*, Davis-Bacon does not set prevailing rates for helpers. If a contractor uses helpers, they must be paid journeymen rates.

My summary, then, remains true now:

> How much does Davis-Bacon cost? A great deal—at least into the Everett Dirksen range of "real money." ("A billion here, a billion there; pretty soon you're talking real money.") But in a way, the cost question is less important than the fact that Davis-Bacon provides so few benefits to society. Only if a law achieves some necessary purpose that can't be achieved another, easier way can it claim that almost no level of cost is too great to sustain it. And although it is true, as someone has pointed out, that Davis-Bacon has been around for sixty-five years [longer, now] and we've learned to live with its costs, this argument, consistently followed, would have us still erecting air raid shelters.

This is significant enough I shall repeat it as a tentative reason for repeal, pending discussion of possible offsetting advantages in the next section.

No. 51. The cost of Davis-Bacon is immense. But the cost question is less important than the fact that Davis-Bacon provides so few benefits to society. Only if a law achieves some necessary purpose that can't be achieved another, easier way can it claim that almost no level of cost is too great to sustain it.

2. Counterclaims: The Benefits of Davis-Bacon

Proponents of Davis-Bacon perceive dire consequences arising from its repeal, with a return to the days of itinerant contractors and roving bands of low-wage workers picking off the choice government jobs. They also suggest that union contractors would be unable to compete for government work, and that union members' falling wages might reduce them to penury. They foresee vastly increased construction injuries and fatalities, declining government tax receipts, diminished opportunities for minority workers, a less skilled construction workforce, lower work force productivity, less-competent contractors and possibly more unsafe buildings, increased cost overruns, and even a larger number of work change orders.

In sum, proponents assert that repealing Davis-Bacon and state prevailing wage laws would be an unmitigated disaster, negatively affecting construction companies, union and nonunion construction workers, taxpayers, and government purchasers. Any savings from repeal would be exceeded by tax losses even if they were not offset by cost overruns. The country would suffer from having to make up the tax losses, from absorbing large new costs associated with workers' compensation claims, from an increased accidental death rate, etc. One study asserted that repeal of Davis-Bacon might *add* $4 billion to $5 billion per year to the net cost of government construction.[18]

None of these counterclaims are supported by data, by actual experience, or by common sense, even in places where prevailing wage laws have actually been suspended or eliminated, but I do not propose to rebut them individually, here, or in detail.[19] As a general rebuttal, however, note that roughly four-fifths of construction work now going on in the United States is being done free from the strictures of

[18] Philips, *et al., op. cit,* fn. 104.

[19] I have done so, among other places, in Thieblot (1995), *Failure of Arguments Support Prevailing Wage.* They have also been debunked in several major particulars by Paul Kersey, "The Effects of Michigan's Prevailing Wage Law," (2007) unpublished, Mackinac Center, pp. 6–14, and elsewhere.

prevailing wage laws. There is no evidence of monopsony, no roaming bands of itinerant low-wage workers driving down local wages.[20] Some private construction work is even being done by unionized contractors using unionized workforces because, despite their higher wage rates and higher construction costs, these firms and individuals have been able to demonstrate their worth to buyers.

With or without prevailing wages, there is an across-the-board trend in the direction of the open shop in construction. Without the government support provided by Davis-Bacon, unions there may well fall to irrelevance as they have in other industries such as mining and manufacturing. But there is always room at the top, and no reason why those at the top should not also be members of unions if they wished. It's just that government in general and Davis-Bacon in particular should have no duty to reverse the trend, even if they could.

Proponents also talk of the necessity for Davis-Bacon to sustain the apprenticeship system and to provide a floor under federal job training programs. Actually, the opposite is true. One positive consequence of Davis-Bacon repeal is that it could actually relieve some of the burdens placed on the anachronistic and underperforming federal and state-sponsored job training systems. It would also induce an automatic shift in providing for the training of a significant number of persons from "joint" programs dominated by unions and designed to keep the number of skilled construction workmen down, to one dominated by the industry and designed to increase the number of skilled workers.

Consider these numbers: Assume there are about 1.4 million construction workers in public construction, of whom 800,000 are employed on federal work in any given year. Assume these 800,000 are 20 percent more efficient because of being paid prevailing wage

[20] There are, to be sure, low wages for unskilled work, some of it done by immigrants or even aliens. So what? Their low wages are, on average, considerably better than they could get in other unskilled jobs (flipping burgers, picking berries, or at home) so they are happy; they accomplish the work required of them, so their employers are happy; and no one suggests that they might be employed at low wages to erect high steel or to operate $1-million trackhoes. If their presence burdens the local polity, perhaps we should make it illegal for employers to hire them. (Wait. We already do.)

rates (a false assumption) and assume the prevailing wage rates are 20 percent above market wages (probably pretty close or a bit low). Under these assumptions, if Davis-Bacon were repealed, the 800,000 workmen being paid wage rates of, say $38 per hour, would be replaced by 960,000 workmen being paid wages in the $30 range. Assuming each does government work for 1,000 hours for a year, the total annual savings to the government would be $1.3 billion, and an additional 160,000 workers would be employed at wage rates of 3–4 times the minimum wage.[21] Furthermore, at no cost at all to the federal government, 160,000 persons (the size of the entire population of the city of Little Rock) would be getting on-the-job training in a good-paying industry.

A. RECURRING THEMES

The three most-often heard themes of Davis-Bacon proponents are that it creates a "level playing field," that it encourages "high skills because of high costs," and that it "protects local workers." All three of these are red herrings.

The Level Playing field

Davis-Bacon, it is said, levels the playing field between union and nonunion contractors bidding for government work by requiring both to have the same high labor costs; this is said to have the side benefit of promoting managerial efficiency by requiring management to control other construction inputs more closely and make investments encouraging labor productivity. Both of these are true, but only in a perverse way. The playing field is leveled in the same perverse way as it would be leveled for minority contractors by writing all of the plans and specifications only in Kanji, the language of a few of

[21] Actual savings, of course, would be greater because prevailing-wage workers are not more 20 percent more efficient just because they are paid 20 percent more. If the 800,000 prevailing wage workmen were simply replaced by 800,000 average-wage workers, the government would save $6.4 billion. In that case, the government could use part of the savings to improve an apprenticeship system freed from union dominance. Or, it could be anywhere in between.

them, but equally accessible to all. Or, the playing field would be leveled in the same perverse way that it would be between a professional basketball team (average player height 6'9") and a high school team by requiring all players shorter than 6'9" to play wearing stilts. The side benefit of promoting managerial efficiency by not allowing it to apply to the one-third of costs that are labor-related is the same kind of perverse logic that encourages personal productivity by raising marginal tax rates.

High costs yield high skills ("You get what you pay for.")

How many more miles to the gallon does your Prius get if the price of gasoline doubles? Does a construction flagger become twice as productive if his pay is doubled? The answers (none, and no) go a long way toward explaining that the high-wage, high-skill paradigm is not transitive: high skills may require high wages to attract them, but high wages do not create high skills. Paying $10 per pound for Spam will not turn it into steak.

Forced Labor Substitution for Higher Quality Buildings

With respect to construction work, some proponents of Davis-Bacon argue that the higher rates required force substitution of higher-priced resources for lower-priced ones. Since the country deserves to have the highest-quality and safest buildings that can be built, only the most qualified construction workers should be used on public works projects; open shop contractors with lesser-skilled, lower-paid workers should be encouraged or required to replace them with the higher-priced ones who will more likely be highly skilled and therefore make better buildings.

Sometimes this argument is accompanied by assertions that union workmen are some percent more efficient than nonunion ones, and therefore, although they command a higher wage rate, produce lower total labor costs. This assertion is not credible for two reasons: first, if it were true there would be no need for unions to support prevailing wage laws or otherwise worry about organizing contractors. Even nonunion profit-maximizing contractors would jump at the chance to lower their total wage bills through the higher union workers' productivity, so the whole industry would quickly become union.

It has not, and, in fact, is going the other direction. Open shop work is an increasing proportion of every construction sector.

Second, studies of private construction cost differentials between union and nonunion construction have found open shop tradesmen to install up to 48 percent more materials per dollar of labor cost, resulting in net savings of total project costs on the order of 6 percent when buildings are built using open shop labor. The claimed efficiencies of high-priced labor are unsupported.

Nevertheless, the question remains of whether higher-priced workmen produce higher-quality output. Although there is a general relationship between price and quality, it doesn't always apply. (Does a Rolls Royce make a better taxicab than a Ford?) The tasks of a flag-person or a common laborer prohibited from using the tools of any trade are but little subject to quality enhancement. Furthermore, there is the matter of quality level desired. Public buildings, like any other product, can be produced to various standards. It is the job of the end user, his architect, and whoever produces the bid specifications to identify and prescribe the quality level desired in the finished product, which may well be less than the highest possible standard. Marble facings and gold faucets, though always possible, are not always necessary. In the event that high quality output is sought, it is up to the specifications, and later the acceptance inspectors, to ensure they are complied with. It should not be up to the DOL. Higher mandated wage rates are far too inefficient a mechanism for the purpose.

Local construction workers need protection

What do local construction wages need protection from that local gas-station attendant wages do not? Or local die-sinkers? Or local providers of construction materials? Why should local writers of labor policy books not have income protection? And if the local construction workers that need protection happen to be highly paid union workers, shouldn't their union be the one protecting them, not the federal government?

3. Compromise: Why Solutions Short of Repeal Won't Work

For those of a certain mindset, it can be amusing to contemplate ways the government could achieve all of whatever protections and benefits the prevailing wage laws are supposed to confer, but without the hash that the USDL and pro-labor legislators and administrators have made of the current system. Here are some possibilities, short of repeal, in no particular order:

- Set rates independently for union and for nonunion workers (or only for nonunion workers) based on surveys of similars. No government job will depress union wages (they are covered by contracts). If the purpose is to protect local workers' wages, there is no reason why what union workers make should enter into the picture. The entire wage determination process could be subcontracted to a company like PAS, Inc., a private provider of wage rate information for the nonunion construction industry. The averages they currently offer, by job title, contract size, and region of the country, are those now used by nonunion contractors to estimate labor costs and prepare job bids on private work. If DOL were to prescribe "nothing less than the average of those," its job would be done and the purposes of Davis-Bacon fulfilled. (DOL already separately identifies union rates in surveys, so would have no trouble with this differentiation.)
- Set rates only for the lowest common denominator of the construction industry, unskilled laborers, and let all others key on those, as is done under the Walsh-Healey prevailing wage law for industrial firms, where the wage rates of janitors are protected. (Skilled workers will always both command and demand higher wages than the unskilled, except in certain perverse prevailing rate determinations.)
- Update the threshold for Davis-Bacon application to some reasonable amount, say $1,000,000, for new construction, and perhaps $100,000 for other construction activities—repair, renovation, alteration, etc. In 1931, when Davis-Bacon was first passed, the average construction worker wage was something south of $.25 per hour and the Davis-

Bacon threshold was $5,000; today's construction wages (including fringes) are about 200 times greater, so a contract threshold of $1 million would be in proportion. For such a system, surveys could be done on an as-needed basis for the menu of jobs to be required, and be better for it.

- Eliminate coverage for residential projects. Almost all private residential work is being done nonunion, without notable labor issues. Government residential projects in any local area are of the same scale as any others, and therefore offer no special impacts from which local workers would need protection.
- Eliminate coverage for heavy and highway projects. None of these projects occur in any given county with sufficient frequency to sustain a dedicated local workforce, so no local wage rates need to be protected.
- Require DOL to use one of the standard, readily available listings of construction jobs, for example from the Standard Occupation Classification (SOC) system of the Office of Management and Budget, or perhaps the more focused system of its own BLS (that has the Occupational Outlook Handbook listing trades for 19 construction specialties plus laborers and helpers, separately), or perhaps the O-Net listing provided by its own Employment and Training Administration that lists 43 construction trades (e.g., Solar Photovoltaic Installers, Terrazzo Workers and Finishers, Weatherization Workers and Technicians) plus 8 helper categories. Setting rates only for a limited number of broader categories of construction workers would ensure that there were rates for all and that all work necessary for any particular job would be represented. Any of these alternatives would cut down on the proliferation of named job categories and increase the chances of having rates available for all workers necessary to build a proposed project.
- Use the existing system but insist upon some minimum number of independent submissions from actual employer payroll records for a rate to be listed; add a category of "not otherwise classified."

- Change the survey method from the current haphazard one to one relying on the Current Population Survey that is conducted by the Census Bureau every month or the National Compensation Survey that, although slightly skewed toward SMSAs and toward larger firms, is both comprehensive and timely. Or contract wage-setting to the BLS or to some outside data-gathering company, like PAS, Inc. Use either the median or the weighted average rates for as fine a geographical area as already exists (regional, statewide, SMSA or not-SMSA, etc.) in the survey chosen.
- Require DOL to treat surveys alike for both union and nonunion wage rates submitted. Currently, DOL treats all union rates for any given job category as identical to the penny even if they differ by as much as 30% to 50% from one another. If all the union rates submitted for a given title can be counted as being the same, then all the nonunion rates could also be counted as the same. Then the existing methodologies for selection of prevailing (majority or weighted average) could be used. The result would be prevailing rates at the union level, at the weighted average of nonunion survey submissions, or at the grand average of union and nonunion survey submissions. (Only the first would escalate automatically; the others would remain until the next survey was performed.)
- Issue no prevailing wage rates for job categories for which no workers or an insufficient number of workers can be found to have worked in the locality. If there were no such workers, there are no workers' rates to be protected; and if no prevailing rate is issued for a category of workers, none should be required. Substitution of determination rates for other categories of workers should be prohibited.
- Require DOL to desist from "updating" determination rates from current union contracts. Leave all rates as established until another survey is conducted. A union contract rate or any other wage rate cannot be said to require protection until such time as it has, at the very least, been paid to someone and identified in a survey. The automatic updating of union rates to make rates "current" simply

disguises the age and likely inaccuracy of underlying surveys.

- Abandon surveys and set some multiple of the minimum wage as the minimum construction wage—perhaps twice or three times the minimum wage. Surely, that would be enough to protect local construction wage earners from the predations of roving government contractors.

Unfortunately, what all of these ideas have in common is that they require DOL to do something it has proved itself loathe to do: abandon or at least modify its dedication to union rates and methods. Any wage determination other than union rate, any determination based on mean, median, or multiple of minimum would result in rates that did not automatically multiply to cover related and lesser jobs mentioned in union contracts and would not automatically be updated with each new union contract issued. Under any of the proposed compromises short of repeal, the likelihood of union prevailing rates, per se, would diminish. And for that reason, if history is a guide, they will fail, regardless of how much sense they might make. DOL will do nothing that lessens union dominance of prevailing rates.

Examples of DOL's unwillingness to undertake even modest attitudinal change arise from the helper controversy (the twenty-year struggle to avoid issuing rates for nonunion helpers, already covered, extensively in Chapter V and Appendix Three), and from DOL's reaction to evaluations of Davis-Bacon administration conducted from time to time by the General Accounting Office (GAO). The earliest of these in my files is from 1979 and between then and 1997, GAO issued 26 "products" (reports) dealing with Davis-Bacon rates and administrative procedures, almost all of them critical.

In the first one, GAO "pointed out that the act appeared to be impractical to administer due to the magnitude of the task of producing an estimated 12,400 accurate and timely prevailing wage determinations." It made suggestions to DOL for administrative improvements, however, and suggested additional funding for the Wage and Hour division, with these results as of its 1994 report: "Since [1979], Labor has implemented regulatory changes that have addressed some of our specific concerns about the process used to determine prevailing wages. For example, rules were changed to generally prohibit (1) including federal contracts in the area wage surveys and (2) mixing prevailing wage data from surveys of urban and rural areas." Then it noted: "Despite these changes, in 1994, we found continuing verification problems with the data that Labor uses to make prevailing wage determinations." In fact DOL had done little but schmooze the GOA with promises of administrative reform.

Another GAO report was in response to the devastating testimony provided to the U.S. House of Representatives by the Oklahoma Attorney General and the Oklahoma Department of Labor, parts of which I have reproduced here in Appendix Seven. That testimony lists massive and blatant fraud, some of it going even beyond what I could impute from the Pennsylvania surveys and determinations.

For example, a plumber's rate for heavy construction in Oklahoma was set based on one contractor's report of 12 union plumbers (out of a survey total of 14 plumbers) making the same rate to the penny on one job for an underground storage tank that was confirmed to have these problems: a) the project did not exist and had never existed; b) the contractor did not file the wage report although it had his name on it; c) the plumbers listed did not work on that job or any like it; d) the report was filed late, beyond the deadline for submissions; e) the wage rate reported to be received by the union plumbers was different from and higher than what was specified by their union contract. In other words, these specific employees identified on this project, were ghost employees on a phantom project whose data should have been rejected. But their rates prevailed and were published for future work. From the hearings: "This indicates to us that there is no accountability and no integrity in the U.S. Department of Labor wage survey process."

In 1995, the Attorney General of Oklahoma became convinced that Davis-Bacon wage determinations for projects in Oklahoma City showed evidence of criminal input, and asked the U.S. Department of Justice to conduct a criminal investigation of the survey process. This led Congress to ask the GAO to not only investigate the particular incident, but also to conduct periodic reviews of the Wage and Hours Division of the DOL, the division responsible for determining rates. These were done, and included many, many examples of erroneous surveys and determinations, resulting in suggestions and recommendations for improvement to survey and wage calculation methodologies. The DOL promised internal review and consideration and, in most cases, went on as before.

Since 1997, Congress has appropriated $22 million for the purpose of modernizing the wage survey process, but as of 2004, another GAO review found "significant inaccuracies in 65 percent of the comparisons of the WD-10 to actual payroll data." Note that this 65-percent error rate is in the easiest part of the entire survey process, the transcription of rates from wage records to survey forms. It does not go to any of the problems uncovered in the Oklahoma situation, above (or in any of the many, many other survey and determination problems highlighted in the Oklahoma review here in Appendix Seven, *q.v.*, or the Pennsylvania analyses covered earlier, for example.) In the period prior to when GAO started its periodic reviews, of 421 WD-10 forms reviewed, errors had been found in 406, an astonishing error rate of 96 percent. After spending a lot of money and hearing a lot of promises from DOL, when GAO reviewed 261 WD-10 forms, it found errors in 257 of them. The error rate had actually increased to 98 percent. By 2004, GAO reported that OIG [Office of the Inspector General] had achieved the ultimate: "OIG found errors in almost 100 percent of verified survey forms."[22]

Errors are only part of the problem. The Office of the Inspector General (an independent review office within DOL), also reviewing the rate determination process, found in 2004 that the DOL survey process continued to produce biased data, not much different from that cited in the 1995 Oklahoma case. It found that continued reliance on third-party non-employer rate submissions, and continued dominance of survey returns by large companies with the resources to employ staff to deal with the WD-10s, set incentives for unions to participate but no incentives for firms uninterested in pursuing government contracts to become involved—all still conspiring to produce biased, unreliable, and erroneous determinations, and would continue to do so even if the reported error rates were all solved.

[22] GAO, "Davis-Bacon Act: Methodological Changes Needed to Improve Wage Survey," March 2011.

In its most recent review (2011), GAO again found problems with Davis-Bacon procedures for surveys and determinations and reiterated its recent findings:

- 1996: Labor had internal control weaknesses that contributed to lack of confidence in wage determinations; also, a difficult appeals process.
- 1997: OIG found much of the data it examined to be inaccurate and potentially biased due to weaknesses in survey methodology.
  (In 1997, Congress directed $3.75 million toward improvements in the wage determination process.)
- 1999: Labor was evaluating options and doing some additional verifying of survey data.
- 2001: Labor agreed it would pursue reengineering to use BLS data for determinations, and add computer systems to make it feasible to survey every area of the country for all four classes of construction every three years.
- 2004: OIG found Labor's reengineering had not solved problems; errors found in almost 100 percent of determinations.
- After 2004: No changes noted.

In summary, since 1979, despite massive efforts by at least two federal oversight agencies, many reviews and analyses, and many promises of reform by DOL, not only has the mechanical error rate associated with survey data collection not improved, the more fundamental underlying problems of determination inaccuracy and outright pro-union bias have not even been approached. And the oversight agencies don't help much, in my opinion. Although the GAO knew about, reviewed, and had explained to them much of the basic material in this book,[23] their 2011 recommendations for "Methodological Changes Needed to Improve Wage Survey" consist of suggesting Congress allow wage rates to be issued for broader civil subdivisions, and that DOL "obtains objective expert advice on its survey design

[23] I know this for a fact, because I did it personally.

and methodology." Oh, and it also recommended "Labor take steps to improve the transparency of its wage determinations," which, it was happy to report, Labor agreed to do. Sadly, Labor also "said obtaining expert survey advice may be premature given ongoing changes."

> No. 52. DOL will brook no change that diminishes the dominance of Davis-Bacon survey or determination processes by union rates and methods. The ills of Davis-Bacon cannot be cured by administrative reform.

4. CONCLUSIONS

From the examples throughout this book, it should be apparent even to readers who have skimmed these sections that prevailing wage determinations are set with improbably high frequency at the union rate; that they fail to reflect either local labor deployment or local wage practices; that they set rates for palettes of workers unrepresentative of local demographics; that they set rates for palettes of workers that are insufficient with which to carry out future projects; and, in general, that they spread illogic in wage administration. As a result, prevailing wages add substantially to public construction costs, add unnecessarily to state and federal tax burdens, interfere with the way that the majority sector of the industry would prefer to operate, and impede changes necessary for the industry to adopt in wage administration, work assignment, and training.

No sentient administrator would deliberately institute a system that would produce such an outcome, so it is a fair question to ask how the system evolved into its present form. The answer lies partly with the way the controlling concepts of prevailing wages are implemented, partly with how the surveys that are supposed to underlie wage determinations are conducted, and partly in how determinations are published and administered. There is no question that the dysfunctionality of the prevailing rate system has come about through the active efforts of DOL to cater to union ways, rates, and practices. And it is quite clear in the failed efforts by some seeking to modernize the system with respect to helper use and rates, for example, that DOL will not easily be made to adopt a more neutral stand.

No. 53. Davis-Bacon is outmoded, unnecessary, and selectively biased towards union rates and methods. It is also broken even under its own terms and it can't be fixed. It should be repealed.

The Davis-Bacon Act and, by extension, the other federal, state, and local prevailing wage laws have long been used by unions to preserve a foothold, at least, in the public sector. They also have enshrined a built-in affinity for union organizational and training systems, particularly the apprenticeship system. This is a highly effective training system for those who appreciate its merits and are willing to abide by its constraints. But like military academies for officer training, or even MBAs for corporate executives, they are not and should not be the only road to achieve fully skilled positions.

By the same token, the prevailing wage systems also attempt to ignore the real and continuing need for realignment of work assignments and job "ownership" in the construction trades, particularly with respect to helpers and similar semi-skilled or particularly-skilled workers who have less than full journeyman status in the skilled crafts. These come in two different types, those who are in the process of picking up the skills of the trade through on-the-job experience and who may someday achieve (and be recognized for having) full journey status and others who know all they need to know about some portion of what used to be one of many things a journeyman would have done in some older craft or is a new construction developments for which there are no established or traditional crafts. In following the union lead and failing routinely to recognize these types of positions, wage specialists for DOL and other prevailing rate administrators are not only bowing to union interests, but they are also forcing nonunion contractors arbitrarily to increase wage rates and inflate construction costs in ways that are not only unnecessary, but also are counterproductive.

Without the support of prevailing provisions (or project labor agreements, which have similar and sometimes even greater effect in the same market segments), construction unions would undoubtedly be following the pattern they have seen in residential and building construction work in the private commercial sector, where their current market penetration is probably in single digits. But in the public sector, which amounts to something in excess of $230 billion a year, unions have higher market penetration, on the order of 30 percent or more. Since this comes at the cost of increased prices for public buildings on the order of $5 billion a year or more, although one can easily understand the unions' desire to maintain their position of dominance in the field, one finds it much more difficult to understand why public agencies are willing to support it with the necessarily higher taxes.

The Davis-Bacon Act single-handedly supports unionization in the construction industry by "leveling the playing field" between union and nonunion work. It removes the union premium, however, not by lowering the cost or improving the efficiency of union labor and methods, but by arbitrarily raising the costs and undermining the efficiency of nonunion labor and methods. Simultaneously, it requires that a major buyer of construction work, the federal government (and by extension, other public polities) pay the increased costs out of tax-supported funding.

Without the support of prevailing wage laws and the related and even-more-union-biased prevailing requirements in the likes of Fair Labor Contracting and Project Labor Agreements, unionization in building construction would undoubtedly fall to a level no greater than that required to support the affinity sector defined in Chapter II, and probably would follow the pattern of unionization in coal mining, garment making, or cigar rolling into obscurity. This would not be a bad thing for the economy or the society: the age of unions, like the age of the robber baron industrialists who inspired them, is past.

The final reason for repeal:

> No. 54. If one believes that the proper public policy should be to obtain the best government construction at the lowest price, the Davis-Bacon Act needs to be repealed.

Appendix One
The Davis-Bacon Act

The Act as Originally Formulated in 1931:

That every contract in excess of $5,000 in amount, to which the United States of the District of Columbia is a party, which requires or involves the employment of laborers or mechanics in the construction, alteration, and/or repair of any public buildings of the United States or the District of Columbia within the geographical limits of the States of the Union or the District of Columbia, shall contain a provision to the effect that the rate of wages for all laborers and mechanics employed by the contractor or any subcontractor on the public buildings covered by the contract shall be not less than the prevailing rate of wages for work of a similar nature in the city, town, village, or other civil division of the State in which the public buildings are located or in the District of Columbia if the public buildings are located there, and a further provision that in case any dispute arises as to what are the prevailing rates of wages for work of a similar nature applicable to the contract which cannot be adjusted by the contracting officer, the matter shall be referred to the Secretary of Labor for determination and his decision thereon shall be conclusive on all parties to the contract: Provided, That in case of national emergency the President is authorized to suspend the provisions of this Act.

Davis-Bacon Act, [Ch 411, § 1, 46 Stat. 1494 (1931)]

Essence of the 1935 Amendments to (Substitution for) the 1931 Act:

The advertised specifications for every contract in excess of $2,000 to which the United States of the District of Columbia is a party, for construction alternation and/or repair, including painting and decorating of pubic buildings or public works of the United States or the District of Columba within the geographic limits of the States of the Union or the District of Columbia, and which requires or involves the employment of mechanics and/or laborers shall contain a provision stating the minimum wages to be paid various classes of laborers and mechanics which shall be based upon the wages that will be determined by the Secretary of Labor to be prevailing for the corresponding classes of laborers and mechanics employed on projects of a character similar to the contract work in the city, town, village, or other civil subdivision of the state, in which the work is to be performed, or in the District of Columbia if the work is to be performed there; . . .

The Davis-Bacon Act, 40 U.S.C. § 276(a) (1982)

Appendix Two

The Construction Industry: Labor Organization and Manpower Use

Organization of this Appendix

This appendix is not a comprehensive review of the construction industry, but rather an explanation of the labor organization within it and the considerable differences between the outlooks of its union and nonunion segments. A more complete, and still largely up-to-date coverage of the industry, the development of construction trade unions, the differences in labor deployment patterns in the union and nonunion segments of the trade, the development of the nonunion sector to be competitive on all classes of construction work, and the decline of unionism in private construction work are all covered in Chapter 1 of Northrup, Thieblot, and Baskin (2008), *Construction Union Tactics*, pp. 1–61.

The first section here discusses why to some extent the organizational patterns of labor in the industry are irrelevant to the industry's final output. The most complex element of the structure is the developing need for levels of construction employees fitting between journeymen, at the high-skill end, and laborers, at the low-skill end. With advances in technologically based specialization, the use of helpers and semi-skilled workers has become increasingly important to the way buildings are built, but their existence is scarcely acknowledged by Davis-Bacon or other prevailing wage laws. This is discussed in Section E, below, and the sordid history of the USDL's failure to confront this issue is the topic of Appendix Three.

A. Fungible Construction Output

Although almost all commercial construction projects differ from one another, construction contractors and workers are fungible with respect to their output. Elaborate systems of security bonding, output specifications by professional designers, penalties for failing to meet schedules, etc. ensure that the final output will not only be acceptable to the construction buyer, but will be indistinguishable from the final output produced by a different contractor using different workers, fraud and malfeasance, of course, excepted. If the low-cost bidder can build a wall that stands up, follow the architect's and engineer's plans, and meets specifications, the personal characteristics, union status, or pay grades of whoever laid it up it are as immaterial as their shoe sizes. It is also immaterial to the construction buyer if the contractor employs three wall builders at $20 per hour or two wall builders at $30 per hour. Provided that the wall gets built to specifications and is completed on time, the details of labor input are (or should be) at the discretion of the contractor. Specifically with respect to union versus nonunion construction workers, regardless of the level their individual skills, training, productivity, quality, experience, or performance, union workers build no better buildings than nonunion workers (although they may do so with greater or lesser efficiency).

B. INDUSTRIAL STRUCTURE: THE UNION PATTERN

The Industrial Revolution in the late eighteenth century substantially bypassed the construction trades, which because of their scattered locations and short job durations, were amenable neither to factory settings nor to the economies of mass production. The ancient European craft guild system that still formed the basis of both work organization and job performance was premised on the notion that all admitted journeymen to any guilded trade had mastered the entirety of that trade's secrets and that all working journeymen were sufficiently (and therefore equally) skilled. Within any locality and time frame, all workers of the same craft would be due the same pay for the same quantity of their labor.

A second premise of the guild system was that the entirety of any construction task could be divided and parceled out to non-competing groups of journeymen handling non-overlapping tasks. The work of each trade was defined by the materials worked and the tools used to work them. Thus, every building project would be completed entirely by groups of journeymen workmen from separate guilds, aided where necessary only by unskilled workers (usually called laborers) who used the tools of no trade, and sometimes by a limited number of apprentices in training to become journeymen. The journeymen of each guild "owned" its work and were responsible for determining who would be allowed to perform what part of it and how many newcomers would be admitted to the guild under what conditions. The guilds were intended to control both the supply and demand for labor within their specialties, and full employment for themselves.

This already-ancient system provided the organizational structure for craft-guild unions at the end of the nineteenth century for any large-scale construction work, because the actual work tasks and processes of the industry had changed very little from when it had been developed years or hundreds of years before. Building construction was simply not amenable to the great advances associated with technological changes of the factory system and the industrial revolution.

When modern building trades' unions began to form toward the end of the nineteenth century and to join the American Federation of Labor, they joined as what amounted to craft-guilds, each having its own bailiwick and the other characteristics discussed above. This was the union organizational model. A second and different model started with small-scale construction for homes and farms. This work was normally performed by homeowners or farmers, themselves, and so was outside the bailiwick of early unions. In this alternative model, individual workers did as many different jobs as necessary, and were not restricted by craft or tools used. They were called thing like "construction workers" or "building constructors." The nonunion segment of the industry, now over 80 percent of the total, developed from this model.

C. INDUSTRIAL STRUCTURE: THE NONUNION PATTERN

From the same initial orientation, job identification, and ownership breakdowns within the nonunion (also known as the "merit shop" or "open shop") sector evolved differently. Because it was free from the need to maintain strict differentiation among competing crafts and between journeymen and persons of lesser skill within any particular craft, the nonunion sector was much more flexible. Each trade could expand both horizontally and vertically, without fear of consequence for overlapping areas of jurisdiction or work ownership.

A nonunion constructor might be able to work in several different crafts (a carpenter's helper, for example, might do framing or roughing-in for carpenters, electricians, plumbers, or for anyone else who needed it, or might help the carpenter with everything from materials handling to final finishing) or could work in entirely new crafts (metal building assembly, drywall installing and finishing, drop ceiling installation, vinyl siding, sprinkler fitting, welding, etc.)—whatever seemed best to meet the changing needs of the industry. Because there was a greater attachment between workmen and their employers, and greater retention of workmen during slow periods, it was also expected that workmen could help out in other, busier, trades or work temporarily at lesser levels, if necessary. Their loyalty was therefore more directed towards their employer than to an individual craft.

The two principal keys were flexibility and the potential for individual advancement, which the nonunion sector generally had and the union sector generally did not. A nonunion laborer might advance to be a carpenter's helper, then a forms carpenter, then carpenter, then carpenter leader, advancing with skill and experience; but a union laborer would always remain a laborer unless he gave up seniority and pay to become a carpenter's apprentice (for several years) before joining the carpenters at their lowest seniority.

As their labor deployment patterns began to diverge, so too did both craft ownership of work and the use of helpers and learners. The more flexible nonunion pattern has tried to keep up with the changing demands of new technologies and evolve as necessary, but many of its developments have been restrained by the operations of prevailing wage laws that have strongly favored the more conservative union methods and practices. But the controversy over helpers, semi-skilled workers, and more specifically, their job titles, is immensely important, and the way controversies have been resolved for these things for Davis-Bacon purposes illustrates perhaps more thoroughly than anything else the degree to which government (DOL) will go to support union views and methods. This deserves further consideration, which will be given in the next few sections and illustrated with examples in Appendix 3.

D. CRAFT UNIONS IN THE AFL

The first organizational meeting of the AFL, held in St. Louis in 1886, had several construction trades in attendance. By 1900, carpenters, boilermakers, bricklayers, plasterers, lathers, electricians, ironworkers, painters, and plumbers had formed and joined as unions structured along similar guild-craft lines, differentiated by their tools and materials used. Hod carriers, asbestos workers, roofers, elevator constructors, and the hoisting-and-portable locals of the operating engineers joined a bit later. All these were on board before 1908, and all but the first of this group, hod carriers, were of the same structural form. Hod carriers (bricklayers' helpers) joined with helpers from a couple of other trades and later became the laborers' union. [1] At the time, it was the only cross-craft union in the construction group.

By 1908, when the AFL established the Building and Construction Trades Council as the industry's labor-coordinating group, 19 building trade unions held seats, and together these provided a close approximation to blanket coverage of all the tasks needed by any commercial construction work being done at that time. Amazingly, 14 survivors (stone polishers and granite cutters had disappeared, some others had merged) still characterized the BCTC when it ceased to be a separate unit of the AFL-CIO in the early 2000s, despite the fact that the general technology of the industry had, by then, changed quite significantly and the industry might have been better served by a different array of trade specialties.

Through the years, however, these same early forming construction unions retained their initial orientations towards their crafts' ownership of work, job assignment, and skill development. But neither the original nor the remaining unions any longer encompassed all the crafts required by modern projects, nor did they reflect the changing skill levels needed within crafts also brought about by new technologies developed during the century—notably with such tasks as handling of sheet rock (wallboard), communications and security wiring, welding, drop ceiling installation, sprinkler fitting, metal building erection, or (more recently) weatherization work, among others. Therefore, most unions have had to make room for craft help-

---

[1] A hod is a pair of boards in a v-shape on a pole, designed to hold and carry bricks and hoist them up to the working level of the bricklayer's scaffold. Hod Carriers carry hods, but also serve as helpers, mixing mortar and performing other functions to assist the bricklayer craftsmen.

ers or journeymen tenders from their own unions, or for laborers, or for sub-craft specialists, all of whom have skills and pay rates differentiable from those of journeymen. Unions are clearly uncomfortable with this change from journeymen-only status and different unions have adopted different ways to handle it.

E. SEMI-SKILLED WORKERS AND HELPERS

Throughout the construction industry, both union and nonunion, there has been growing need to spread fully qualified craftsmen a little thinner. This takes two forms: first, some fully qualified craftsmen have been replaced by craftsmen specialized in more narrow applications of the craft's skills (e.g., "Cement Block Layer" instead of "Mason"); second, craftsmen have been increasingly aided by persons who assist them by doing a variety of tasks that may include heavy lifting and the service work of fetching and toting, but who also can assist in performing some of the lesser or more repetitive craft tasks (e.g., "Mason Tender"). Both of these are threatening to the journeymen of established trades when they represent the development of new levels of skill between the laborer and the fully qualified journeyman. No area of construction has generated more controversy in union construction than the creation of these proliferating levels of semi-skilled workmen, and the controversy has persisted since the construction unions were first formed.

The helper who picks up the trade threatens the skilled craftsman. He not only provides competition for jobs in a business in which job scarcity consciousness is a way of life, but if the former helper is not accredited and admitted to the craft union, he is a potential replacement for the journeyman as a nonunion worker. More commonly today, helpers are part of nonunion teams vying for the available work with union apprentice-trained journeymen. The determination of construction unions to eliminate such competition has been at the heart of union policy toward helpers for more than a century.

The Union Paradigm for Semi-Skilled Work

The problem is especially acute for helpers, as such. Although the nature of the work might require a helper to toil close to the craft job and to the journeymen performing it, in the union view, regardless of how much the helper who is alert and ambitious might learn to perform the skilled work and be qualified to advance to journeyman status, he should not be allowed upward mobility except through the apprenticeship route. Learning remains the exclusive province of the apprentice, and helping of the helper. On-the-job training is not part of the system.

It is not a new problem for unions, but a solution has proved elusive from the start. Already by the end of the nineteenth century, construction unions were experimenting with several approaches to what they considered even then to be "the helper problem." Various policies were tried, including attempting to forbid the employment of helpers entirely, encouraging helpers to form separate unions, and admitting them to their unions either as auxiliaries or as full members. None of these policies worked well alone, so the final solution was a pastiche of all three.

After experimenting unsuccessfully with separate helper unions, some early unions decided to admit their own helpers in order to control them. Consequently, the word "helper" was added to the name of some unions. For example, the boilermakers, which became (after some further mergers) the International Brotherhood of Boilermakers, Iron Ship Builders, Blacksmiths, Forgers, and *Helpers* clearly added that name and status. Elevator constructors, although they do not use the word helper in their union's title, have always admitted and used helpers, too.

Initially, some other craft unions admitting helpers placed them in auxiliary organizations in which they had few, if any, rights of self-government or control of their bargaining. Understandably, helpers rejected such arrangements, and in most cases the auxiliaries were disbanded and the members admitted into the general membership at reduced status, except where they were used to discriminate against black workers, as was done by the sheet metal workers. The electrical workers and the plumbers and steamfitters, however, from their inception, largely barred both helpers and blacks from their organizations until the civil rights revolution of the 1960s forced a policy change toward minorities.

The survivor was the laborers' union, originally the International Hod Carriers, Building and Common Laborers Union, now the Laborers International Union of North America. The reason for its success is partially in its separateness, partially in its diversity, and partially in the fact that its members do not move up to become journeymen in the craft trades to which they may be related. Being a complex body of unskilled workers from different trades and backgrounds, laborers assert their jurisdiction over no particular trade, but rather over certain classes or levels of work.[2]

The organization of laborers into the Hod Carriers left the skilled tradesmen in the rest of the construction industry free to continue undisputed ownership of their respective trades. Furthermore, the separated laborers' group saved the unions from having to give national charters to other helpers which, especially in the case of the trades requiring higher levels of skill development, might have provoked division of jurisdiction between journeymen and helpers, with a high likelihood of endless jurisdictional disputes.

Today, the laborers' union segregates helpers and laborers from journeymen and tends to prevent helpers who might pick up a trade through job experience from becoming journeymen without first becoming apprentices. With changing technology in the industry as a whole, however, and increasingly large gaps in coverage by the original craft designations with respect to modern work needs, the jobs of various laborers have diverged, and only a small portion of them remain doing "grunt work." Indeed, there exists the odd anomaly that the laborers union, originally designated as a union of individuals using the tools of no trade, now provides an apprenticeship program and also confers upon its members the oxymoronic status of "journeyman laborer."

It should be noted, however, that many of the tasks performed by "laborers," such as welding, torching, or demolition, do in fact require greater skill development, precision, and complex tool use than for other laborer's tasks like materials handling or flagging, or than several of the traditional specialty crafts like painting, roofing, or tile

[2] The laborers' union is not quite the CIO to the AFL's construction trades group, because it is not structured as an alternative to craft unionism, but rather is a cross-specialty support union as well as a semi-vertical catch-all for developing trades that were not represented among the original AFL affiliates.

setting. This has led to great problems with the equitable administration of wage rates in prevailing wage administration, in which everyone with the same job title is presumed to be equally skilled and entitled to equal pay, and in which skilled workers expect to be paid better than unskilled ones.

The creation of the laborers union did not entirely eliminate jurisdictional disputes between helpers and craftsmen, even in the bricklaying segment (bricklaying journeymen v. hod-carrying helpers). When the craft unions were still young at the start of the twentieth century, they were already expanding their job claims to include unskilled or other sub-journeymen's work associated with their specialties and denying the less skilled workmen jobs that actually required little or no skilled training. Concrete mixing, rough form building, erection of scaffolding, cleaning brick walls, handling materials, and (a bit later) laying cement block were among the many tasks whose ownership could be disputed by bricklayers, masons, and laborers. The attempted takeover of unskilled and semi-skilled work by the unions of skilled craftsmen thus has a long history.

Nonunion Practices with Respect to Helpers

Nonunion work developed the relationship of learners and helpers along different lines. For a long time, however, there was not much need for analysis, because the majority of construction work beyond homebuilding was performed by union contractors, while in small-scale nonunion work there was little need for job title elaboration or designated steps for advancement within a craft. But as nonunion contractors made increasing inroads into the union strongholds in commercial, industrial, and heavy and highway construction work, they developed needs for greater system in these areas.

By 1960, when the unions still controlled the majority of construction work in the U.S., unions with the help of governments had accomplished their objectives of controlling training and limiting job advancement, eliminating or curtailing helpers. In this way they maintained for their skilled craftsmen not only high wage rates when doing craft work but also ownership of the semi-skilled and much of the unskilled work in their trades, where craftsmen were paid the same high wage rates for doing unskilled, ancillary tasks. This may have suited journeymen unionists very well, but its inefficiencies opened the way for nonunion forces to underbid them competitively and take on ever-larger projects in the private sector. Open shop builders, who already performed the bulk of the home building, low-rise apartments, and smaller commercial work, now moved into large-scale commercial and industrial construction, and became a factor with which the unionized contractors needed to reckon. In this competition, open shop labor deployment and training, including the use of helpers and other semi-skilled workers in job teams led by skilled journeymen, has a clear economic edge.

For a typical job involving, for example, electricians, a union contractor might use a work crew composed entirely of three to five journeymen. These high-priced, skilled workers would perform their skilled work, but also do the menial tasks of nailing up conduit, pulling wires through conduit, or carrying materials. For the same job, a nonunion contractor would be more likely to deploy one senior journeyman, whose compensation might be equal to, or even above, the union rate, and either two helpers and one or two laborers, or just one helper and the balance laborers. Helpers might be graded "A" or "B" depending on their experience, and helpers, journeymen, and laborers would probably be compensated at different rates within grade as well as between grades. Regardless of the details, the nonunion combination would usually produce a substantial cost advantage in comparison with the union deployment pattern.[3]

The Prevailing Rate Complication

An additional complication for the unions when it came to the use of helpers was created by the Davis-Bacon Act and other prevailing wage laws that specified particular minimum wage rates for indi-

[3] An analysis performed by the author of labor costs of constructing a large electrical distribution and transmission facility in Alaska in the mid-1990s estimated the cost of wage and productivity differences between all-union and merit-shop (nonunion) bidding to be between 8.6 and 18.8 percent. *See,* Herbert R. Northrup and Armand J. Thieblot, "Cost Review for Contracting Alternatives for Transmission Facilities in Alaska," (1996) unpublished, Prepared for Chugach Electric Association. (Copy available from the author.)

vidually named job titles. So long as the job titles were standard journey-level ones ("Carpenter" or "Elevator Constructor") and unions had a majority presence in the construction strata most used for public works, unions had no problem winning wage surveys and forcing nonunion competitors to comply with the same two-level skill system (all journeymen equally skilled, assisted by unskilled laborers) within each trade. (Apprentices were automatically allowed at reduced wage rates if registered, or excluded if not, and were neither surveyed for nor listed in prevailing rate determinations.)

Once unions started adding job titles designating additional skill levels (e.g., "helper" or "tender"), however, they opened themselves up to risks at both the survey and the determination levels of prevailing rate administration. First, they might have to actually demonstrate the "prevailing-ness" of their own use of particular semi-skilled job titles in order to get reduced rates determined for their own employees, and second, they had to do it such a way as to prevent nonunion competitors from either using the same ones (that might lead to rates determined at the not-union level) or from being allowed to use their own, differently named ones (that might lead to prevailing rates being determined just for them). Either possibility would open the door to merit-related wages that would no longer protect the high-wage union journeymen and might even result in something like a two-tiered prevailing rate system, one for union job titles and one for nonunion job titles. This would be an outcome that, in the unions' view, would miss the whole point of prevailing rates, and would allow nonunion employers to maintain their labor cost advantage for a large portion of their workforces.

As the nonunion sector of the industry grew and the union "only-two-levels-of-skill" model became increasingly obsolete and uncompetitive, prevailing wage administrators were forced into bizarre accommodations to try to carve out niches for the union use of semi-skilled job titles while continuing to prevent the nonunion use of similar nonunion ones. To date, it has been successful. With the usual help from government agencies, unions seem to have beaten back the challenge to their dominance of prevailing rate determinations, but it has not been an easy task. The importance of the issue to both sides can be judged by the ferocity and tenacity with which they acted during the "Helper Rate Experiment," which involves too lengthy a discussion to be entered into here, and so is covered in detail, below, in Appendix Three.

F. UNION AND NONUNION WAGE RATES, AND THE UNION WAGE RATE DIFFERENTIAL

The idealized labor model of Frederick W. Taylor and Henry Ford (among others), is one in which high wages exist simultaneously with low labor costs. It is the model that all modern business embraces and that unions, in particular, strive to achieve for their members and employers. If high wages can be offset by capitalization for greater labor productivity, by reduced wastage, or by superior performance, then high wages and low labor costs can occur simultaneously to mutual benefit and satisfaction.

At the time this idealized labor model was developed, it involved just wage rates, because the notion of fringe benefits and of differential terms-and-conditions costs between various categories of labor performing the same tasks had not yet become a factor. These details are now very much a factor, and it is important to understand that wages are only part of the broader category of employment costs, and that these are what count. Nevertheless, the two most important components are wages and fringe benefits, and for my purposes here, I shall ignore the others. Before returning to the greater discussion of whether unions have achieved both ends of the Taylor trade-off or only the high-wage part, it is necessary to determine how union and nonunion wages rates actually compare.

Nonunion Wages and Fringe Benefit Amounts

In private work, the union contractor does not have to worry about the market rate for wages, because it is irrelevant to him. As a union contractor, he must pay union rate. This is also true on prevailing rate jobs. It is often overlooked that union contractors must pay union rates regardless of what wage rates might be determined as prevailing. If a prevailing wage rate is set below the union rate, or at a nonunion average, or at the minimum wage, or even at zero, the union contractor must nevertheless pay the contract rate for the union from which he must draw his workforce. A prevailing wage is not determinative—it is a minimum. A prevailing wage would affect his pay rates only if it was above the union scale, and that is rare.

Paying the union rate on a private job in a new territory is expensive, but it does have the side benefit that the union contractor knows what his wage rates will be when he bids the job. A nonunion contractor in the same circumstance must anticipate what the market rate for his employees will be, and he has no contract to refer to. For this reason, firms exist to sample the market rates for construction workers in various craft specialties in different parts of the country for different types or scales of project. One company is PAS, Inc., which compiles such data and sells it by subscription to nonunion contractors to help them estimate prospective labor costs of various trades in the locality of the upcoming work.[4]

For its current survey (2011), PAS surveyed 1,200 contractors who provided data on 74,909 nonunion laborers and 30 different craft specialties including all of the usual building trades (e.g., asbestos worker, bricklayer, electrician, operating engineer, plumber, sheet metal worker, etc.) and several that are not generally recognized AFL unions of their own (acoustical workers, drywall finishers, low voltage installers, insulators, metal building mechanics, riggers, sprinkler fitters, welders). The national average rate for the craft journeymen in these specialties for commercial, industrial, and institutional construction was found to be $20.45. Their fringes benefits averaged 20.3 percent of gross wages, for a total effective wage of $24.60. (As a matter of convenience, although Davis-Bacon determinations always state wages and fringes separately, I shall generally combine them.) Here are some details:

- For residential work, the average was about $1.00 lower, for heavy and highway work, $1.00 to $2.00 higher. There were slight differences among crafts and in different regions of the country, but the variances were small.
- Laborers' average wage was $15.61, plus 19.1 percent fringes ($18.59 total) for residential work, a bit lower in commercial, industrial, and institutional work, a bit higher in heavy and highway work.

[4] PAS, Inc., "2011 Merit Shop Wage and Benefit Survey." <www.pas1.com>. The author is grateful to PAS, Inc. for making the proprietary information from the survey available for this book.

- Helpers, of whom 6,218 were included in the survey, averaged $18.32 compared with the journeymen's rates in corresponding crafts of $31.65. As a generality, most helpers were paid 50 to 60 percent of what their corresponding journeymen were receiving. Helpers were identified with 11 trades—HVAC mechanics, bricklayers, carpenters, cement masons, electricians, ironworkers (reinforcing), ironworkers (structural), painters, pipefitters, plumbers, and sheet metal workers.

Union Wages and Fringe Benefit Amounts

Despite the fact that union contractors always know what they need to pay under their contracts, union contract rates are surprisingly variable even within the same type of construction and in the close geographic proximity to one another. It is too large a data-collection task to compile all current union wage rates from their contracts, but I have done so for the 694 union journeymen rates, the 151 union laborer rates, and the 80 union helper and semi-skilled rates that appear in the prevailing wage determinations for commercial construction in the state of Pennsylvania, current as of mid-2011. Of the 1,017 wage rates that appear in the compilation of Pennsylvania determinations, only 92 (9 percent) were not-union, although 81.1 percent of construction workers in the state are known to be nonunion. Table A2–1 gives the results. Union journeymen's rates (including fringes) ranged from $34.00 per hour for truck drivers to $63.18 for elevator mechanics. The astonishing range of wage rates within individual crafts (e.g., $38 to $69 per hour for unionized sheet metal workers within the state) give the lie to the notion that the union wage is a monolithic wage. There is, in fact, more variation in union wages from polity to polity in Pennsylvania than there is in nonunion or market wages for the same crafts, or between union and nonunion wages by craft. Taken together, union journeymen's rates averaged $48.53 for the 18 trades that appeared in the determinations.

Union laborers also worked for a wide rage of contract wages, from $27 to $47 per hour, averaging $39.14. Helpers and semi-skilled union operators averaged $37.70.

Table A2-1

Range and Average of Union Determination Rates By Craft

Commercial Construction, Pennsylvania 2011
(Including Fringes)

Craft	*Range*	*Average*
Asbestos Worker	$47-$72	$52.16
Boilermaker	53-67	63.17
Bricklayer, Stonemason, Cement Mason	20-57	43.00
Carpenter, Millwright, Floor Layer	35-67	45.60
Electrician	41-76	52.79
Elevator Mechanic	61-70	63.18
Equipment Operator	33-73	47.58
Glazier	31-58	38.37
Iron Worker (Structural)	41-73	53.55
Painter	32-54	37.88
Pile Driver	43-67	57.63
Plasterer	25-56	37.60
Plumber, Pipefitter	34-69	55.97
Roofer	36-56	44.29
Sheet Metal Worker	38-69	53.16
Sprinkler Fitter	39-67	52.44
Tile Setter	39-42	41.20
Truck Driver	31-43	34.00
Journeymen, Grand Range and Avg.	$20-$76	$48.53
Laborer	$27-$47	$34.69
Helpers and Semi-skilled	$24-$58	$37.70

Source: Compiled by the author from Davis-Bacon prevailing wage determinations for commercial construction, state of Pennsylvania, 2011

In comparison with the merit shop rates, the union wage differential was near 100 percent higher for all three categories of workmen. Union wage rates (with fringes) are thus just about exactly twice as high as could be found on the open market. These figures are tabulated in Table A2-2.

Table A2–2

Union Wage Differential By Level of Worker

Commercial Construction, Pennsylvania 2011
(Including Fringes)

Level of Worker	*Union Wage Rate*	*Nonunion Wage Rate*	*Union Differential $/hr*	*Union Differential %*
Journeymen	$48.53	$24.60	$23.93	97%
Laborer	$34.69	$18.59	$16.10	86%
Helpers and Semi-skilled	$37.70	$18.81	$18.89	100%

Source: Compiled by the author from Davis-Bacon prevailing wage determinations for commercial construction, state of Pennsylvania, 2011, and PAS, Inc., "2011 Merit Shop Wage and Benefit Survey."

Wage differentials alone, however, do not define what I call here the union premium.

G. THE TOTAL UNION PREMIUM

The residual cost differential between union and nonunion labor that continues to exist even after skill, experience, and productivity factors are taken into account is the true union premium. Higher union wages and fringe benefits are only part of the story, because there are some union offsetting productivity gains on the one hand but additional employer costs associated with hiring union personnel on the other that on balance increase the cost difference substantially.

Union contracts often require a specific number of work breaks, or make-ready time and clean-up time, require employers to pay for union stewards to do union business of company time, require specific (low) ratios of apprentices to journeymen, require special overtime rates that are twice or even three times straight wages, allow unions rather than employers to select workers for hire, require large numbers of paid holidays, require employers to collect and administer union dues from members, require payment of up to a half-day for show-up time in the event of bad weather, and many other minutia. By some estimates, union work rules can add as much as another 25 percent to the effective union wage costs.

It is this total union premium, not just wages, that becomes the component of labor cost that must be offset by higher union productivity or performance to achieve total union labor costs equivalent to those of nonunion competitors. Although individual union journeymen are well characterized as being among the most skilled practitioners of their trades, and are widely accoladed for their knowledge, skills, training, experience, and dedication, their additional productivity, efficiency, or performance is insufficient to overcome the economic penalties associated with their higher wages, benefits, and other employment costs.

Pro-unionists often recite the mantra that, "you get what you pay for" in justification for the admittedly higher wage rates caused by Davis-Bacon. The clear implication is that high wages and benefits are necessary to attract the best workers, and, by transitive implication, that offering lower wages and benefits will attract only lower-grade workers. The open market of nonunion construction understands this fully well—it being the very basis of the free markets—but also understands the basic precept of economic efficiency that requires you to pay only for the skills and skill levels you actually need.

Union labor is outside of the open market and actually fails on both the premise and the precept: it fails on the premise because all union journeymen, regardless of any manifest difference in skill or individual ability, must be paid the same rate—the union wage; it fails on the precept because, regardless of whether there are menial parts of the jobs that journeymen "own" that could be done equally well or even better by semi-skilled or unskilled persons at lower cost, all aspects of the job must be paid for at the high-skilled journeyman's rate and performed by journeymen. Union members, in other words, do not command their uniformly high wages because they are worth them or because all aspects of the jobs they own actually require their developed skills, but simply because they demand them. In union work the better premise is, "you pay for whatever you get," and you do so at the union rate.

In construction, therefore, unions have achieved only the first part of the idealized labor formula, the high-wage part; they have failed the second. Not only do union members have high wage rates, but their employers also have high labor costs in comparison to their nonunion alternatives. This residual additional union labor cost, expressed as a totality or on a per-hour basis, is the residual union premium—the extra cost of union labor that remains after the added benefits of union training, skills, productivity, etc. have been taken into account. That such a union premium actually exists can be seen in the fact that unions have been able to win a smaller and smaller percentage of jobs over the years in competitive markets where labor costs matter.

The prima facie evidence that union productivity and other benefits are unable to overcome the union cost differential lies in the fact that unions actively seek political or coercive rather than economic means to find work, by persuading or coercing construction buyers to enter into Project Labor Agreements (PLAs) or to prefer or to deal exclusively with unions (solutions that requires the buyers to ignore their own best interests in achieving lower costs). If the total package of employment costs and satisfactions that unions presented equaled that of their nonunion competitors, unions could rely on having an equal chance of being employed solely on the basis of net economic efficiency and would not need the help of a coercive government.

Because of the inherent fungiblity of building construction work, the consequence to union employers and workers of the existence of large union premiums is less work and fewer members in any freely competitive market for construction work. The statistics verify this, showing that unions and unionized construction workers have literally became the victims of their own success. Union density (coverage) in construction reached a high point of over 87 percent of the industry in 1947, then declined asymptotically towards the current level, falling from something still over 80 percent in the 1940s, to about 55 percent in the 1950s, 40 percent in the 1960s, 30 percent by the beginning of the 1980s, 20 percent in the 1990s, and finally to about 15 percent, now.[5] The union position in the construction marketplace thus fell from near monopoly control after World War II to near insignificance at the present time except in a few highly specialized segments and in protected affinity and prevailing wage market segments where construction buyers have been persuaded to ignore economic efficiency in favor of union advantage.

H. TYPES OF CONSTRUCTION MARKETS

Two discussions are relevant to the topic of construction markets. The first has to do with the identification of markets by characteristics or degree of difficulty for the purposes of setting different prevailing wage rates for construction workers having the same title (e.g., carpenter or laborer) working in the various sectors. The second has to do with the delineation of construction markets by the type of competition that exists within them. The second is more significant than the first, but I will discuss them in order.

Work Classifications for Davis-Bacon Purposes

The Davis-Bacon Act requires predetermination of prevailing wage rates for "project of a similar character" to those from which the wage survey was drawn. According to the U.S. Department of Labor *Davis-Bacon Resource Book*, "As a matter of longstanding policy, the Department has distinguished four general types of construction for purposes of making prevailing wage determinations: building construction, residential construction, heavy construction, and highway construction."[6]

These definitions are, of course, not discrete, and it can be a matter of some importance if a proposed project of, say, 4-story military apartment units is classified as residential or as building construction. (Usually the difference in this case is resolved not by the number of

[5] *See* Northrup, (2008) *Union Tactics*, Figures 1-5.

[6] Taken from the 2002 edition of the Resource Book. If more recent versions have been printed, they have been issued under some different title that I have not been able to identify, but it is unlikely substantive changes have occurred.

units to be built or the total scale of the project, but by whether or not elevators are to be installed.) Residential rates are often only a fraction of building rates, especially for mechanics, as opposed to laborers. In those rare surveys that reflect the actual 80–85 percent dominance of residential work by nonunion contractors, the differences can be much greater.

In many states (Pennsylvania is an example), heavy and highway determinations are merged, perhaps because both are based on statewide or even on multi-state surveys. This leads to such anomalies as finding plumbers' or drywall finishers' rates for application to highway work and, in general, a lot of unnecessary rate detail in determinations for this sector.

Of greater concern is the emergence of specialty surveys and determinations whose purpose seems to be to settle jurisdictional arguments among unions for control of specialty labor. For example, in the early 2000s, a large percentage of the new surveys actually performed by the Department of Labor each year were devoted to setting rates for landscaping work, apparently because various locals of teamsters' unions and of laborers' unions laid claim to the same work and wanted their local rates protected. More recently, similar disputes have given rise to special surveys for weatherproofing work, and special determinations have been made for "water and sewer only," and others. Within surveys, one can also find differentiations of carpenter rates, for example, requiring different prevailing rates for work on projects valued at above or below some contract amount despite the fact that these differentiations are not sanctioned by the law, itself, or even its administrative manual.

The distinctions and classifications of type of work for which the DOL makes surveys and issues wage determinations is, in short, arbitrary.

Work Classification by the Nature of Its Market Sector

The majority of building construction is awarded to the lowest-cost, competent bidder in the free-market sector characterized by price-elasticity and open competition. I estimate the freely competitive sector of the broad construction marketplace and of the building and heavy sectors to be on the order of 60 percent of the total. Residential construction is perhaps 80–85 percent freely competitive;

highway construction considerably less so, mostly because of the paucity of private buyers. However, the free-market sector is only one of three major sectors that exist.

A second sector, the affinity sector, is one in which building construction is awarded to the lowest-cost bidder but all bidders must be unionized, or even be unionized by particular locals. This sector is characterized by price-inelasticity with respect to input costs, limited competition, and some level of indifference on the part of the construction buyer to the possibility of cheaper prices from other equally competent but politically or fraternally unconnected suppliers.

A common example of a price-inelastic affinity would be buildings built for the use of unions, themselves, in solidarity with common principles of their fraternal organizations, though it is not unknown for construction unions to graciously respond by having their members work at less than posted union rates. The second main affinity connection is between, for example, a unionized industrial company and unionized building trades to limit bidding opportunities for new building projects to union signatories so as to avoid the spread of any labor unrest from the construction site to the industrial one. The third type of affinity market is private construction that may take place in union-dominated urban areas. Although affinity projects are price-inelastic with respect to labor input costs, even these projects remain price elastic in the broader sense that the higher the labor costs (and therefore the total costs of the projects), the fewer projects will be undertaken.

The third sector, and the most important protected one with respect to prevailing rates, is the public works sector. In this sector, building projects may be awarded by virtue of low-cost bid to either union or nonunion contractors, but every successful bidder must pay above-market wages because of the prevailing rate requirements that are part of public works contracting at the federal, state, and (sometimes) local levels. Where prevailing rate requirements exist, they compel employers to pay politically derived wage rates rather than economically derived wage rates, all of which are above market rates and most of which are set to current union collective bargaining agreements.

Another form of protected, price-inelastic construction labor market is contracting under the terms of Project Labor Agreements, which require not only union wage rates and fringes benefits, but also union work rules, labor deployment patterns, and dues-equivalent payments from nonunion employees. The Boston Big Dig was such a PLA and they are important variations on labor contracting. Nevertheless, with the exception of Copeland Act considerations that might impact such union initiatives as job targeting, a PLA requirement and a prevailing rate requirement have the same economic implications and I will not differentiate between them.

About 26 percent of all building construction in the United States is for public owners at federal, state, or local levels, much of it subject to the requirement to pay prevailing wages. It is not widely understood, but all prevailing rates, whether set by reference to union contract rates or by survey, are above market at the time they are issued. In even the least obtrusive formulation of prevailing rates—the weighted average of an all-nonunion survey—the minimum wage set will require higher payments to the lower 50 percent of the of the survey that composed the average, while ordinary market forces will ensure continuation of higher rates to the 50 percent that were the top half of the survey.

Thus, unless they have become obsolete, prevailing rates always increase labor input costs, even if they are not set at the union rate, and even if they are set at a purely nonunion rate. The single exception is if the prevailing rate is set at the minimum wage by the 50-percent rule.

All prevailing rates on public works are union rates or above-market rates. The great majority of prevailing rates, vastly disproportionate to unions' proportion of the construction labor force, are set at the union wage. I estimate that although unions represent less than 20 percent of the construction labor force, union rates are found to prevail in 80 percent of the tens of thousands of individual rates published in wage determinations. Any individual determination of union prevalence (50 percent or more) by fair sample from a population less than 20 percent union is unlikely, and finding union prevalence repeatedly in 80 percent of all tens of thousands of separate determinations is vanishingly improbable. Yet, that is what prevailing rate determinations do, so something other than fair sampling must determine the actual outcome.[7]

Thus, the important characteristics of prevailing rate jobs with respect to prevailing rates are: 1) that the wage rates set by prevailing rates are politically rather than economically derived and are set at levels that are demonstrably excessive and usually at the union rate; 2) that prevailing rate work is price-inelastic with respect to labor input costs; 3) that nonunion competitors are deprived of their most powerful economic weapons—their ability to produce equivalent construction output more efficiently and cheaply because of their lower total labor costs.

---

[7] *See* Thieblot, (1995) "The Twenty-Percent Majority."

Appendix Three

Proliferating Semi-Skilled Job Titles and the Helper Controversy

One of the most significant tests of the Davis-Bacon system and its possibilities for reform came with respect to the proliferating semi-skilled job titles and the rising use of helpers among nonunion firms seeking an alternative to the journeyman-and-apprentice system long held sacrosanct by unions and reflected in the prevailing rate determination process. On-the-job training and the possibility of advancement through skill development and differential pay for differential performance became increasingly necessary as the old apprenticeship system ossified and new labor deployment paradigms arose.

In 1982, after much discussion, federal legislators agreed to institute new rules for Davis-Bacon administration that, among other changes, eliminated the 30-percent rule in favor of majority determination of prevailing rates, eliminated the importation of urban wage scales into rural areas, excluded wages paid under previous Davis-Bacon determinations from most new surveys, and included the use of helpers in the ratio of two helpers for every three journeymen provided that the use of helpers was an "identifiable" practice in the area of the survey.[1]

Before the new rules were introduced in 1982, prevailing rates had generally been set only for journeymen and laborers, although

---

[1] The ratio requirement limiting helper use to two helpers per three journeymen is a strange one, and seems to have no precedent other than that the use of apprentices is similarly constrained. The named helpers and tenders used in union construction had never been constrained in any similar way, however, whether they were separately named in determinations or not. Also unprecedented was the requirement that helper use had to be an identifiable practice in the area of the survey. It brings up an entirely new definitional controversy: one can presume that union use of helpers is "identifiable" if they appear in union contracts; but how could their use be identified in non-union work other than through the rate determination process?

there were exceptions for helpers in crafts such as elevator constructor or boilermaker where the helper designation was traditional in union work. The new rules brought no change to union practice, but they were considered a great step forward by nonunion contractors, whose helpers had never been acknowledged by Davis-Bacon administrators. Nonunion contractors hoped the new rules would bring an end to determinations that, by ignoring rate-setting for the semiskilled employees they called helpers, had required them to choose between not using such employees or paying them as journeyman regardless of their proficiency. One of the characteristics of all prevailing wage laws is that only rates found in their published determinations can be paid: if no rates are published for a particular type of work, fence erection for example, then whoever does that work must be paid at the closest journeyman's rate, probably a carpenter's rate in this case or perhaps an ornamental ironworker's rate.

Unfortunately, the new rules did not bring the desired relief because, over the next 20 years, they were in effect for a total of 21 months, and while in effect they were both unheralded and generally ignored.

1. The 20-Year Death of Helper Regulation Reform

(Note: the boxed headline, below, and the similar ones that will be found throughout this appendix, repeat information summarized in the text in Chapter 2 at the corresponding box number. They serve here as an index to where the detailed discussions very briefly summarized in Chapter 2 are found.)

No. 18. The Department of Labor's victorious 20-year struggle to quash modest reforms setting wage rates for construction helpers, even in constrained circumstances and defined settings, shows undue bias towards union wages and work patterns.

New Regulation Stalled (1982–1985, years 1–3)

Although the change embodied in the 1982 rules that received the greatest publicity was the change to the "50-percent rule" (from the "30-percent rule," reflecting the higher proportion of rates "the same to the penny" needed to be found in order for that rate to be designated as prevailing), this in fact had relatively little economic or operational impact, for two reasons: First, survey collection still heavily favored union contract rates (and they did not really need to be the "same to the penny"); and second, prevailing rates based on weighted averages still drove up nonunion costs when they became the new required minimums.

The part of the change that went relatively unnoticed by the general public was the modest and entirely reasonable extension of the existing rules to cover the previously neglected helper designations. This threatened the ownership of semi-skilled work by journeymen, and was vehemently resisted by unions, who immediately sought and won from Judge Harold Greene, United States District Court, Washington, D.C., a permanent injunction against the implementation of all the changes except that involving the 30-percent rule.[2]

Judge Greene based his decision on the novel premise that although the Act gave the Secretary of Labor complete control over administrative procedure, all previous secretaries had failed to make these changes, and thus established a negative precedent preventing the current one from making them also. The Greene decision was overturned on appeal, but the appellate court, also delimiting the secretary's control without apparent justification, limited the use of helpers and the determination of the wage rates for them to areas in which

[2] Building and Construction Trades Department, AFL-CIO, v. Raymond Donovan, Secretary of Labor, 543 F. Supp. 1282; 553 F. Supp. 352 (D.D.C. 1982).

they were a prevailing, not just an identifiable practice.[3] In 1984, the Supreme Court rejected the union request to grant certiorari.[4]

Although Judge Greene had thus been successfully overturned, astonishingly, he did not lift his injunction against implementing the new rules (other than the 30-percent rule change, which he had not earlier enjoined) until 18 months after the appellate court reversed his decision and 11 months after the Supreme Court declined to review the appellate court decision. Even then, he frustrated the proposed reform by refusing to rescind the injunction against the helper rule and to permit the DOL merely to substitute the words "prevailing practice" for "identifiable practice." Rather, the judge required that "if DOL wanted to ease the rules for helpers, even if they form a prevailing category of workmen, it . . . [would] have to start all over again with a notice of intended rulemaking."[5]

Judge Greene Concedes (1985–1990, years 3–8)

The DOL did not immediately respond. In January 1985, it implemented the other Davis-Bacon modifications without the helper provision and shelved development of a new helper regulation until finally issuing one four years later, at the end of January 1989. The new regulation provided that contractors would be permitted to use helpers at wage rates lower than those for journeymen when the practice was found to be prevailing on local construction projects, but only in limited numbers and proportions to journeymen.[6]

---

[3] This completed the two-step Catch 22: helper rates could only be found to be prevailing if they were certified to be prevailing before being found.

[4] Building & Construction Trades Department, AFL-CIO, v. Raymond Donovan, Secretary of Labor, 712 F.2d 611 (DC Cir. 1983); *cert. den.*, 464 U.S. 1069 (1984)

[5] Building & Construction Trades Department, AFL-CIO, v. Raymond Donovan, Secretary of Labor, 102 CCH Labor Cases, 34,648 (D.D.C. 1984).

[6] *Labor Department Issues Final Regulation Allowing Helpers on Davis-Bacon Projects,* Const. Lab. Report (BNA), February 1, 1989, at 1227–28, 1263–73. Needless to say, no similar use restrictions applied to named, semi-skilled union workers.

The regulation was scheduled to be effective 60 days after Judge Greene actually lifted his injunction, but he delayed lifting it while considering another AFL-CIO suit asking for continuation. Finally, on September 24, 1990, he ruled that the new regulations were not contrary to the Davis-Bacon Act's statutory purpose and lifted the injunction.[7] Thus, the again-revised helper regulations became effective on December 4, 1990.

Second Phase – Congress, President, and the Supreme Court Act (1990–1992, years 8–10)

The construction unions, however, had not yet given up. Even while DOL was still in the preparation phase of implementation and before it had actually done a survey or issued a rate including helpers, they again maneuvered to derail their inclusion. While AFL-CIO lawyers appealed Judge Greene's decision to the Court of Appeals, District of Columbia, its lobbyists induced Congress to act. In March 1991, before the Court of Appeals could render a decision, the Democrat-controlled Congress came through with a rider to a supplemental appropriations bill forbidding the DOL from spending funds to implement the helper rule.[8] The House of Representatives rejected an amendment to delete this provision, as did the Senate, largely along party lines. On April 10, 1991, President George H.W. Bush signed the legislation to which the rider remained attached, thus returning the helper issue to limbo.[9]

Persistence reigned on both sides of the issue, however, and in his proposed budget the following year, President Bush announced that labor market regulations planned for 1992 would once again al-

---

[7] Building & Construction Trades Department, AFL-CIO v. Elizabeth Dole, Secretary of Labor, 29 BNA Wage Hour Cases 1607, 116 CCH Labor Cases ¶35,395 (D.C.C. 1990).

[8] Congress was unaware that the "additional funds needed for implementation" were largely imaginary. As will be discussed later in this Appendix, there is no inherently different or more expensive aspect to finding and administering prevailing rates for helpers than for any other category of worker or job title.

[9] "Bush Signs Bill with Prohibition of Helper, Apprenticeship Funding," 37 Const. Lab. Rep. (BNA) (April 17, 1991).

low the use of helpers, in a ratio of two helpers to three journeymen. Simultaneously, the DOL announced that the ban on spending funds for its helper regulation was no longer in effect.[10]

Again the unions went to work, and their friends in Congress moved to prohibit the DOL from lifting the ban, but rather to make it permanent instead.[11] Before this could be achieved, however, the Court of Appeals, District of Columbia Circuit, handed the unions a double-barreled defeat. It ruled that the 1991 ban on use of funds to institute the helper regulation was indeed no longer in effect, and furthermore, that with minor change, the DOL's revised helper regulations were valid.[12] The Supreme Court was, of course, petitioned to review this decision, but declined.[13] Accordingly, the additionally revised regulations went into effect shortly thereafter, 11 years after having originally been approved.

Period of Non-suspension (1992–1993, years 11–12)

This period, also, would prove to be short lived. It lasted for 20-3/4 months, from January 29, 1992 to October 21, 1993, and has aptly been characterized as the "period of non-suspension." During it, the DOL actually conducted 78 wage surveys, a small number and many of them deeply flawed, but which did include at least the possibility of determining prevailing wage rates for helpers.

Congress and a New President (1993–1996, years 12–15)

The brief period of non-suspension came to its end in October 1993 when Congress enacted another rider to yet another appropriations bill, once again prohibiting the enforcement of the revised regu-

[10] "Congressional Ban on Helper Rules No Longer in Effect, DOL Tells Agencies," 37 Const. Lab. Rep. (BNA) (February 5, 1992).

[11] "Ban of Helper Rules May Be Reinstituted in DOL's 1993 Spending Bill, Harkin Says," 90 Daily Lab. Rep. (BNA) (May 8, 1992).

[12] Building & Construction Trades Department, AFL-CIO v. Lynn Martin, Secretary of Labor, 961 F.2d 269 (D.C. Cir. 1992).

[13] *Id.*, *cert. den.*, 464 U.S. 1069 (1992).

lations.[14] This new prohibition, accepted by President Clinton, was extended in 1994,[15] and as a result of these Congressional actions, the DOL suspended its regulations again since they could not be enforced.

Last Phase – The Department of Labor Acts Unilaterally (1996–2000, years 15–20)

The final phase began on April 26, 1996 when (to the surprise of many) President Clinton signed a new appropriations bill passed by Congress that lifted all pending restrictions connected with the new helper regulations, thus returning the state of the law to that which existed in 1992 after the 1991 appropriations rider had lapsed.[16] Thus, as of April 26, 1996, there was no statutory obstacle to enforcement of the revised regulations, which had never been repealed.

Now it became the Department of Labor's turn, however, to decline to implement its own regulations. On August 2, 1996, DOL published a new notice of proposed rulemaking that acknowledged the lack of any bar to proceeding, but nevertheless declined to proceed. Instead, it requested public comment on a proposed "continuation" of the suspension of the regulations, without acknowledging that the suspensions was, or should have been, no longer in effect.[17]

DOL, itself, thus brought about a new suspension of the helper rules, and formally proposed to keep them in suspension until some unspecified date in the future when it might or might not amend the rules or propose something different. Of the four reasons it gave for denying implementation in the meantime, the most compelling was that doing so would create uncertainty among federal agencies and

[14] Pub. L. No. 103–112, § 104 (Oct. 21, 1993).

[15] Pub. L. No. 103–333 (Sept. 30, 1994).

[16] Pub. L. No. 104–134 (April 26, 1996). There is speculation that President Clinton at this time was "moving to the center" as part of his election campaign of that year.

[17] The DOL is an agency under federal control. Its actions may have also been part of the same election-year maneuverings, allowing President Clinton to have his cake and eat it, too.

contractors due to the possibility that the regulations would be further amended—a wonderfully circular logic.[18]

After receiving public comment, DOL issued its final rule, published in the *Federal Register* on December 30, 1996, which restated DOL's concerns, acknowledged countervailing opinions about all of them, and summarily rejected all contrary views.[19] The final rule contained no analysis of the regulatory cost or impact of the proposed new suspensions, as apparently required by law, but the department demurred based on the logic that although application of the regulations might produce cost savings estimated at $600 million a year, suspension of the application of the regulations would not involve a cost *increase*, and therefore would have no negative budgetary or cost impact.

Final Regulation, November 22, 2000.

A lingering problem for both DOL and the unions during this long struggle had been to find a way to carve out a protected niche for the few unions that had traditionally used workers identified as helpers, especially the elevator constructors and boilermakers. When, following yet additional public comment on proposed rulemaking, DOL issued its Final Davis-Bacon Act Helper Regulation on November 22, 2000, it "amend[ed] the regulations to incorporate [what it called] the Wage and Hour Division's longstanding policy of recognizing helper classifications and wage rates only where: (1) their duties are clearly defined and distinct from those of journeyman and laborer classifications in the area; (2) the use of such helpers is an established prevailing practice in the area; and (3) the term 'helper' is not synonymous with 'trainee' in an informal training program."[20]

[18] The other three reasons, in brief, were: (1) helpers were not as widespread as had originally been thought; (2) the regulations might encourage abuse in classifying individuals; and (3) apprenticeship training programs might be affected in some unspecified way. (*See* 61 Fed. Reg., at 68641.)

[19] 61 Fed. Reg., at 68644–46.

[20] "Labor Department's Final Davis-Bacon Act Helper Regulation," 46 Const. Lab. Rep. (BNA) (Nov. 22, 2000).

This built fences around traditional union helpers about as tightly as could be arranged, but still presented some difficulties. As would be seen in subsequent determinations, helper rates were simply not issued independently for even the established classes of helpers. Instead, DOL's published determinations generally allowed the unions to rename their helper rates as, for example, "70% probationary elevator constructor" and include them by automatic addition to the basic trade rates (a practice discussed in detail here in the text in Chapter II).

Thus, DOL effectively returned the status of recognition of helpers in prevailing rate determinations to where it had been 20 years before, and effectively took the issue off the table into the foreseeable future, ending the saga of the attempt to reform helper regulations, and with it, reform the prevailing wage process. Despite clear evidence that it was becoming more and more difficult even for unions to avoid open recognition and use of helpers and semi-skilled workers, or to keep them from learning anything extra while they are on the job, or from advancing by jumping ship to journeyman status in a nonunion firm rather than stay in dead-end subordinate positions within their union—the unions desperately wanted to keep helpers and semi-skilled workmen dominated by their union's eponymous trade journeymen. By rejecting the helper reforms, DOL continued to assist them in this. The degree to which DOL was willing to go to do so is the subject of the next sections.

2. Lessons about Helpers and Semi-Skilled Workers from the Period of Non-Suspension

A side effect from the helper regulation controversy was that details that would otherwise not be available concerning the wage survey process for implementing the Davis-Bacon Act became available, much of it from the surveys conducted during the 21-month period of non-suspension. The WD-10 survey forms, the WD-22A compilation forms, and the resulting determinations were all reviewed for what they could tell about the difference in the way submissions were handled and rates determined for job titles within the union domain in comparison with those in the nonunion domain. The results are enlightening, and yield additional insight into DOL bias. Some of them are evident in the rationales DOL used to avoid helper reform.

A. DEPARTMENT OF LABOR'S FLAWED CASE FOR NOT IMPLEMENTING NEW HELPER REGULATIONS

Concerning the brief period of non-suspension, DOL made strong assertions to the effect that the idea of helper rates had been adequately tested in the surveys conducted then, and was inherently inapplicable because of five additional problems. It asserted that helper rates were difficult to compile, difficult to identify for job content, and difficult to administer. It also asserted that helpers were not found with sufficient frequency to merit determinations and that even if they were, establishing rates for them would not affect construction patterns or costs. And finally, it asserted that issuing rates for helpers would open the door to contractor manipulation of the system, require costly additional enforcement mechanisms, and detract from the apprenticeship system. These items will be treated in turn.

Test Period Adequacy

No. 19. The Department of Labor's assertion that the viability of helper rates was adequately tested by the 78 surveys during the period of non-suspension is clear evidence of bias towards union rates and work methods.

DOL's position that the period of non-suspension gave an adequate test of the new rules was not supported by data from wage surveys made then. For example, the 78 surveys actually performed during these 21 months were far from an adequate, being about 90 times fewer than would be needed for a comprehensive test. Furthermore, the number of "real" surveys performed, that is the number of independently conducted surveys using different data was closer to 58.[21]

Tens of billions of dollars of construction work is done each year that is subject to prevailing wage laws, and this work is performed in geographically diverse areas all around the country. Both local wage

[21] *See* discussion at footnote 29, Ch. III, in the main text.

rates and local work delineations are involved. Because it may or may not be the prevailing practice in Adams County, Ohio, for sheet metal workers to do HVAC duct work, (which might also be done by plumbers or carpenters or laborers or HVAC mechanics) and the journeymen may or may not use helpers to assist them, there is no easy answer to establishing what is and ought to be protected in that county without actually surveying it. If it turns out to be the particular practice in Adams County is for this work to be done by sheet metal workers, the rates paid to those workers become the prevailing rate, and all who would do similar work on covered projects would do it using sheet metal workers at the determined rate, because this was the prevailing practice there.

The tradition within the DOL, however, made a special exemption for nonunion construction worker titles, especially those of helpers. Without the specific goad such as that attached to the new helper regulations to survey for helper use patterns in the same way other work patterns were surveyed, the prevalence of helper use in this particular trade in this particular county would be ignored, regardless of how common it might be, and no rates would be issued for helpers. Surveys performed during the period of non-suspension would correct the oversight, but because the pattern of helper use might vary from county to county, a comprehensive analysis would require surveying for the purpose in all counties. It would also require that either the DOL proactively search for helper use or at least broadly disseminate the information that helper rates submitted to the new surveys would not be routinely ignored.

Thus, to cover the differences in prevailing local job delineation and payment practices adequately, surveys would be needed in each of the 3,000 or so counties for each of four sectors of construction over some reasonable period of time—say over 3 years. This would require some 4,000 surveys per year. During the 21-month period of non-suspension, DOL conducted a total of only 78. At least 20 of these surveys were not independent, but even using the claimed total, this amounts to fewer than 40 surveys a year—one hundred times fewer than needed for adequacy.

Under strict interpretation of the regulatory requirement, this process could not be shortened by using a structured or unstructured random sample. The intent of the Davis-Bacon act is to reflect local practice, whatever it is, and there is no such thing as a national local helper-use practice, any more than there is a national locally prevailing tile-setter wage rate. Nevertheless, it might be argued that the standard practice of DOL has come to define "locality" in broader terms than "county" so as to ease administration of the act, and this practice was followed by DOL in surveys conducted during the period of non-suspension. Setting aside arguments about the validity of DOL's present patterning, which is haphazard, if a full set of surveys for national coverage were conducted with locality groupings proportional to those used in the surveys carried out during the period of non-suspension (but eliminating the 4 "landscape only" and 3 "water and sewer only" surveys as meaningless), an average of 35 counties per survey would be covered by highway surveys, 1.9 in the building sector, 3 in the residential sector, and 5.3 in the heavy construction sector. Applying these same ratios across the board, for reasonable currency and proper evaluation of whether using helper categories were the prevailing practice in local construction around the country, 333 residential surveys, 526 building surveys, 28 highway surveys, and 190 heavy surveys, a total of 1,077, would be required each year of a 3-year cycle.

Even under these broadened conditions of defining locality, no reasonable conclusions about the use of helpers or their prevailingness in local construction practices could possibly be drawn from the very few surveys that were actually performed—1,000 per year short of full coverage. Furthermore, among the surveys actually performed there was massive concentration in a very few parts of the country: 12 of the 16 highway surveys were in a single state; 17 of the 34 building surveys were in only 3 states; all 5 of the heavy surveys were done in 2 contiguous states; and 10 of the 14 residential surveys were done in only two states. Thus, not only was the number of surveys actually performed grossly inadequate, their geographical concentration made them even more so.

Furthermore, the time during which the period of non-suspension applied was too short to provide a meaningful test. Details of the temporal horizons of DOL's 78 listed surveys during the non-suspension period are not available, but typically the time over which rates are collected for survey purposes extends back 18 months to 2 years, or even longer. An example is provided by a survey and determination made shortly after the period of non-suspension ended. This survey for building work in Montgomery County Maryland, 94 MD 022, was conducted in October 1994 based on work performed in the county (selected from the Dodge Reports, as is the common DOL practice) between July 1993 and August 1994. The determination was actually issued 15 November 1995. Thus a time span of more than 2 years applied between when rates were actually paid and when the determination was issued for new work.

Since it may be presumed that allowing helper rates on Davis-Bacon work would encourage the use and reporting of helper rates on non-Davis-Bacon work, also (and thus influence the basis of survey submissions), a minimum of 18 months to 2 years of implementation of the revised helper rule would be needed before a fair assessment of the change could be begun.

This was possibly reflected in the surveys that were actually performed during non-suspension. Among residential and building surveys dated 1992, 18 of 25 (72%) did not have any helper rates established (other than for the traditional union category of elevator helper), whereas in residential and building surveys dated 1993, 11 of 17 (65%) did have such rates. Whether or not the simple passage of time was a factor (there are other possible explanations), it is quite clear that inadequate time was allowed by DOL to test the revisions, especially as there is no evidence that DOL made any particular effort to inform contractors or others of the non-suspension.

Compiling Rates for Helpers and Semi-skilled Construction Workers

> No. 20. The Department of Labor's assertion that helper rates were difficult to compile is clear evidence of bias towards union rates and work methods.

DOL had suggested that it experienced great difficulties in implementing the revised regulations, but it gave no explanation of what those difficulties could have been. In fact, there are no apparent differences between identifying and collecting survey data for helpers of various types and doing the same thing for, say, employees engaged in hanging and taping drywall.[22] It has long been the practice of DOL to accept whatever rates and job titles for such employees as are used by the contractors who paid them.

In even the small number of surveys performed during the period of non-suspension, more than 220 job title variations were submitted, and 78 different job titles were found to be prevailing. They were in this following list:

Exhibit A3-1

Some Job Titles Submitted to
Prevailing Wage Residential or Building Surveys on Forms WD-10
on One or More of the 78 Surveys Performed
During the 21-Month Period of Non-Suspension, 1992–1993
(Titles in Bold Face Were Found Prevailing)

Acoustical Ceiling Mechanic
Acoustical Installers
Aluminum Siding Installer
Air Balance Technician
Air Compressor
Air Tool Operator
Asbestos Laborers
Asbestos Removers
Asbestos Workers
ASP Distributors
Asphalt Distributor
Asphalt Paving Machine Operator
Automatic Door Installer
Backhoe
Bidwell Operator
Blasters

[22] *See* discussion, below, at footnote 9, Appendix Five, concerning the substantially endless variations in job titles for drywall work. These occur principally because drywall work—like work associated with heating and air conditioning installation, alarm and telecommunications wiring, metal building erection and metal studding, concrete block, concrete slip form and machine finishing, and a number of others—was developed after the building trades were organized into their established crafts, and "ownership" of it by particular unions varies from place to place.

Boilermaker
Bobcat
Bricklayer
- Bricklayer's Apprentice
- Bricklayer's Helper
- Brick Mason Tender

Broom Operator
Bulldozer
Carpenter
- Carpenter's Apprentice
- Carpenter Helper
- Carpenter Tender

Carpenter, Acoustical Only
- Carpenter, Acoustical Helper

Carpenter – Cabinet
Carpenter (Drywall Only)
- Carpenter, Drywall Hanging Helper

Carpenter, Drywall Also
Carpenter, Drywall & Acoustic
Carpenter, Excluding Drywall
- Carpenter, Excluding Drywall Apprentice
- Carpenter, Excluding Drywall Helper

Carpenters, Including Carpenters, Excluding Acoustic Ceiling Mechanics
Carpenter, Excluding Drywall, Batt & Acoustic
- Carpenter Helper, Excluding Drywall, Batt & Acoustic

Carpenter Formsetting Only
- **Carpenter Formwork Helper**
- Carpenter Formwork Apprentice

Carpenters Including Drywall & Batt Insulation
Carpenter, Insulation Also
Carpenter, Insulation & Acoustic Also
Carpenter, Insulation & Forms Also
Carpenter, Only
Carpenter, Overhead Door
Carpenter, Piledriverman
Caulkers
Cement Mason
- Cement Mason Apprentice
- Cement Mason Helper
- Cement Mason Tender

Cherry Picker
Concrete Finish Machine
Concrete Flatwork
Concrete Finishers
- Concrete Finishers Helper

Concrete Workers
Cranes
Drillers
Drill Rig
Drywall Finisher
- Drywall Finisher Helper

Drywall Hanger
- Drywall Hanger Helper

Drywall Hanger
Drywall Mechanics
  Drywall Mechanics Helper
Electrician
  Electrician Apprentice
  Electrician Helper
  Electrician Trainee
Electrician, Alarms
Electrical, Excluding HVAC Control Wire
Electric – Low Voltage Also
Electronic Technician
Elevator Constructor
  Elevator Constructor Helper
  Elevator Constructor 70%
  Elevator Constructor Probationary Helper
Elevator Mechanics
  Elevator Mechanics Helper
Fence Erectors
Fork Lift
Formsetter
Front End Loader
Garage Door Installer
  Garage Door Helper
Glaziers
  Glaziers Helper
Grader
Gutter Installers
Heat & Frost Insulator
  Heat & Frost Apprentice
Hoist Operator
HVAC Mechanic
  HVAC Mechanic Helper
HVAC Mechanics Duct Work
  HVAC Mechanics Duct Work Helper
HVAC Mechanic – Pipe, Duct
HVAC Mechanic – Wiring / Startup / Unit
Insulators, Batt
  Insulator Helper, Batt
Insulator, Batt & Blown
  Insulator Helper, Batt & Blown
Insulator, Blown
  Insulator Helper, Blown
Insulators, Pipe
  Insulator Pipe, Apprentice
  Insulator, Pipe, Helper
Ironworkers
  Ironworkers Apprentice
Ironworkers, Ornamental
Ironworker, Reinforcing
Ironworkers, Structural
  Ironworker, Structural Apprentice
Jackhammer Operator

Landscape Laborer
Landscape Operator
Laborers
Laborer, Common
Laborers, Landscaping Also
Laborers, Landscaping Only
Laborers, Semi-Skilled
Laborer - Skilled
Laborers, Unskilled
- **Mason Tender**
- **Mason Tender, Brick**
- Mason Tender, Cement

Mechanic
Millwright
Mortar Mixers
Oiler
Painters
Painters, Brush
- Painters Brush, Helpers

Painters, Brush & Roller
- **Painter's Helper, Brush & Roller**

Painters, Drywall Also
Painters Excluding Drywall
Painters Only
Painters, Spray
- Painter / Wallpaper Apprentice

Paperhangers
Pavers
Piledrivermen
Pipe Coverer
Pipefitters
- Pipefitter's Apprentice
- Pipefitter's Helper
- Pipefitter Trainee

Pipefitters, HVAC Also
Pipefitters, HVAC Only
Pipefitter – Fire
Pipefitter - Irrigation
Pipefitter, Pneumatic
Pipefitter, Sprinklerfitter
Pipelayers
Plasterers
- Plasterer Tender
- Plasterer Helpers

Plumbers
Plumbers, Including HVAC Pipe
Plumbers / Pipefitters
- Plumber / Pipefitter Apprentice
- Plumber / Pipefitter Helper

Plumber, HVAC Only
Plumbers Only
- Plumber's Apprentice
- Plumber Helper

Pump Operators
Raker
Refrigeration Mechanic
Roller, All Types
Roofers
    Roofer Helper
Saw Man – Brick, Block
Screed Operator
Sheet Metal, Duct & Set Unit
    Sheet Metal, Duct & Set Unit Apprentice
    Sheet Metal, Duct & Set Unit Helper
    Sheet Metal, Duct & Set Unit Trainee
Sheet Metal HVAC Only
Sheet Metal, Including HVAC
    Sheet Metal, Including HVAC Apprentice
    Sheet Metal, Including HVAC Helper
Sheet Metal Workers
Sheet Metal Workers (Only)
    Sheet Metal Apprentice
    Sheet Metal Helper
Sheet Metal Worker, Metal Building
Shingler
    Shingler Helper
Shover Dozer
Skidder
Soft Floor Layers
    Soft Floor Layer's Apprentice
    Soft Floor Layer Helper
Sprinklerfitter
    Sprinkler Apprentice
    Sprinklerfitter's Helper
Stone Mason
Tile Setter
    Tile Setter Helper
Tile Setters / Mechanics
Trackhoe
Trailer Driver
Truck Drivers
Truck Drivers – 1X
Truck Drivers, 2 Axle
Truck Drivers, 3 Axle
Truck Drivers, 4 - X
Truck Drivers to Site Only
Truck, Lowboy
Vinyl Siding Installer
Waterproofers
    Waterproofer Helper

It should be noted that this list is far from comprehensive of all 78 of the surveys. It leaves out the job titles associated with highway and heavy determinations that would increase the total by about 50 percent. These are of little interest to questions involving helpers, since they are mostly improbably precise lists of equipment (sometimes by brand name) in various sizes that can be driven by operating engineers (or sometimes by truck drivers or specialty laborers).[23]

Obviously, there was nothing special about those job titles that were designated as being for helpers of one sort or another (e.g., "Carpenter Formwork Helper," "Drywall Mechanic's Helper"), nor

[23] The specificity at times defies credulity and at times is impenetrable. A Maryland (building) determination MD 960002 based on union rates is brief, but contains instances of both. In that determination, truck drivers are divided into 7 groups, each paid separately. Group 6 establishes the specialty rate that will apply to driving the following list of equipment of exactly 50 tons capacity (since Group 6 applies to "over 49 ton capacity to 59 ton capacity" while Group 7 applies to "over 50 ton capacity"): Dump trucks over 15 yard capacity, bottom and end dump euclids [a brand name, and a category made redundant by the category next in the list], all other euclid type trucks, turnarockers, ross carriers, athey wagons, A frames, mechanics, utility drivers [two categories that cannot reasonably have a capacity], semi-trailers or tractor-trailers, lowboy trucks [already covered by semi-trailers], asphalt distributor trucks, agitator mixer, dumpcrete or batch trucks, specialized earth moving equipment [concrete pump, concrete mixer, and earth rollers are also assigned to two different wage categories of power equipment operators], off-highway tandem back-dump [already covered as a euclid type], and double hitched equipment (where not self-loaded) [leaving one to wonder how to handle double-hitched equipment that is self-loaded]. Another example is from the New Jersey general determination NJ 950002, where in some counties truck drivers are divided into two groups and others into four. Different rates are set by group. In the four-group set, Group 1 contains, among others, flats, floats, water sprinkler, road oil, stringer, transit mixers, agitator mixers, winch trucks, stringers [again], asphalt distributors, seeding, mulching, tractors, and wagons. Group 3 also contains, among others, flats, floats, water sprinkler, stringer, road oil, transit mixer, agitator mixer, winch trucks, etc. [entirely duplicated, though not in the same order, without distinction].

any reason why DOL might have had any more difficulty accepting them on form WD-10 than it did to accept any of the other job titles that also appeared in the survey listings (e.g., "Carpenter, Drywall Only," "Elevator Constructor 70% Probationary," or "Sheet Metal, Duct and Set Unit,") all of which were not only accepted in the survey, but were actually found to be prevailing.

Another example is provided in the recent (after 2008) presidential decision to promote weatherization work as a national priority and to require that such work be subject to the Davis-Bacon Act. At the time this was announced, no prevailing rates existed for weatherization workers because no construction workers in the country actually used any of the newly invented job titles. In this case, however, DOL was undeterred by the necessity to establish prevailing rates for the new job titles for every county in the country out of whole cloth. By one means or another, DOL "surveyed" all 3,000 counties (and a few territories and independent cities as well) establishing prevailing rates for three levels of weatherization job titles in 2009 and apparently again in 2010. Not only was this a literally impossible task (given the total lack of possible input data), it was done without whining by DOL about the attendant difficulty or expense. Certainly the much easier task of setting rate for construction workers their employers called helpers in the ordinary process of conducting ordinary surveys could have been accomplished as well.

Determining Job Content of Helpers and Semi-skilled Construction Workers

No. 21. The Department of Labor's assertion that helper rates were difficult to identify for job content is clear evidence of bias towards union rates and work methods.

The legitimacy of work content associated with a given job title is not something that DOL is authorized to assess. The "Davis-Bacon Construction Wage Determinations Manual of Operations" is the document that establishes procedures for collecting and evaluating wage data. It is almost entirely silent about selecting or evaluating job titles, contenting itself with noting that:

> . . . the proper classification of work performed by laborers and mechanics is that classification used by firms whose wage rates were found to be prevailing in the area.

In other words, whatever gets submitted, if the rates prevail, so does the work. It is not up to the wage specialists to analyze job content, only to record it. Thus, prevailing job titles and work delineations in determinations have included such things as gutter installer or, from a 1995 Montgomery County, Maryland, determination, a category of plumbers defined as one that worked on,

> Apartment Buildings over 4 stories (except hotels), schools, colleges, and speculative office buildings, strip shopping centers, churches, water coolers, room air conditioning units, appliances, packaged ice machines, and light commercial refrigeration and/or air conditioning systems serving a single business in a single story building and not to exceed 5 h.p. or tons, self-contained package unit up to and including 5 h.p. or tons.

In the survey, itself, the rates for a person holding this job would have been submitted as plumbers' rates, and the fine distinctions would have been added later in the determination process. But historically, the only place helpers' rates were similarly treated was with respect to elevator constructor helpers, a title that had been traditional in union work for many years.

Issuing Wage Rates for Helpers and Semi-skilled Construction Workers

No. 22. The Department of Labor's assertion that helper rates were difficult to administer is clear evidence of bias towards union rates and work methods.

Just as DOL has no mandate to establish job content beyond identifying what prevails in a locality, it has no mandate to establish "ownership" of various pieces of construction work by one trade or another, or to impose union systems of job delimitation on nonunion contractors. Therefore post-determination administration should be no more difficult for helpers than anyone else. In the 78 wage determinations that resulted from the surveys made during the period of non-suspension, a total of 343 different job descriptions were found to be prevailing and to have rates issued for them.

This is a larger number than the number of job descriptions submitted to the surveys because these job titles found in determinations were not necessarily submitted independently to the surveys or found to be prevailing on their own. In most determinations, if a generic union job title is found to be prevailing, when the determination is issued based on this, lesser and related specific job titles associated with the generic one are simply imported into the determination from union contracts, along with slight or significant variances in pay rates required to go along with them, and are either added to or substituted for the generic one. The job content of each of these is indeterminate and may depend on local practice.

In Exhibit A3-2, job titles are listed that were specifically identified in one or another of the determinations performed during the period of non-suspension as being prevailing and having their own specific wage and fringe benefit rates issued. Some of these, underlined in the exhibit, are for helper or helper-like jobs, but there is no evidence that any more than one or two of them came about because of the non-suspension of the helper rules. The rest would be as likely to appear in any other set of determinations of similar size before or after the period of non-suspension.

Exhibit A3-2

Construction Laborer Job Titles Found To Be Prevailing in One or More of the 78 Wage Determinations Issued As a Result of Surveys Performed During the 21-Month Period of Non-Suspension 1992–1993

(Helper and helper-equivalent designations found within the listing are underlined. Those set in bold font are designations identified in at least one determination as "skilled." Indented titles represent different skill levels of the same job.)

Adzeman
Air Blasting
Air Tool Operator
Air Trac Operator
<u>Air Track Helper</u>

Air Tamping Hammerman
Arc Welding (in connection with laborer's work)
Asbestos Removal Labor
Asphalt Belly Dump Lay Down
Asphalt Headerboarder
Asphalt Ironer
Asphalt Lute Person
Asphalt Raker
Asphalt Rubber Distributor Bootperson
Asphalt Tamper, Smoother, and Raker
Asphalt Workers (Shovelman, Plant Crew)
Astro Turf Layer
Backfiller
Bander
Bellmen
Bio Filer (Pressman, Installer, Operator)
Bit Grinder, Drill Doctor (in field)
Blacksmith Tender
Blaster
  Blasterers Helper
Block/Bricklayer Tender
Blocklayer Tender
Bobcat Operator
Boring Machine Tender
Brick Cleaner (jobsite only)
Brick Paver (Asphalt Block Paver, Asphalt Block Sawman, Asphalt Block Grinder; Hastings Block or Similar Type)
Bricklayer Tenders
Brush Cutters
Bucket Dumper
Buggymobile Operator
Burner Planer Operator
Burning and Cutting Torch
Button Setter
Caisson Workers
Camp Maintenance Laborer
Carpenter Tenders
Carpet Layer Tender
Caulker
Cement Dumper
Cement Finisher Helper
Cement Finisher Tenders
Cement Mason Tender
Cement or Lime Dumper or Handler (sack or bulk)
Cemetery Laborers
Certified Hazardous Waste Worker
Cesspool Diggers and Installers
Chainman, Rodman, Grade Marker
Change House Attendant
  Changehouse Person
Chainsaw Operator
  Filer
Chat Box Man
Chemical Grout Jet Person
Cherry Picker Person

Chipper (clearing and grubbing)
Choke Setters
Choker Splicer
Chucktender (wagon, airtrack and hydraulic drills)
Cleaner, Lumber, Brick
Cofferdam Worker
Compactors of all types
Concrete Burning Machine Operator
Concrete Chipper
Concrete Core Cutter
Concrete Curer
Concrete Cutting Torch
Concrete Finisher Tender
Concrete Forms Cleaning and Handling
Concrete Grinder and Sander
Concrete Gunman (pneumatic)
Concrete Laborers (power buggy, concrete saws, pumpcrete nozzleman, vibratorman)
Concrete Laborer (curb and gutter, chute handler, grouting, curing, screeding)
Concrete Laborer (belt, pipe and/or hoseman)
Concrete Liquid Hardner
Concrete Mixer
Concrete Nozzleman (pneumatic)
Concrete Pipe Cutter
Concrete Puddler
Concrete Sawyer (hand guided) (Concrete Saw Operator)
Concrete Sealer
Concrete Shute Handler
Concrete Vibrating Machine
Conduit Layer (Conduit Layer, telephone and electrical)
Conveyor Operators used in tending Bricklayers, Plaster Tenders, and Window Cleaners
Corrugated Metal Culvert Pipe Layer
Covering of tanks, structures & material piles with tarpaulins
Creosote Material Handler Craft Tender
Cribber (Cribber and Shorer)
Crocklayer
Crusher Plant Laborer
Curb Asphalt Machine Operator
Cutting Torch Operator
Deck Hand
Demolition Laborer
Diamond Driller
Ditch Digger
Ditch Witch Operator
Dredge Hand
Drillers (wagon drills, air-track drills, hydraulic drills, other)
Drill Doctor and/or Air Tool Repairman
Dry-Pak-It Machine
Dry Packing of concrete, plugging, filling of she bolt holes
Dump Man
Electrician Laborer
Electric Tool Operator
Environmental Laborer (asbestos, hazardous and toxic waste, oil spill)
Environmental Laborer (marine work)

Excavator
Fence Installer
Final Clean-Up Labor
Fine Grader
Fire Watch Laborer
Flagman (Flag Person, Flag Waver, Flagger)
Floor Sanders (concrete)
Forklift Operator
Foam Gun or Foam Machine Operator
Form Blower
Form Builder
 <u>Form Builder Tender</u>
Form Oiler
Form Raiser
Form Setter
 <u>Form Setter Tender</u>
Form Stripper
Gardner, horticultural and landscape laborer
Gabion Setter
General Laborer
Grademan
Grade Setter (pipeline)
Grating and Grill Work for Drains
Grout Gun Person
Grout Mixer Person
Grout Pump Person
Green Cutter (dam work)
 Guardrail Laborer, Bridge Rail Installer
 Guardrail Machine Operator
Guinea Chaser
Gunnite Gun
Gunnite Industrial Fume Stack
Gunnite Laborer
Gunnite Operator
Gunnite Nozzle and Rod
Gunnite Rebound
Heater Tender
Heat Welder of Plastics
High Rigger and Tree Topper
High Scaler
<u>Hod Carrier</u>
Hook Tender
Hookup Men
House Mover
Hydraulic Jacks and Similar Mechanical Tools
<u>Ironworker Tenders</u>
Jackhammer or Pavement Breakers (more than 45 pounds)
Jacking of Pipe
Jackleg Miner
Jetter
Jumbo Person
Kettleman - tarman
Hydro-Seeder Nozzleman
Laborers (building)
Laborer, General Clean-Up

Laborers working for mechanical & electric contractors (including but not limited to digging of all trenches, ditches, holes, paving of concrete & cleaning of all trash)
Lagger
Lagging, sheeting, whaling, bracing, trenchjacking, lagging hammer
Landscape and Planter
Landscape Laborer
Laser Beam Operator
Layton Box Spreader
Leverman
Line Construction Linemen
Line Construction Equipment Operators & Cable Man
Line Construction Groundman
Line Construction Inexperienced Groundman
Line Construction Driver Groundman (Material)
Line Construction Driver Groundman (Class I and III)
[each of the above Line Construction laborer titles had separate rates issued.]
Lighting Installer
Licensed Powdermen
Logloader
Magnesite, epoxy resin, fiberglass, mastic worker (wet or dry)
Man Mixing Cement for Cement Finisher
Mason Tender and Mud Mixer (sewer work)
Mason Tender
Mason Tender – Brick
Mason Tender (Brick/Block)
Mason Tender (Concrete)
Masonry Forklift Operator
Material Handlers
Material Hose Operator (walls, slabs, floors, and decks)
Membrane Vapor Barrier Installer
Metal Pan Handler
Masonry Tender
Mechanic Tenders
Men directly tending lathers, masons, cement masons, and plasterers
Miners
Miners Helpers
Mortarman for Mason & Plasterer
Mortar Mixers
Mortar Mixer used in connection with hose for gypsum roofs (roofer's tender)
Mortar Mixer used in connection with plastering
Mortar Mixer used in connection with fiber and soundproofing
Motormen
Mucking Machine Operators
Multi-Trade Tender
Nipper (Outside Nipper)
Packing Rod Steel and Pans
Paving Breakers
Pioneer Drilling and Drilling Off Tugger (all types drills)
Pipelayer, Pipe Builder, Plastic Welding
Pipelayer's Backup (coating, grouting, making of joints, sealing, caulking, diapering and including rubber gasket joints, pointing and any and all other services)
Pipelayer Tender
Pipe Caulker and/or backup man – pipeline

Pipe Cutter
Pipe Doper
Pipe Wrapper
Plastic Pipe Layer
Plasterer Tender
Plasterer Clean-Up Laborer
Plasterers Helper
Plumber Laborer
Pneumatic Gohper
Pneumatic Powder Person
Pneumatic or Power Tools Operator
Porta Shot Blaster
Portable or Chemical Toilet Serviceman
Post Hole Digger
Pot Tender
Powderman (Powder Blaster)
　　Powderman Tender
Power Broom Sweeper
Power Saw Operator
Power Tool Operator
Power Type Concrete Buggy
Powderman & Chuck Tender
Precast Manhole Erector
Precast Slab Layer (Floors, Roofs, Walks, Curbs)
Pressure Pipe Tester
Primer Person
Pump Man or Mixer Man
Railroad Bull Gang Trackman
Railroad – Mechanical Equipment (includes Spiker, Puller, Tie Cleaner, Tamper, Pipe Wrapper, Power-Driven Wheelbarrows, Operators of Hand Derricks, **Towmasters, Scootcretes, Buggymobiles,** and similar equipment.)
Railroad Switch Layout Laborer
Railroad Track Laborer
Rammer
Reinforcing Iron Worker Tender (carrying and hauling of all rods and materials for use in reinforcing concrete construction)
Reinforced Steel Handler
Retimber Person, wood or steel
Rigger
Rip Rap Stone Man
Rock Slinger
Roofer Tenders
Rotary Scarifier
Roto Scraper and Tiller
Roustabout
Salamander Heater, drying of plaster, concrete, mortar.
Sandblaster
Sandblaster Tailhoseman
Scaffolds and Staging for masons and plasterers
Scaffolds: Erection, planking and removal of all scaffolds used for support for lathers, plasterers, brick layers, and other construction crafts.
Scaffolds: (Specially designed by carpenters) laborers shall tend said carpenter on erection and dismantling thereof.
Scaffold Building and Erecting
Scale Man

Septic Tank Digger and Installer
Signalman
Sewer Caulker
Sewer Plant Maintenance Man
Saw Tender
Screeder (asphalt or concrete)
Sewer Cleaner
Sewer Pipe Layer
Sewer Pipe Wiper & Pot Person
Sewer Pipe Yarner
Signalman (including traffic control)
Sign Erector
Single-foot Tamper
Slip-Form Riser
Sloper
Slurry Seal Squeegee Man
Slurry Work (Mixer Operator, Applicator, Squeegee Man, Shuttle Man, Top Man)
Soil Test Operations
Spaders
Spikers
Spotters Trucks
Stake Hopper (Stake Jumper)
Steam Point or Water Jet Operator
Steam Cleaner Operator
Steel Form Raiser and Setter
<u>Stonemason Tender</u>
Striper, concrete or other paved surfaces
Stud Gunner
Street Cleaner
Swamper
Tailhoseman (water)
Tamper
Tank Cleaner
<u>Tenders, All Crafts</u>
<u>Terrazzo Tender (Terrazzo Tile Tender)</u>
Thermal Plastic Applicator
Thermit Welder
Tile Layer
    <u>Tile Layer Tender</u>
Timber Bucker
Timber Feller, chain saw operator
Timberman
Tool Dispatcher or Checker (Tool Crib, Tool House Laborer)
Torchmen
Towmaster Operator
Tree Climber
Traffic Delineating Device Applicator
Trencher (hand operated)
Turbo Blaster
Truck Drivers (flatbed up to 2-1/2 tons)
Truck Driver (refuse and garbage disposal, job site to dump)
Truck-spotter Dumper
Utiliwalk and Utilidor Laborer

Vibrascreed, bull float
Vibrator Operator
Victualic or similar
Wagon Drill Operator
  Wagon Drill Helper
Walk-type Mech. used in tending plasterers and bricklayers
Waterboy (Water person)
Waterproofer
Watchman
Welder
Well Point Installer
Winch Handler
Window Cleaner
Wire Mesh Puller
Wire Winding Machine Operator
Work of an unskilled and semi-skilled nature
Work on and/or in bell hole footings and shafts thereof, and work on and in deep footings (15 feet or more in depth)
Work pertaining to or in connection with & Repair of Stove, Blast Furnace, Basic Oxygen Process Furnace, Steeple & Stack, Annealing Process Furnace, Kiln, Soaking Pit, Coke Battery on Industrial Work
Wrecker – Laborer
  Wrecker – Semi-Skilled
  Wrecker – Skilled
Wrenchers – creosote tiemen
Yard Maintenance Person
"&Etc."

It bears emphasis that all of the job titles found in this exhibit are for construction laborers, alone, and all were found in the 78 determinations issued during the period of non-suspension. No individual determination had all of them, and the titles presented in the exhibit did not all have independent prevailing rates issued. But they are all titles specifically used for categories or subcategories of laborers and are all separately identified in one or more of the determinations and are therefore recognized by the DOL. In some determinations there was only a single rate for undifferentiated construction laborers. In others, various combinations of these construction laborer titles are grouped into 2, 4, 6, 7, 10, or 11 different wage categories, differently defined and based on fine gradations in skill. In these latter groups, which are the great majority, all of the titles are union titles.

These are the very determinations to which the DOL decided adding rates for nonunion construction helpers would make administration of prevailing rates complex, imprecise, and excessively burdensome. Although DOL apparently has no trouble issuing prevailing rates for an "Asphalt Rubber Distributor Bootperson," a "Cement or

Lime Dumper or Handler (sack or bulk)," or "Laborers working for mechanical & electrical contractors (including but not limited to digging of all trenches, ditches, holes, paving of concrete & cleaning of all trash)," it balks at issuing them for a nonunion "Carpenter's Helper," or something as complex as an "HVAC Helper." But surely, if current administration methods can handle wage and job content administration for the actual union job titles found in Exhibit A3-2, they should be able to stretch themselves to administer a handful of nonunion helper titles, also.

Size of the Helper Class Overlooked by Prevailing Rate Determinations

> No. 23. The Department of Labor's assertion that helpers are not a sufficient construction class is clear evidence of bias towards union rates and work methods.

Unlike some of the job titles found above, the nonunion helper job title is not rare. Concerning DOL's contention that the actual number of helpers (as found by their surveys) was far fewer than expected—and therefore inferentially inconsequential—the Department seems to have manufactured the data to its own liking and disregarded those that are readily available. The Current Population Survey ("CPS"), maintained by the Bureau of Labor Statistics, estimates that as of 1995—around the time of this survey—there were approximately 2.3 million wage-earning journeymen in the construction industry, plus 744,000 laborers, and 54,000 trade apprentices. It also found that there were 940,000 construction helpers. Far from being inconsequential, persons called helpers constituted 23 percent of the wage-earning workmen in the industry.

If all the helpers had the same title (as union laborers often do for survey purposes, despite their various assignments), their total would outnumber laborers substantially, be more than ten times the number of apprentices, and outnumber journeymen in 10 of the 16 trades listed by CPS, *combined*: Tile Setters, Carpet Installers, Drywall Installers, Plasterers, Glaziers, Insulation Workers, Paving and Surfacing Workers, Roofers, Sheet Metal Workers, and those not otherwise classified.

In a 1980s analysis, DOL expected that if helper rates were allowed, they would be found in two-thirds of all rate determinations. But during the period of non-suspension in "only 20 of the 78 surveys conducted, covering only 52 of 328 counties surveyed, were any open shop helper classifications found to prevail,"[24] and excluding the union helper categories (e.g., elevator constructor helper), only 2.7 percent of the 1,763 classification were in the nonunion sector. "This is particularly noteworthy," said DOL, "because it had been assumed in the past that helpers would almost always be found to prevail for classifications in the nonunion sector."[25]

The disappointment was surely feigned, because here, DOL had created a straw man by both overstating the expectations of helper use and by selectively reporting the helpers (and their proportions) actually found in the surveys. In fact, analysis of the data from the period of non-suspension reveals that in surveys of nonunion areas, where helpers are most likely to be used, at least one helper category actually was found to prevail in over 10 percent of the determinations. Furthermore, helpers are not used in all classifications, e.g., laborers do not ordinarily have helpers. Eliminating these categories yields a more realistic count of helpers in the jobs and areas where they most likely to be found and a determination that such job titles prevailed in about 14.5 percent of all classifications where they reasonably could have been expected to have been found. So the numbers found were actually several times those reported by DOL. Nevertheless, helpers were clearly not found in the proportions that DOL said they anticipated.

The reason why more were not found may be linked to two further things: First, as already covered above, the surveys were not designed to test for the prevailing-ness of helper categories; no special call was issued to contractors to now submit rates for helpers, nor

[24] Procedures for Predetermination of Wage Rates; Labor Standards Provisions Applicable to Contracts Covering Federally Financed and Assisted Construction and to Certain Nonconstruction Contracts, 64 Fed. Reg. 68 (1999) (to be codified at 29 C.F.R. §§ 1, 5) (proposed April 9, 1999), at 17,446.

[25] *Id.* at 17,448.

any call to solicit information only on helpers. Second, subjective selection by wage specialists rather than to a lack of data may have led to disproportionate dismissal of helper job titles and survey submissions.

B. DOL'S QUESTIONABLE IMPLEMENTATION OF HELPER USE IN SURVEYS DURING THE PERIOD OF NON-SUSPENSION

Evidence from the surveys done during this period of non-suspension raises the question of whether DOL wage specialists may have been applying different and more stringent standards in selecting categories of helpers to have prevailing rates set for them than in selecting other categories of construction workers doing work of similar nature and skill requirement but having different job titles.

At the time the surveys were made, the early 1990s, construction workers who were called "helpers" existed almost exclusively in non-union work. The exceptions include "Elevator Constructor Helper," a title of long tradition in both union work and nonunion work, and "Boilermaker Helper," a title used mostly on the union side.[26] Most unions, however, typically used the alternative title of "tender" instead of "helper," though there is no differentiation other than name.

Both union and nonunion contractors also employ semi-skilled persons who may have been doing helper-like work with specialty laborer titles, such as "Form Setter," or "Latherer," or "Terrazzo Finisher," although some of the more common ones (e.g., "Hod Carrier," "Cement Finisher," or "Electrical Groundman") were more prevalent in union work. And finally, both union and nonunion contractors used specialty titles for various semi-skilled workers who might otherwise

[26] During the helper controversy and for some time thereafter, there was a trend towards renaming "Elevator Constructor Helpers" as either "Elevator Constructor – 70 Percent" or "Elevator Constructor, Probationary." As the controversy has receded into history, the traditional titles seem to have resurfaced, since the most-recently revised helper regulations of the DOL were drafted specifically to allow traditional union titles uniquely to be recognized.

have been classified as laborers or helpers. Examples of this last are "Acoustical Ceiling Mechanic," "Fence Erector," "Waterproofer," or "Roller Operator."

An evaluation of how DOL reacted to and handled survey data on these various job titles during the period of non-suspension is enlightening. Persons called helpers had demonstrably different success ratios in having their job titles recognized and prevailing wages issued for them. Persons doing similar kinds of helper-like semi-skilled work and persons doing similar kinds of helper-like laborer work, both carrying titles more closely associated with union than nonunion characterizations also met with different levels of success. And so did (union) tenders in comparison to (nonunion) helpers.

For all four categories of job titles—helpers as such, semi-skilled operators performing helper-like functions, laborers performing helper-like functions, and tenders performing the same functions as laborers—survey rates were submitted for possible prevailing rate determination for their categories that could be differentiated based on probable union status.[27] In all cases, the WD-22a forms recorded the number of individual worker's rates submitted in response to the survey request and the number of different construction projects they were drawn from. Although DOL has no hard-and-fast rules for how many rates from how many projects are enough to form the basis for a prevailing rate, there are obvious low-point cutoffs (a rate submission from a single worker on a single project is certainly insufficient) one might expect a linear relationship between larger numbers of rates and projects producing a higher probability of a prevailing rate being found.

Success Ratios by Job Title: Helpers Named As Such

No 24. The Department of Labor's disproportionate rejection of helper rates in surveys is clear evidence of bias towards union rates and work methods.

[27] Given the small number of surveys, the profusion of titles is remarkable for which at least some survey data were submitted.

The helper category, as such, had 295 survey rates submitted for 53 job titles (exclusive of the two elevator helper titles that are traditionally union) in the 78 surveys during the period of non-suspension. Each one of the separate helper job titles had between 1 and 69 rates submitted. Sometimes, based on those numbers of rates a prevailing rate was determined, and sometimes one was rejected. Although one might suppose that a rate would be rejected if a survey contained only a single submission of it, in 6 instances a rate was determined to prevail even in those circumstances. It might be noted that 4 of the 6 single submissions, the rate in question was for elevator helper, a title known to be used in union construction. (For the other two, a painter's helper and a pipe insulator helper, the union affiliation is unknown.) But the differentiation of interest here is not that between union and nonunion helpers, named as such, but between helpers of all kinds and other types of construction workers. As a surrogate, consider the number of instances in which helper rates were rejected above and beyond the traditional criteria (a total of at least three rate submissions from two different employers) despite a relatively large number of rates submitted to the survey, and compare it with the much smaller number of instances in which they were accepted following the normal rules. (The identity of employers was not available, so I assumed that on the rejection side, a normal rejection would have occurred if fewer than 3 rates were submitted.)

In the table, for each job title listed, the first numerical column shows how many wage rates were submitted in one or more surveys where the job title was found to be prevailing, and the second shows how many wage rates were submitted in one or more surveys where the job title was not found to be prevailing, and were therefore ignored. (Blank entries should be read as 0 submissions.)

Exhibit A3-3

Disposition of Wage Rate Survey Information for Helpers in the 78 Wage Determinations Issued As a Result of Surveys Performed During The 21-Month Period of Non-Suspension 1992–1993

HELPERS SUBMITTED	*# in Survey, Rate Issued*	*# in Survey, Rate Ignored*
Automatic Door Helper		2
Batt Insulator Helper		2
Bricklayer Helper	12	6, 10, 5, 4
Cabinet Installer Helper		1
Carpenter('s) Helper	14, 27, 9 (found prevailing, but no rate issued), 9	9, 10, 14, 35, 5,13, 14, 16, 22, 7, 5, 41, 20, 14, 7, 1, 61, 22, 4, 1, 13, 10, 9, 1, 3, 21, 15
Carpenter, Acoustical (Acoustic Tile) (Acoustical Ceiling) Helper		6, 10, 2
Carpenter, Acoustical Partition Helper		2
Carpenter, Excld Drywall Helper		3
Carpenter, Formwork Helper		11
Carpenter, Metal Structure Erector Helper		2
Carpet Layer Helper		6
Carpeting & Resilient Floor Helper	3	
Cement/Concrete Finisher Helper		5, 9
Cement Finisher Helper		2
Cement Mason Helper		2, 2, 8, 3, 3, 4
Concrete Finisher Helper		3
Drywall Finishing Helper		1, 1, 2
Drywall Hanger & Studs Helper		14, 1
Drywall Hanging Helper		2, 2, 7, 1, 3, 1, 6
Drywall Mechanic Helper	14	4
Drywall Taper Helper		6
Electrician Helper	5, 5, 10, 18, 5, 69, 10	3, 3, 5, 23, 4, 84, 13, 2, 5, 27, 38, 20, 14, 2, 2, 3, 7, 7, 1, 3, 2, 7, 1, 1
Elevator (Constructor) (Mechanic) Helper	8, 4, 5, 4, 2, 32, 1, 1, 1, 1	2, 1, 2, 2, 7, 1, 5, 1, 8, 1, 4, 1, 1, 2, 2
Elevator Constructor – 70%	4, 4	
Elevator Constructor (Probationary) Helper		2
Fabric Awning Installer Helper		1

Fence Erector Helper		4
Garage Door Helper		1, 1
Glazier's Helper	18, 4, 4	1, 6, 3, 1, 2, 3, 2, 6, 5, 1
Heat & Frost Helper		2
HVAC Installer Duct Helper	27	5, 1
HVAC Mechanic Helper	8	17, 2
Insulator Helper		1
Insulator Helper - Blown		27, 2
Insulator Helper - Batt		27, 2
Ironworker, Ornamental Helper		2
Ironworker, Reinforcing Helper		1, 1, 1
Ironworker, Structural Helper		2, 2, 3, 1, 1
Landscape Laborer Helper		1
Marble Setter Helper		1, 3
Metal Building Erector Helper		3
Painter Helper	1	1, 1
Painter, Brush Helper		5, 3, 3, 1, 6
Painter - Brush, Roller Helper		2
Painter – Roller Helper		1
Painter, Spray Helper		2, 1
Pipe Insulator Helper	6, 1	1, 1
Pipe/Steamfitter Helper		2
Pipefitter's Helper	8	1, 4, 10, 7, 1, 1
Plasterer's Helper		1, 2, 2, 2, 7
Plumber Helper	16, 24, 15	4, 2, 7, 11, 2, 5, 2, 26, 5, 20, 3, 2, 4, 2, 3, 3
Plumber/HVAC Helper	23	
Plumber/Pipefitter Helper	2	8, 19, 32
Resilient Flooring & Carpet Laying Helper		3
Roofer Helper	4, 4, 11, 6	10, 3, 7, 13, 3, 5, 2, 1, 4, 8, 11, 4
Sheet Metal Worker Duct/Set Unit Helper		2
Sheet Metal (Worker) Helper	9, 3, 3	4, 14, 30, 8, 1, 1, 3, 2, 3, 3, 11, 9, 4
Sheet Metal Worker HVAC Helper	5	9, 23, 4, 1
Soft Floor Layer (/Carpet) Helper	3	1, 2, 3, 3, 1, 1, 2
Soft Floor Layer (exc. carpet) Helper		1
Sprinkler Fitter Helper	4, 11, 11	1, 16, 3, 2, 5, 5, 3, 2, 1, 2, 1, 7, 1, 1, 3
Sprinkler Fitter (Irrigation) Helper		3
Steamfitter – HVAC Unit Helper		1, 1
Steel Fabricator Helper		1

Terrazzo Helper		1, 5
Tile Helper		12, 5, 3
Tile Setter Helper	10	2, 2, 2, 2, 1, 4, 9, 3, 7, 11, 1, 1, 1, 1, 1
Tile Terrazzo Helper		7
Waterproofer Helper		2, 3, 12, 2

Source: Derived by A.J. Thieblot from USDL survey documents.

For the helpers represented in the surveys and shown in Exhibit A3-3, 53 instances occurred where the rate was found to be prevailing (regardless of how many survey submissions there were), whereas 148 rates were rejected although at least 3 survey rates had been submitted. Thus, for helpers, the success ratio was only slightly higher than 26 percent. The average number of rate submissions for a helper category to be determined to be prevailing was 9.7; the average number of rate for a helper category to be rejected for a prevailing rate was almost as great, 8.4. Some were rejected although they were supported by 20, 30, 40, and even up to 84 rate submissions. Although it is possible that each of these high-count submissions was from single projects and was excluded for that reason, it seems unlikely. Furthermore, as we have already seen in the case of rate submissions in the Montgomery County, Maryland, determinations, those based on single large-project submissions are not unknown in ordinary prevailing rate practice and were routinely accepted as controlling.

Success Ratios by Job Title: Semi-Skilled Workers

> No 25. The Department of Labor's higher acceptance of semi-skilled rates in surveys where union orientation is not known, than of helper rates where it is known to be nonunion, is clear evidence of bias towards union rates and work methods.

The category of semi-skilled helper-like journeymen or specialty craftsmen had 116 survey rates submitted for 32 job titles. Most of these titles are unable to be readily identified as to whether they derived from the union or from the nonunion sector. These were the job titles of the semi-skilled helper-like journeymen or specialty craftsmen: Acoustical Ceiling Mechanic, Carpenter Acoustical, Carpenter Form Work, Carpenter Who Also Does Drywall, Fabric Awning Installer, Fence Erector, Installer of Mini Blinds, Sign Erector, Window Covering Installer, Batt Insulator, Blown Insulator, Carpenter—Non-Mechanical Insulator, Insulator (Batt, Blown), Seal Coater (Concrete), Waterproofer, Air Compressor Operator, and 16 additional titles for equipment operators of specific types.

Exhibit A3-4

Examples of Wage Rates Set For Semi-Skilled Helper-Like Journeymen

SEMI-SKILLED OR SPECIALTY CARPENTERS WHO MIGHT ALSO BE HELPERS	*# in Survey, Rate Issued*	*# in Survey, Rate Ignored*
Acoustical Ceiling Mechanics	3, 9, 19, 69, 20	2, 2, 2
Carpenter–Acoustical	53, 198, 137	3
Carpenter–Form Work	86	37, 5
Carpenter Who Also Does Drywall	211	
Fabric Awning Installer		1
Fence Erector	22	1, 10, 4, 10, 6, 2, 1, 1, 2
Installer – Mini Blinds (Blinds, Chalkboard)		1, 2
Sign Erector		6, 25
Window Covering Installer		7

SEMI-SKILLED OR SPECIALTY INSULATORS WHO MIGHT ALSO BE HELPERS	*# in Survey, Rate Issued*	*# in Survey, Rate Ignored*
Batt Insulators	3, 17, 15	4, 3, 3, 2, 6, 2, 2, 2
Blown Insulators	15	2, 2
Carpenter – Non-Mechanical Insulator	198	
Insulators, Batt, Blown	42, 21, 96	3, 21
Seal Coater, Concrete		8
Waterproofer	7	2, 2, 4, 3, 2, 3, 3

SPECIALTY EQUIPMENT	*# in Survey, Rate*	*# in Survey, Rate*

OPERATORS WHO MIGHT ALSO BE HELPERS	*Issued*	*Ignored*
Air Compressor		1
Bobcat		3, 2, 6, 1, 1, 2
Broom Operator		2, 5, 1
Cherry Picker		4
Compactor		1, 1
Forklift		1, 1
Hoist Operator		4, 1
Gannon Tractor		2, 1
Landscape Operator		1, 1
Oiler	6	5, 1, 1, 1, 1
Oiler, Crane		3
Oiler, Drill		2
Oiler – PEO		1
Pickup Truck Operator		2
Roller, Roller/Compactor	19, 9, 3, 3, 3, 4, 3	20, 8, 1, 1, 1, 1, 6, 2, 1, 2, 1
Roller – Hot Mix	8	1, 1
Tractor Operator		4, 3, 1

Source: Derived by A.J. Thieblot from USDL survey documents.

Using the same criterion as in Exhibit A3-3—that a rate should be properly rejected if fewer than 4 survey submissions were made for it—for this list of semi-skilled workers who might also be called helpers, there were 29 instances in which the rate was accepted as prevailing, and only 23 instances when it was rejected despite having 3 or more survey rates submitted. Therefore, the success ratio for this kind of job title was 44 percent, considerably higher than the 26 percent success ratio of helpers named as such. Here, again, the union status of the persons holding these job titles is generally unknown, whereas persons holding helper job titles are generally in the nonunion sector.

Success Ratios by Job Title: Helper-like Laborers

> No 26. The Department of Labor's disproportionate acceptance of union helper-like laborer helper rates in surveys is clear evidence of bias towards union rates and work methods.

Exhibit A3-5 gives a similar picture for categories of workers who might be called "hidden helpers." These are categories used by both union and nonunion contractors for specialized categories of laborers who, like tenders, have as the principal duties the support of either trade journeymen or more skilled laborers, but who are not always called laborers. In nonunion work, it is much more likely that these individuals would be called either helpers to the related trade journeymen or simply laborers, although some of the rates submitted for this group may be for nonunion workmen. This group has a much higher level of acceptance given similar numbers of rate submissions to the survey than did either the nonunion helpers or the mixed semi-skilled workers. The success ratio for this group was slightly more than 50 percent. Helper-like laborers are shown with their most likely trade superior in Exhibit A3-5.

Exhibit A3-5

Disposition of Wage Rate Survey Information for Helper-Like Laborers Submitted to Prevailing Wage Residential or Building Surveys During Period of Non-Suspension

HELPER-LIKE LABORERS SUBMITTED	*HELPER TO*	*# in Survey, Rate Issued*	*# in Survey, Rate Ignored*
Asphalt Distributor	Paver	3	1, 3, 1
Asphalt Luteman	Paver		2
Asphalt Raker	Paver	38, 5,6	1, 6, 36, 30, 2, 7, 5, 3, 4, 4, 1, 1
Asphalt Screedman	Paver	6	5, 2, 2, 3, 5, 4, 1, 2, 1, 1, 1, 1, 2
Asphalt Wacker	Paver		3
Asphalt Worker	Paver	6	3, 10
Caulker	Waterproofer	22, 5, 4	6, 2, 11
Cement Block Layer	Mason	63	10
Cement Finisher	Mason	66, 42, 31, 5	
Concrete Finish Machine		2	1, 1
Concrete Finisher	Mason	11	4
Concrete Pumper	Mason		11, 1, 1
Concrete Worker	Mason	13, 8, 28, 66	4, 4, 11, 1

Electrician Trainee	Electrician		2
Electrical Groundman	Electrician	4	3
Form Setter	Mason		2, 2, 2, 5, 4, 8, 5, 5
Glazier Finisher	Glazier		1
Laborer – Hod Carrier	Bricklayer	16	
Lather	Plasterer	33, 3	
Materials Handler, Pipefitter	Pipefitter	12	
Mortar Mixer	Mason	7	1, 10, 1, 1, 2, 1, 3, 5, 5, 8
Pipe Insulator	Pipefitter	22, 5	2
Saw Man (brick, block)	Mason		1
Semi-skilled Laborers	Various		2
Pipefitter Trainee	Pipefitter		2
Scaffold Builder	Mason		3
Sheet Metal Worker Duct Set Trainee	SMW		2
Sheet Metal Worker Set Unit Trainee	SMW		2
Terrazzo Finisher	Terrazzo Setter		5
Tile Setter Finisher	Tile Setter	6, 12	4, 1, 9
Tile Terrazzo Finisher	Tile or Terrazzo Setter	9	
Tool Material Handler – Pipefitter	Pipefitter		3
Tool Material Handler – Plumber	Plumber		6
Tool and Material Handler	Unknown		3
Trenching Machine Operator	Pipelayer		5
Trowel Machine Operator	Mason	20	1, 1, 1

Source: Derived by A.J. Thieblot from USDL survey documents.

For the 36 job titles in this category, all of which can be assumed to be union, the success ratio was even higher than for the semi-skilled workers. There were 31 instances of the rate being accepted regardless of the number of submissions, and only 30 of it being rejected, a success ratio of 51 percent. Thus the pattern is consistent: increasing likelihood of union affiliation brings increasing likelihood of rates being accepted as prevailing.

Success Ratios by Job Title: Union Helpers Called Tenders

> No. 27. The Department of Labor's disproportionate acceptance of union tender rates in surveys is clear evidence of bias towards union rates and work methods.

The final exhibit in this series shows what happened to the acceptance or rejection of rates for the category of workers who are called tenders. A tender (e.g., a carpenter tender) in union work is the exact equivalent of a helper in nonunion work, and just as few helpers named as such are used in union construction, few tenders named as such are used in nonunion construction.

Exhibit A3-6

Disposition of Wage Rate Survey Information for Tenders Submitted to Prevailing Wage Residential or Building Surveys During Period of Non-Suspension

TENDERS SUBMITTED	*# in Survey, Rate Issued*	*# in Survey, Rate Ignored*
Brick Tender		11, 8
Carpenter Tender		1
Cement Block Tender	56	
Hod Carrier/Brick Tender		8
Laborer, Brick Mason Tender	32	
Laborer, Mason Tender	6, 4, 4	
Mason Tender	14, 29, 85, 5, 4	14, 20, 3, 2, 1
Mason Tender, Brick	7, 19, 14, 14, 41, 31, 16, 17, 18, 7	1, 6, 12
Mason Tender, Cement	24, 23	2, 1, 3, 2, 3, 2, 4
Plasterer Tender	11, 1	7, 28, 2

Source: Derived by A.J. Thieblot from USDL survey documents.

In this instance, although the total number of rates submitted was considerably less than for the other categories, the success ratio was extremely high: 24 acceptances of the title as prevailing and only 9 rejections of it when it was supported by at least 3 submissions. The success ratio (union) tenders named as such was therefore 73 percent—more than 2-1/2 times higher than the rate for (nonunion) helpers named as such.

Summary of DOL Handling of Helper and Helper-Like Rates

The results of what proportion of helper and helper-like job titles were found to be prevailing are arrayed in Exhibit A3-7, grouped according to the likelihood of the title in question being used by union contractors, nonunion contractors, or both. The generally nonunion helpers are in the first column, those with the equivalent union title of tenders are in the second column, and the other semi-skilled titles used by both camps are in the third. Only 20 of the (generally nonunion) helper titles were found prevailing in at least one determination, a success ratio of only 37 percent, whereas 9 of the (generally union) tender titles, were found prevailing, a success ratio of 75 percent. Thirty-two of the semi-skilled journeyman and helper-like laborers' titles (used by both sides) were found to be prevailing and their success ratio was between the other two, at 47 percent.

Table A3-7

Acceptance and Rejection of Survey Rates
for Variously Named Semi–Skilled Workers
During Period of Non-Suspension of Helper Regulations

	"Helper" (title used in nonunion work)	*"Tender" (title used in union work)*	*Specialty Laborers, Semi-Skilled (mixed use)*
Titles within category found in survey	79	12	70
Total number of individual rate submissions	323	49	231
Number (percent) of different titles found prevailing in at least one survey	53 (16.4%)	24 (49%)	61 (26.4%)
Number (percent) of instances when no rates were issued despite 3 or more individual rate submissions	95 (29.4%)	9 (18.4%)	41 (17.8%)

Source: Derived by A.J. Thieblot from USDL survey documents.

As seen in Table A3-7, in the surveys taken during the period of non-suspension of the helper regulations, without especially looking for them, DOL found almost as many of the generally nonunion helper job categories (79) submitted to the survey as the combination of semi-skilled workers, subspecialty journeymen, union helper-like laborers, and union tenders put together (82). It also found that there were more rates submitted to the surveys for helpers (323) than for those other job titles combined (280).

On the other hand, DOL found a far smaller number of the nonunion helper titles to be prevailing (53) compared with the others (85). It also rejected far more nonunion rate submissions despite their being supported by 3 or more survey submissions much more frequently (95) that the likely union ones (50)—30 percent of the time compared with only an average of 18 percent of the time. Nonunion categories that seemed to have especially large number of survey rates ignored were bricklayer helpers, carpenter helpers, electrician helpers, plumber helpers, and sheet metal worker helpers.

In summary, DOL's failure to find helper rates prevailing during the period of non-suspension seems to have had more to do with what type of surveys it conducted, where it conducted them, and how it interpreted the results than with how many persons actually worked in the construction area as helpers. Furthermore, because there is no apparent statistical basis for these results, they must be attributable to some other causality, either anti nonunion bias or pro union bias on the part of the prevailing wage administrators.

Unintended Consequences of Issuing Rates for Helpers with Respect to Employer Manipulation of Job Assignments

No. 28. The Department of Labor's assertion that helper designations in prevailing rate determinations would lead to contractor manipulation of job assignments is a red herring and a false basis for public policy.

Prevailing wage administration is no harder when helper rates are in effect than when they are not. If unscrupulous contractors, given the availability of helper rates, might misuse them by paying for work that otherwise might be done by laborers or journeymen at higher rates, there is no identifiable prevailing wage issue, provided that paying such wages on private work in the area is also the prevailing practice. The same is true with respect to contractor use of persons with various other job titles.

DOL had expressed concern that unscrupulous contractors, given the availability of helper rates, might misuse them, presumably by paying workers whose work might also be done by laborers at rates other than laborers' or by paying workers doing semi-skilled trade work at rates other than the journeymen's rates for that trade. What misuse this actually entails, if paying such wages on private work in the area is the prevailing practice, is difficult to quantify, but no doubt ensuring against this might require difficult and arduous work. It is not work DOL has undertaken for other craft-specific or semi-skilled jobs.

Only with respect to helpers named as such does DOL express a concern for the task differentiation that it does not apply to other categories. But if it is the prevailing local practice for drywall mechanics to use drywall helpers, it should not matter to DOL if the job of those helpers contains work that would otherwise be done by laborers, any more than it matters that cement block tenders, mason tenders (brick or cement) or plasterers tenders also do jobs that could otherwise be done by laborers, as do asphalt rakers, caulkers, cement finishers, form setters, pipe insulators, or pipefitter material handlers, to name a few at random. It also should not matter to DOL if it is the local practice to employ helpers in semi-skilled categories where they are doing sub-journeymen-level work at less than journeymen's rates, because this is also the case with respect to frame setters and form builders, acoustical ceiling installers, drywall hangers, fence erectors, or metal building studders, to again name only a few, all of whom are sub-journey-level carpenters who are typically paid less than full carpenters' rates. DOL may spend its time evaluating job content and auditing it with respect to helpers, admittedly difficult work, but there is nothing in Davis-Bacon administration that compels it to do so, nor anything that makes doing it for helpers any different from doing it for the other jobs mentioned or for many others similar ones. DOL has no mandate to establish job content beyond identifying what prevails in a locality, or establishing "ownership" of various pieces of construction work by one trade or another, or of imposing union systems of job delimitation on nonunion contractors. Therefore post-determination administration should be no more difficult for helpers than anyone else.

Possible Unintended Consequences of Issuing Rates for Helpers with Respect to Special Enforcement Problems

No. 29. The Department of Labor's assertion that helper designations in prevailing rate determinations would cause special enforcement problems is another red herring and a false basis for public policy.

The enforcement issue is closely related to the contractor malfeasance one and yields to the same counterpoint. The DOL assertion is false, with no basis in fact. DOL has no duty to enforce the use of one category of workman over another or even a lawful right to do so. Its mission is to ensure payment of wage rates specified in determinations, so if the determinations list a rate for carpenter's helper at a certain sum, its enforcement duties stop at making sure that sum is dispensed by employers to carpenter's helpers, in exactly the same way as it would if the determinations listed a rate for "elevator mechanic, probational 70%."

It is true that some variations of the originally proposed helper regulation had maximum ratios of helpers to journeymen, added in deference to union rules limiting the number of apprentices to journeymen in many trades, but it was only after these proposals were removed that DOL voiced its objections based on enforcement difficulties. The original proposal would, indeed, have been difficult to administer, but also was none of DOL's business.

Impact of Helper Rates on Apprentices

No. 30. The Department of Labor's assertion that helper designations in prevailing wage determinations would adversely affect apprenticeship programs demonstrates clear bias towards union rates and work methods.

During the helper controversy, DOL expressed concern that were it to approve rates for nonunion helpers, the apprenticeship system, the traditional formal training system of the industry, might be harmed in some way. The mechanism by which this might occur was not elaborated, and why DOL felt it was a proper concern for prevailing wage rates was not explained, but the fear was misplaced in any event. Revised helper rules might have allowed more semi-skilled, informal, on-the-job training to take place in both union and nonunion construction, and therefore might have encouraged rather than discouraged upward mobility.

In union work, laborers and even semi-skilled tenders and helper-like journeymen have dead-end jobs and are not permitted to aspire to full trade journeyman status. But helpers in nonunion work who use the tools of the trade under supervision of a journeyman can aspire to elevating themselves in the same way that persons in almost all other skilled fields elevate themselves—by accumulating enough on-the-job training and wisdom to advance. Rather than bemoan the potential negative impact on apprenticeship programs, unions should have welcomed the possible new ways to add to the number of journeymen.

The premise that helpers (or tenders, or other semi-skilled workers, regardless of their job names) may never rise to journeyman levels is demonstrably false, even in union work. Although estimates vary somewhat, it is generally agreed that no more than one-third to one-half of the journeymen in the bigger construction trades (carpentry, electrical work, plumbing) achieved their status by completing formal apprenticeship programs, and the proportions rising that way in many of the smaller trades (ironwork, glazing) is even smaller. Those who achieved journeyman status by other means did so through military experience, on-the-job training, or self-instruction. Thus at least a measurable proportion of helpers and semi-skilled workers can be expected to move up, and the existence of helper categories facilitates this.

Furthermore, the present system that prohibits helpers and therefore (by DOL logic) provides maximum support for the system of apprenticeship and formal training, is incapable of supplying a sufficient number of new journeymen to sustain the needs of the industry. The Bureau of Labor Statistics estimates that the construction trades grow about 1 percent per year in normal years. The Current Population Survey estimates total employment in the skilled construction trades (counting the incorporated self employed, who can be presumed to have journeyman status) number 3.3 million. Thus, the industry's needs for new journeymen can be estimated by the needs for replacement and the needs for growth. Assuming an average working life of a journeyman after achieving journeyman status of, say, 40 years, a turnover of 1/40th of 3.3 million per year creates an annual replacement demand of 82,500. The 1 percent industry growth rate, if it resumes after the housing collapse of 2008 and subsequent recession, will add another 33,000, for a total of 115,000 new journeymen needed annually.

The same source estimates that there are currently somewhere between 51,000 and 54,000 construction apprentices, and it is known that almost all of these are in four-year programs or longer. Even neglecting the estimated 20 percent drop-out rate (much higher, by other estimates), the maximum number of new journeymen who can be produced by the "official" joint state apprenticeship program is that number divided by 4—less than 14,000 per year, which leaves a massive shortfall of skilled and trained journeymen of almost 100,000 per year. Alternatives to reaching journeyman status beyond formal apprenticeship training are not only advantageous to all, they are necessary and should be encouraged.

As it stands today, and stood in the early 1990s when the helper controversy was active, there are insufficient apprentices in the structured system to satisfy the future needs for journeymen even in the union segment where approved apprenticeship programs are more readily available, and certainly not enough to satisfy identifiable need for the industry as a whole. Formal apprenticeships are an anachronism of the guild system, and although they continue to exist not only in construction but also in many other industries, they are of vestigial interest everywhere but in construction. In construction, their continued reliance impedes industry advancement by giving too many participants too much of a vested interest in old technologies absorbed in ancient ways.[1]

[1] *See* Northrup, (2008) Construction Union Tactics, Ch. 7, for a more complete discussion of the apprenticeship problem.

Summary of the Helper Controversy

DOL's failure to find helper rates prevailing during the period of non-suspension had more to do with what type of surveys it conducted, where it conducted them, and how it interpreted the results than with how many persons actually worked in the construction area as helpers. The few surveys that were done in nonunion areas, like western Virginia, Florida, Texas, parts of Maryland, or Tennessee, found a great deal (proportionately) of helper use. Not surprisingly, highly union areas, like New York, New Jersey, Massachusetts, or Wisconsin, found little.

If DOL had actually been interested in finding out the degree to which helper categories were (and still are) used in nonunion construction so as to form a better estimate of how they might impact Davis-Bacon determinations in the future, it had four options: 1) It could have continued to conduct surveys until the entire country was covered. Since the entire country has never been surveyed for Davis-Bacon purposes in its 70-year history, however, that probably was never a viable option. 2) It could have conducted the surveys it did do in a more balanced fashion, including more sunbelt and fewer rust-belt areas, especially since the sun belt is where most construction activity takes place. 3) It could have done specially focused surveys in depth (with follow-up phone calls, etc.) in selected areas in the same way it did surveys for landscape concerns. 4) It could have interpreted helper job titles and helper rates in the same way it interpreted titles and rates for tenders and various gradations of laborers and semi-skilled workmen that it administers on behalf of unions.

But DOL did none of those things. Instead, it made every possible choice and took every possible option that favored union wages and practices and obfuscated its choices with a series of bogus arguments in justification of what it did. So today, despite an ever-growing coterie of helpers (and helper-equivalents in union work), its prevailing wage administrators continue to pretend that Davis-Bacon reflects local practice by ignoring them.

Appendix Four

Anomalies in Projects Used by DOL in Conducting Wage Survey 94-MD-022

The degree of credulity prevailing rate specialists are willing to exercise in conducting wage surveys for rate determinations is shown to be very large in these examples from a Montgomery County, Maryland survey. This survey allowed bizarre rate submissions to be included that, although not all necessarily improper, should have caused suspicion of the adequacy of the rate setting and review process:

- Project #294, said to be of $30,000 value, showed 4 carpenters, 1 sheet metal worker, and 50 electricians working in its peak week—a most unusual combination.
- Project #197 reported employing simultaneously 2 union glaziers at each of the following hourly rates: $13.50, $13.75, and $14.00, all plus $1.61 in fringes. Another project, #80, reported simultaneously employing 1 union glazier at $13.00, 1 at $13.75, and 2 each at $14.00, $14.75, and $15.00, all plus fringes of $1.16 (not $1.61). These are unusual variations to be found on single jobs at union rates.
- Project #275 separately identified 68 structural ironworkers and 68 ornamental ironworkers, but both groups had the same rates of pay and fringes. These were probably the same individuals, since structural and ornamental ironworkers are commonly joined.
- Project #240 had 16 roofers paid at 13 different rates ranging from $8.00 to $16.50. Although nonunion, it is unusual to have this much wage variation and this many roofers on a single job.
- For three Sears store renovations, done successively by what appears to have been the same crew going from one job to another, there were about 20 carpenters, 2 electricians, 3 carpet layers, and 4 resilient floor layers. All were paid at consistent union rates, all likely worked for the same

general contractor, and all seemed to have had their wage rates tallied successively for each assignment. Realistically, such persons were not participating in the labor market for each job and should not have been counted repetitively. (At least two rate calculations might have changed from majority to average if this sort of apparent duplication had been eliminated.)

- Project #42, said to be of $900,000 value, employed a single, nonunion laborer (one) in its peak week.
- Nine jobs showed total employment of from 2 to 5 sheet metal workers, and 10 jobs showed total employment limited to from 1 to 6 sprinkler fitters and helpers. This probably demonstrates more about what trade representatives participate more actively in surveys than it does about wage rates paid construction workers in the county.
- Project #275 was so large ($275 million) that it dominated the survey, providing 21 percent of the total number of survey wage rates and having a controlling majority in 7 job categories, 3 of them exclusively. Such a project is fundamentally different from a $200,000 school repair job or the typical building project. Davis-Bacon administration calls for different rates for different types of construction; but this job, a "resource recovery facility," was not differentiated from schools and office buildings, whose wage requirements would nevertheless be influenced by it for years.

Source: Thieblot *Fraud* (1997).

Appendix Five

Mechanics of Wage Determination: The Pennsylvania Example[1]

Data collected for the Pennsylvania survey of the six-county area around Pittsburgh in 2002 and the resulting residential and commercial wage determinations that now cover various combinations of those counties revealed that there is much more to wage determination surveys than simply collecting existing wage rates and applying some count or arithmetical calculation to see which wage rate "prevailed." Indeed, there are many levels of data transmutation that take place more or less routinely, but well out of public view, in almost all prevailing rate determinations. This appendix uses the actual documentation from the six-county survey to illustrate the degree to which every step of the process of rate collection, rate consolidation, rate determination, and rate dissemination to favor unions or union ways.[2] There are at least eight distinct levels at which the process of rate-setting impacts, transforms, and sometimes even transcends the actual data found in surveys to produce "prevailing rates."

It is difficult not to be impressed by how far DOL will go to accommodate complexities unique to union organizations, such as inter-union jurisdictional disputes, local and regional differences in job-naming conventions, pay grades, fringe benefit differences, and the like. It is also difficult not to be impressed by how little the output of the wage determination process resembles the input wage data.

The first step in the transformation that will be discussed below has to do with how DOL identifies rates found in a wage survey that

[1] Some of the material in the Appendix was previously published in Thieblot (2005) "The 20-Percent Majority," and Thieblot (2006) "Perspectives," but it has been updated where appropriate, here.

[2] The discussion here and in following sections concerns only the federal wage-setting process. Things similar to those discussed happen on the state level as well, but are overlooked here to avoid the added confusion.

are "identical to the penny." There are actually several steps that occur even before this—having to do with how the surveys are conducted and who is allowed to submit wage rates to a survey and such matters as whether the same rate paid to the same person on a succession of short jobs counts as one rate submission or many—that are questionable in application, but it will be enough to see how the data are transformed even after they are collected.

Mechanics of Determinations: The Monotonic Union Rate Assumption

> No. 36. DOL arbitrarily transmutes union rates found in surveys, treating all of them as identical to the penny, even if they differ by many dollars. This prejudices rate determinations towards union rates, and demonstrates clear bias towards union rates and practices.

Conventional wisdom about collectively bargained rates is that they are monotonic (as in, "*the* union rate"). This may once have been generally true, but if so, it was long ago. Union rates in the present day are not only not identical one with another, they are often not even close. Nor can they always be seen to relate in identifiable ways, as for example, a base rate rising over time as contract escalators kick in, or rates being higher in metropolitan areas than in rural ones. Neither are they different because of class differences found within union contracts in some trades, especially operating engineers, laborers, and teamsters, where rates may vary with class. Nevertheless, although union rate uniformity has disappeared in fact, it remains in the fiction of rate-determination practice, perhaps because the original concept of prevailing rate perpetuation depended on it. Whatever the reason, DOL's wage specialists routinely excuse union rates from actually having to be the same in order to be counted as identical.

One way this is done is by conflating widely differing union rates submitted to wage surveys, tallying them as though they were identical regardless of their actual differences. This is a formidable example of widespread pro-union administrative bias. DOL had developed elaborate explanations for why they do it, involving such things as the time line over which survey data are collected and the fact that union rates change with contracts that may have changed during the same period, but these are simple rationalizations. The fact of the matter is that nonunion rates also change over time, but the same rationalizations are not advanced with respect to consolidating differing nonunion wage rates.

Both unions and the DOL are sensitive to the fact that if union rate differences in surveys were treated the same as others, the likelihood of union-majority rate determinations would be lessened, and in the final wage determination average rates, not union ones, would obtain more often. Rate consolidation is done exclusively for union data, and it is done routinely. It is also done in the absence of any enabling Davis-Bacon administrative regulations and in clear violation of the spirit of prevailing wage laws. But it is only the first of what will turn out to be many levels of arbitrary data consolidation and transmutation that will be explained subsequently.

How this first transmutation works is easily seen in the Pittsburgh-area survey where the fact that the determination established a union-majority rate instead of an average (not-union) rate for certain trades depended entirely on it. For the trade of drywall finishing in that survey, for example, DOL received a total 74 wage-rate submissions, and its wage specialists asserted that 42 of them, a clear majority, were union rates, so the union rate became the prevailing rate. Fair enough.

But in this instance, no more than 16 of the 74 rates submitted were actually submitted at the same amount. The 32 nonunion rates were all widely different, as might be expected, ranging from under $12 per hour to around $19 per hour. More surprising, however, the 42 union rates had almost as much variation, ranging from around $21 per hour to around $30 per hour. Furthermore, although all of the union workers on any given project received the same hourly wage amount, the amount was different on each of the five union projects submitted. Among union rates for drywall finishers, there were 7 at $21.08, 12 at $21.11, 4 at $28.90, 3 at $28.96, and 16 at $29.64.

Only by counting all of these varying union rates as identical to each other would the selection heuristic (majority paid the same rate to the penny) allow "union rate" to be called the majority, but that is what was done. It could not be argued that the differences were trivial ones that could be ironed out to achieve the outcome, because neither the 19 union rates around $21 per hour nor the 23 rates around $29 per hour were enough to form an independent majority. The outcome could only have been reached by counting $21 an hour to be the same rate to the penny as $29 an hour—a very long stretch.

The conflation of union rates for this craft is far from unique. Other union rates in the same survey were compounded in similar ways. Counted as identical to the penny were: 5 different union rates for carpenters; 6 different union rates for cement masons; 8 different union rates for electricians; 9 different union rates for bricklayers; and 10 different union rates for painters. Within the same craft, rates $14 apart were counted as identical, as were rates differing from one another by more than 40 percent.

Nor did the recorded rates represent rates along a time line, increasing with changing contract terms. The five different union rates for drywall finishers, for example, are shown in Exhibit A5-1, along with the dates of the projects from which they were drawn. They show no time-line correlation.

Exhibit A5-1

Drywall Finishers' Submitted Survey Rates Held To Be Identical to the Penny by DOL, and the Date of Their Project Completion

Project Completion Date	Project Number	Number of Rates Submitted	Wage Rate Submitted	Fringe Benefit Amount	Total Wage Rate
03/10/01	522	4	19.630	9.270	$28.90
05/10/01	154	3	19.630	9.330	$28.96
08/28/01	360	7	15.250	5.830	$21.08
02/28/02	152	12	15.250	5.860	$21.11
05/01/02	151	16	19.990	9.650	$29.64

Source: A. Thieblot, compiled from USDL survey documents.

For setting the determination rate, not only was $21.11 counted to be identical to the penny with $28.90, the differences between them could not possibly have been explained by changing contract terms, as the higher figure preceded the lower one by almost a full year, judging by the project completion dates. Nor could they have been class related, because this specialty group related to carpenters in these counties is not further divided by class, and all drywall finishers are supposed to have the same pay.

Much of the difference here probably has to do with the fact that different locals of union workmen have different contracts, and more than one local may be involved in work in any one county or area, partly because of where the lines of geographic demarcation of local unions fall and partly because unions use travelers, that is, workmen imported from other locals when the local demand exceeds local supply. (There may also be recording or transcription errors. The survey summary forms are filled with omissions and improbable juxtapositions.) But counting these disparate rates as identical for survey and determination purposes is in clear violation of the letter and spirit of the Davis-Bacon Act. Administration reform would not change this because current administration rules already prohibit it. Only repeal of the underlying law would cure it.

Survey Mechanics—Arbitrary Union-Centric Job Title Acceptance

> No. 37. Collecting manipulated survey data by union-supplied job title or consolidating it DOL-supplied job title is an example of obvious bias, and unfairly favors union rates and practices.

Union contracts have become more and more cumbersome and identify many fine distinction in job title, work assignment, and pay within each broader category of workmen. Furthermore, the distinctions are different between different locals of the same union. Just within the state of Pennsylvania, laborer unions' contracts may differentiate unskilled laborers into anywhere from one to six groups for residential work, and one to 11 groups for building work. Here are the contract terms with respect to the division of laborers doing residential work in Monroe County, Pennsylvania in 2011, and their required rates of pay:

Exhibit A5-2

Union Contract Labor Rates and Classifications Applicable to Residential Construction, Monroe County, Pennsylvania, 2011

Laborers:	Rates	Fringes
GROUP 1	$ 22.84	14.39
GROUP 2	$ 23.87	14.39
GROUP 3	$ 23.44	14.39
GROUP 4	$ 23.44	14.39
GROUP 5	$ 25.44	14.39

LABORERS CLASSIFICATIONS

GROUP 1: Cleaning, scrubbing, washing and polishing of floors, furniture and windows, stripping, dismantling, oiling and moving of concrete forms, loading, unloading and carrying of reinforced steel, handling and distribution of lumber of all other building materials, unloading, carrying, distributing and laying of pre-cast concrete slabs and planks in accordance with decisions of record, wrecking, moving and demolishing, underpinning and shoring of all structures, signal person and flag person, landscaping and nursery work, toolroom person, operators of salamanders, smudge pots, propane gas and kerosene burners and all other heating methods. Cleaning of precipitators, operating of jackhammers, busters, drills and all other pneumatic and electric hand tools, wagon drills, air and hydraulic, on or off tracks, power buggies, concrete mixers, pump and vibrators, walk-along compacting equipment, vibrating and tamping, gunniting machines (including the nozzle), operation of steam jennies, sandblasting (filling the pot, cleaning up of sand, use of nozzle), pumps 2: or under conveyors, vacuum cleaners, all types (ride or walk-along), concrete saws and cutting equipment, burning and welding torches, dynamite blasters and blaster tenders, swing scaffolds, slings and bosun chairs. Laying of non-metallic (clay, ironstone, terra cotta, vitrified concrete and plastic) pipe and making of joints for same, walk-along lifts and similar machines, pouring and placing of all concrete and related materials, all concrete curing applications.

GROUP 2: Asbestos removal, hazardous and toxic waste removal, all work in connection with handling, control, removal, abatement, encapsulation or disposal of asbestos and/or toxic waste will be assigned to the member of the Laborers' International Union of North America not to be limited to the erection, moving, servicing and dismantling of all tools and equipment normally used in the handling, control, removal or encapsulation of hazardous material, this Agreement covers work tasks associated with any and all safety requirements and final clean-up and disposal of such hazardous waste material.

GROUP 3: Mason tenders, mixing of mortar, plaster and mortar pumps, plaster tenders, caisson work, blast furnaces, coke ovens and all related work, erection and dismantling of all scaffolding, including tubular frame, manual and powered climbing scaffold, swing scaffolds, slings, bosun chairs, and all associated safety protection including barricades, nets and ropes, scaffold weather enclosures; shoring; mortar buggies; concrete pumps; walk-behind forklifts; electric welders torches, compressors, generators and the repair and maintenance of same; jackhammers, tampers; cut-off saws & other power equipment required for demolition; rotary-hammer drills, electric & pneumatic hand-tools; transit, levels & lasers; tempering mortar; stocking scaffolds with masonry materials including brick, block, mortar, teera cotta, architectural pre-cast concrete, natural stone, insulation & mastic, flashing, anchors & ties, grount; mobile lifting platform scafforing powered by any power mode or method ; cleaning of all masonry debris.

GROUP 4: Skid-steering loader and folklift laborers. Operation of rough terrain forklifts, skid-steering loaders.

GROUP 5: Undefined. [Curiously, although there is a specific rate identified for Group 5 laborers, there is no definition or identification of the job contents covered by this group in the contract as reproduced in the Monroe County federal prevailing wage determination.] [All sic.]

Source: Laborers Union Local 1174 contract negotiated May 1, 2011, as reproduced in Prevailing Wage Determination PA120060, Monroe County in

> Pennsylvania Except Tobyhanna (Including Tobyhanna Army Depot) Residential Construction Projects.

This listing of labor groups and jobs, may have been different in small or large ways in the contract or contracts covering laborers in the 6-county region in 2002, and the wage rates in it were undoubtedly lower. But the Laborers' contract, then, would have contained some similar differentiation of job duties and wage rates among unskilled laborers, and therein lays the rub for Davis-Bacon survey administration. Form WD-22a does not specify job titles for which wages should be submitted, and the DOL has only internal guidelines as to what a full range of job titles should be for residential, commercial, and the usually-combined heavy and highway construction regimes. The handling of job titles at the front (survey) end of the wage determination process and again at the back (distribution) end is a clear illustration of pro-union DOL bias.

In the case of the 6-county survey, the survey summary forms WD-22a associate all laborer wage rates with a particular category called "Laborers, Unskilled." Although two different wage rate for union laborers appeared in the survey, in any given submission all of the laborers covered appear to have been paid identical amounts (24 at $23.41 and 18 at $23.22). There is no variation in job title and no variation in rates within the job title depending on the exact work performed, as demanded by the union contract.

Therefore, there are only two possibilities, both involving wage fraud: either the union agents reported fictitious wages and job titles so that they would appear to have a large number of workers paid the same rate to the penny, or the DOL consolidated the wage rates and titles on behalf of the unions. (A later transmutation by DOL would further consolidate union laborers' wage rates by recording the two already fictional submitted wages, $23.41 and $23.22, as identical to the penny, thereby inflating the sameness and possible prevailing-ness of union rates.)

Similar fraudulent recordings occur in every wage survey I have reviewed that contains union wage rates for trades that are commonly divided by unions into groups or categories for wage purposes, including especially laborers, teamsters, and operating engineers, but also to a lesser degree electricians, plumbers, cement masons, painters, and sheet metal workers, among others. The union contracts for all these trades specify different wage rates for different skills, specialties, and job contents that almost never appear with their corresponding wage differences in the surveys.

The opposite effect, disaggregating and repackaging common job titles and rates, is illustrated by the contract of the Greater Pennsylvania Regional Council of the United Brotherhood of Carpenters and Joiners of America with its union employers that was in effect at the time of the Pittsburgh area residential survey. This contract provided a single rate for journeymen carpenters doing not only routine carpentry work but also forms building, concrete pouring inspection, countertop handing and installation, ceiling installation, and other tasks, all described together as carpenter/lathers; it also established separate rates for floor-laying carpenters, millwrights, and piledrivermen. What it did not provide was a rate for carpenters described as "carpenters, inc drywall & siding." Nevertheless, this is the only carpenter rate found in the WD-22a's of the survey. Twenty-six carpenters were reported working on one single Allegheny County project and 28 on another, all at the exact same union rate and appearing in the survey with the exact same job title; it is impossible to know if any of them were actually doing millwright or floor-laying or piledriving work, but it's pretty certain that at best only a few of them could have been engaged in the specific task of "carpentry (including drywall and siding)." Yet, not only were all carpenters reported with this specific compound job title, carpenters on these two projects pretty well set the prevailing rate for all six counties, in the process applying the urban rates of Allegheny County to the rural areas like Fayette in the initial determination. (There was also one companion carpentry-associated specialty in the survey, that of drywall finishing, already described.)

At the start of the process, the collection of rates for WD-22a, rates that may be supplied by whatever source are apparently consolidated and compiled into a limited number of DOL-decided job categories regardless of how they were supplied. This can make a huge difference because the compilations may be used to decide rates for several narrowly defined job titles or for a smaller number of broadly defined ones, and this in turn may alter the union or nonunion character of the outcome. In actual practice, union contractors tend to prefer narrow titles if their union segregates them, because union contracts typically specify slightly different rates for workers doing slightly different things within broader categories. Laborers doing welding, for example, may command different contract rates if they are welding for carpenters or sheet metal workers, and laborers doing cement handling may command different rates from laborers handling concrete block. Therefore, union contractors providing rate information to surveys based on actual payroll records should be expected to have corresponding differences, but any such differences are rare enough in the surveys that I have never observed them. On the other hand, nonunion contractors, who expect greater flexibility on the part of their workers, might well call all such persons, simply, laborers but pay them all differently, dependent on their skill or experience, and each nonunion contractor would arrive at a different pattern. The former have a much higher chance of being determined to be prevailing than the latter because either the unions or the DOL consolidates the former but not the latter when recording them on the survey.

If all carpenter rates submitted by either union or nonunion sources were submitted as "Carpenters Including Drywall & Siding," all painters as "Painters, Brush & Roller," all cement masons as "Cement Mason/Finishers," all crane operators as "Cranes" (regardless of capacity), etc., and all were paid the same listed rates, then such reports must be fraudulent, because they do not reflect either reality or the pay requirements of their contracts. And if unions did submit their wage reports accurately, with all of their variations in title and pay that exists in the contracts, then the consolidation was fraudulently performed by the DOL. Either case makes the entire prevailing wage identification practice a sham, and judging from the helper situation, there seems to be no possibility of responsible correction. The only alternative is to junk the present system and start over, or better yet, forget about it.

Survey Mechanics—Inadequate Screening of Duplicative Data

No 38. The combination of voluntary rates from various sources may result in duplicative submissions that unduly color the final results, and unfairly favor union rates and practices.

DOL wage specialists collect survey data on the forms called WD-22a. These forms are physically compiled from raw data, and are then re-compiled onto the wage summary sheets from which the determinations are prepared. They list the project name and value, the job categories of the subject wage rates, the number of persons working on the project "in the peak week," and their wage rate and fringe benefits paid. A review of what these look like in detail is neither pretty, nor indicative of any attempt at accuracy.

The WD-22a's collected for the Pennsylvania residential surveys provide a case in point about problems with voluntary rate submissions. There is no way of knowing how many solicitations for wage data went out or how many were returned by employers as opposed to non-employers for those surveys, because such data are not shown and are not easily accessible.[3]

What is known, however, is that whatever the source, only wage rates from about 380 different projects from across all six counties were found in the survey. In comparison the number of building permits issued in those six counties in 2009 (a time when the construction recession was already in full bore) totaled 2,980. In the busier construction climate of 2001, the 380 projects found in the residential survey would have represented only about 10 percent of the total of any one year. Actually, it was substantially less, because rates included in the survey were drawn from a time period that spanned June 2000 through July 2002, two full years. Furthermore, some of the projects are identified as being successive units in the same real estate development that would have been built under a single building permit. These projects were clearly not random or chosen from a structured plan.

Furthermore, many of the project reports contained obvious anomalies, such as far too many or too few workmen in relation to the value of the projects, or evidence of multiple reporting of the same workmen's wages on successive, small jobs. Indeed, many of the projects represented gave evidence of being merely a succession of different houses on the same streets, or even from different residential

[3] At least I've never been able to get them. They tend to be "pencil on yellow pad" numbers.

units in the same complex that were probably covered by single building permits. Five successive WD-22a project wage summary reports for Butler County, were for 5 of at least 14 numbered single family houses in a residential complex named Hidden Meadows, each unit of which had a total project cost of $250,000. Four of these projects were completed in the same week of 2001, and one was completed two weeks later. On the record, the only employment during the peak week on these projects was of bricklayers: 5 bricklayers on 4 of the projects, and 4 on the fifth.

It is obvious even from project names that these were not independent employment events, but rather one bricklayer contractor or one union agent reporting on a crew of 5 workmen going from house to house to do a small job of specialty brick work. Curiously, some of the crews were paid at different union rates—on three projects all 4 individuals at $30.31 per hour, and on 2 projects at $0.60 more, $30.91. (Neither of the higher-rate projects was the outlier job that finished two weeks after the rest.) When these survey rates were consolidated on to form WD-10, the two different union rates were consolidated with 2 other, different union rates paid to 22 other union bricklayers in other counties on similarly duplicative jobs to arrive at a union-negotiated majority determination.

In addition, too few showed acceptable amounts of craft diversity for them to have been submitted in response to a project data request. Nor is this the only problem. Fifty-nine of the 71 total rates in the survey for bricklayers were reported to be on projects where the only workers were bricklayers. More than half of the rates collected by the survey for ornamental ironworkers, plumbers, sheet metal workers, crane operators, elevator constructors, carpenters "including drywall and siding," and soft floor layers were also rates from single-craft projects.[4]

[4] Not all of these were necessarily submitted by unions. A single nonunion contractor employing a total of 2 sheet metal workers on each job may have submitted rates for them separately working on 18 single-trade projects in Westmoreland County. These 36 rates (probably from only 2 actual employees), a majority of the total for the trade in this particular county, would

Survey Mechanics—Flexible Survey Boundaries

No. 39. Accepting data from outside the established time frame of the survey, from other polities, or from jobs previously performed under prevailing wage mandates biases the results, and unfairly favors union rates and practices.

It should not be necessary to go beyond established survey geographic or time parameters or to accepting previous, self-perpetuating Davis-Bacon rates in new survey inclusions. DOL does it only because it so often finds itself with too few survey submissions to support even a rudimentary list of job titles in a wage determination, even by its most relaxed standards for how many survey rates from how many different sources are sufficient to justify a new rate issuance. But by doing so, it violates its precept of finding and preserving "whatever rates actually prevailed" in the locality of new work. They come from outside the locality, or they were not normal, market-driven rates.

The 2002 Pennsylvania residential survey was designed to cover the time period from September 1, 2000 through August 31, 2001. Most of the project reports do carry dates from within this period, but a surprising number also carry more recent dates, including several in 2002 and one in 2003, times after the determinations based on them were issued. (They may have been dates erroneously recorded, or they may have been projects in their very early stages of completion, but if the latter, they were not supposed to be included.)

The number of late-dated rates for bricklayers, drywall finishers, plasterers, and carpenters was large enough to have produced different determination rates than would have obtained without them. For example, 86 percent of the plasterers' rates and 62 percent of the drywall finishers' rates were submitted from dates outside the established contract range. In all cases, these added rates were union rates.

---

have set the rate for rate for the entire six-county area were they not balanced by a large influx of union sheet-metal rates from Allegheny County found late in the survey period, rates perhaps similarly derived.

The residential survey does not show obvious evidence of rate inclusion from previous Davis-Bacon jobs, but only because such evidence is difficult for an outsider to discern. Relatively few of the projects listed in the residential survey, however, have names that would indicate they had been performed under prevailing rate dictates. But some may have.

Mechanics of Determinations: Arbitrary Union Rate Selection

No. 40. DOL arbitrarily selects which local union's rate prevails. This increases the arbitrariness of wage determination outcomes, and while demonstrating clear bias towards union rates and practices, helps render published determinations meaningless.

A second transmutation occurs once a plurality has been established by conflation of the various union rates in surveys. Having decided that the (combined) union rate prevails, DOL's wage specialists must then select a single union rate that will be called "prevailing." It would seem better if this rate bore some relationship to one or more of rates actually submitted, but there are no known guidelines. The rate finally selected might be significantly higher or lower than some or even all of those in the survey (or any statistic drawn from their distribution). One wage specialist might decide to record all the rates as though they were the highest, arguing that these might best represent the most recent union contract, but another specialist might decide to record them all as though they were at some other rate that he or she felt might, for whatever reason, be more representative, regardless of its plurality within the survey. If there is a conflict of union locals that had submitted different rates, perhaps the wage specialist simply selects the one he or she knows best or likes the most. There are simply no guide rules.

When not-union rates are selected as prevailing, their survey average is published, and whatever that is, will remain until another survey is performed for the same area in some future year. When union rates are selected as prevailing, they are always listed in the wage summary sheets as having a rate of "$.000." In the case of the drywall finishers, I do not have access to historical iterations of prevailing rate determinations, so I am unsure of what rate was initially set in 2002. But because the amount said to prevail two years after the first issuance, in 2004, was $22.44, the original determination must have been more clearly aligned with the lower group of rates than with the higher one, despite the fact that the lower group of rates numbered only 19, while the higher group numbered 23. So the selected rate was apparently aligned with a minority within the union section, much less within the entire survey.

There had also been 34 nonunion rates submitted to the survey. If the different union rates had been treated as different, which they in fact were, the prevailing rate would have been established by weighted average instead of arbitrary majority as a not-union rate, and would have been set at $20.86. Had that been the case, the prevailing rate on determinations would have remained $20.86 to this day.

Prevailing rates set for a number of other trades in this determination also seem to have been based on minority, lower, or earlier-dated entries among the union survey submissions.

Mechanics of Determinations: Arbitrary Union Rate Publication

> No. 41. If DOL finds a union rate to be prevailing, the rate published in the determination may be considerably different (invariably higher) than that found, and will reflect current rates published in some union contract. This increases the union orientation of wage determination outcomes, demonstrating clear bias towards union rates and practices.

The 4th iteration of the original six-county residential determination was published in 2004, newly shorn of Allegheny County, which had been given its own, separate determination with no rate designated for drywall finishers. This now 5-county determination is the one that shows the union rate of $22.04 for drywall finishers, the one aligned with the lower survey rates. Over time, however, it did not matter that the initially established union rate was based on the lower number, because once established, like all union determination rates, it rose over time with each successive union contract (or was reallocated to a local union with higher wage rates). By 2011, when the original 6-county determination had been split again, now into 4 pieces conditioned on findings in the original survey and perhaps some additional rates added with respect to Allegheny County, Allegheny County was determined to have a nonunion drywall finisher's rate of $18.48; the combination of Beaver, Fayette, and Washington counties, however, also now had a nonunion rate of a couple of dollars more; and Westmoreland County now had a determination with no rate specified for this trade. But Butler County retained the original union determination, and the rate had now risen to $35.66, almost exactly double the nonunion rate. (This rate may have been re-keyed to the higher-priced union locals who had supplied the original union survey rates in that county. It is also pretty close to the building—as opposed to residential—rate that was $38.20 for all six counties in 2011.[5])

Mechanics of Determinations: Arbitrary Union Rate Updating

> No. 42. If DOL publishes a union rate as prevailing in a determination, that rate is automatically updated to reflect the collective bargaining contract wage, in perpetuity. Determinations containing such information are called "updated," or "current." These automatic increases affect only nonunion contractors, since union contractors pay the union rate, regardless. Following this practice increases the union orientation of wage determination and demonstrates clear bias towards union rates and practices.

By this point, any resemblance between the rates published in the determinations and those actually submitted to the survey was due either to happenstance or to a connection made by the thread of a wage specialists' perceptions of union preference. It also should be clear that, once a union determination rate is specified, the amount does not remain static. All union rates published in wage determinations are updated to the current collective bargaining contract cover-

[5] Few union contracts specify different pay grades for their craftsmen depending on the type of contracts they are working on, although many have escalators for contracts above a certain cost, or for handling hazardous materials, or for using equipment of a larger capacity. How DOL decides on which union rate to honor in determinations is a bit of a mystery, except for laborers, operating engineers, and teamsters, where it simply regurgitates whatever detail the contracts provide.

ing it for each new contract iteration, in perpetuity, until a new survey is conducted. (There is not even a requirement that the contract rate actually be paid to anyone or that any union members actually receive it before it is specified.) All 26 prevailing wage determination for building work in Pennsylvania and most of those set for residential work, 5 of the 6 heavy and highway determinations, and all determinations set by the state for building work under the Pennsylvania prevailing wage law, show evidence of this sort of transmutation because all of these have at least some union rates that are routinely updated by means of current contract escalators.

This practice is sanctioned by Davis-Bacon administrative procedures (though why this should be so is lost to history), and to carry it out the DOL maintains a large file of union contracts. This does not, however, make it less unfair or less false to the spirit of prevailing wage determination, which was based on the idea of continuing and protecting whatever individual wage rates had been paid in the past, not on insuring that the latest union rates would be the current minimums imposed on union and nonunion contractors alike.[6]

The frequent updating of union rates in determinations allows DOL (or state agencies) the pretense that the determinations in which the most recent union rates are published are made current thereby, masking the need for new surveys that might test their underlying validity. As discussed below, one result is that genuine updates based on surveys are rare, and most determinations are hopelessly outdated.

[6] It is worth repeating that the impact is felt exclusively by nonunion contractors. There is no need, from a union contractor's standpoint, for prevailing rates to be up to the minute, as the governing union contract will take precedence over any lower prevailing rate. Up-to-the-minute rates also don't affect union members' employability by nonunion contractors, as union members are not allowed to work for them. So the only impact is exclusively to increase the wastage by nonunion contractors paying nonunion employees at the latest, and undoubtedly highest, above-market union rates.

Mechanics of Determination: Illustration of Rate Consolidation, Redetermination, and Routine Upgrading for Pittsburgh Area Drywall Finishers

A good example of how all the various DOL machinations discussed earlier in this appendix is provided by shepherding details of the relatively minor trade of drywall finishing, already discussed in some of its particulars, through the survey, rate selection, and publication process. The choice of trade is essentially random. Substantially the same patterns existed in the process establishing rates for painters, laborers, carpenters, equipment operators, plumbers, and others in this area, and for many other trades reviewed by the author in surveys for other parts of the country. In late 2001, the federal survey was undertaken of residential projects in a six-county area of Southwestern Pennsylvania comprising Allegheny, Beaver, Butler, Fayette, Washington, and Westmoreland counties, that resulted in the determinations already introduced.[7]

The survey time period covered the year ending August 31, 2001.[8] In the project area, union drywall hanging was done by a named subset of carpenters at the journeymen carpenters' rate,9 and the taping and finishing of drywall was done by a named subset of painters called "drywall finishers" but at a lesser journeymen's rate.

[7]It resulted in a General Determination (PA020013) in April 2002, that was subsequently updated several times and then broken into two parts in late 2003, one for Allegheny County and another for the other five counties. Subsequently, it was re-fractured into four parts covering four different county groupings. Details of the determination numbers and coverage are shown at footnote 2 in the main text.

[8]Pennsylvania Project Wage Summary Survey 01–PA–015, dated 12/05/2002. (The survey date may be incorrect, for it is later than the dates of the determination that was issued as a result of it, PA020013, which is dated 04/18/2002.) Furthermore, a large number of WD-22a survey summary sheets show project dates from outside the designated time range, mostly more recent than the survey cut-off would seem to allow. Some of the anomalies can be put down to typos, but the author has been unable to learn why others are off.

Although the hangers were surveyed as a compound category (usually rendered as "carpenters, including drywall and siding"), the finishers were surveyed separately and rates were collected for drywall finishers, as such.[9]

Contractors, unions, and other non-employers submitted survey data on drywall finishers for 24 projects in the 6-county area. Eighteen of these were nonunion projects that had recently employed 30 drywall finishers in Allegheny County at various rates from $10.10 to $19.05 per hour, averaging $15.93.[10] Westmoreland County also had

[9]When the building trade unions were originally established, walls were plastered and gypsum board (drywall) had not yet been invented. Plasterers thought the new product a threat to their expertise and shunned it. Hence no particular union, then or now, "owns" either the hanging or finishing of drywall. In some areas, by some contractors, persons who hang and finish drywall might be called carpenters and be paid as such; in others, they might be called specialty carpenters (e.g., carpenter, drywall mechanic) and paid at a different rate from other carpenters; or the hanging might be done by either of the above and the taping done by persons called laborers or specialty laborers, journeymen or specialty painters, or journeymen or specialty plasterers. In actual practice, both the hanging and the finishing is increasingly done by specialized contractors called drywall contractors, who operate the right kind of lift-trucks for transporting the product and who are adept at handling up to 12-foot sheets, making minimal seams, and working on stilts to avoid having to scaffold. Crews larger than 4 are seldom needed, especially on residential projects, and they work for only a few days on any given project. There is little evidence from these or other surveys of such specialty contractors participating in the wage-setting process, and as a result, in large parts of the country few independent prevailing rates are published for either sub-set of drywall work. Nevertheless, the specialty already would have relatively strong presence in prevailing rate savings because each short job qualifies as another rate submission when forwarded by, for example, a union representative on behalf of union contractors.

[10]For simplicity, except where there is cause to separate them, wage rates and fringe benefit amounts are combined to a single total rather than reported independently. In this particular case, for example, the actual range was $9.50 to $16.75 for wages, plus $.81 to $3.60 for fringe benefits, but the lowest wages did not correspond with the lowest fringes, nor the highest with the highest.

one nonunion project with two workmen whose rates averaged $14.48. All of the union rates came from only 5 additional projects: two in Allegheny County that employed, respectively, seven persons at $21.08, and three persons at an entirely different rate of $28.96; one in Beaver had 4 persons employed at $28.90; one in Butler had 16 persons employed at $29.55; and one in Washington had 12 persons employed at $29.11. Each of the 5 union projects paid its employees at different union rates, and the not-insignificant difference among them was $8.47 per hour.[11] None of them formed an independent majority of either all of the rates submitted or of all of the union rates. Nevertheless, the 5 different union rates were all consolidated and treated as "the same to the penny," with the result that there were 42 "identical" union rates across the 6 counties, and only 32 nonunion rates. The union rates were therefore established as the majority, and prevailing rates were consequently established for all six counties at (an arbitrarily chosen) union rate. These are summarized in Exhibit A5-3.

[11]Also to be noted, 19 of the 42 union rates represented rates that were both later than others and lower, and so would not have reflected contracts changing over time. A related note is that 28 of the rates (the effective majority) were dated from 6 to 8 months after the close of the survey period. If these dates were correct, the rates should have been eliminated from the survey; but if the dates were typed incorrectly, then there would have been 19 rate submissions on the same day at 2 different amounts, and 24 additional examples of earlier, though higher, rates.

Exhibit A5-3

Residential Survey Rates for Drywall Finishers
Pennsylvania Project Wage Survey Summary 01-PA-015 (12/05/2002)

Six Counties, Southwestern Pennsylvania

	Allegheny	Beaver	Butler	Fayette	Washington	Westmoreland
21 Nonunion Projects, Rates Paid, Per Survey:						
......Under $14.00	4	-	-	-	-	1
.....$14.00–$17.99	12	-	-	-	-	1
....$18.00 and over	14	-	-	-	-	-
Average Nonunion Rates	$15.93	-	-	-	-	$14.48
5 Union Projects, Rates Paid, Per Survey:						
..... $21.08	7	-	-	-	-	-
..... $21.11	-	-	-	-	12	-
..... $28.90	-	4	-	-	-	-
.....$28.96	3	-	-	-	-	-
.....$29.55	-	-	16	-	-	-

Exhibit A5-3 summarizes all of the 74 rates collected for drywall finishers in the survey. Forty-two of those were at union rates averaging $25.62, and 32 were nonunion rates averaging $15.84. A clear majority (57 percent) were therefore union, but without the active intervention of the DOL it would have been very difficult to say which one was the correct union prevailing rate, because 5 different union rates showed up in the submissions. A simple or a weighted average of the union rates might have been chosen—the simple average is $25.92, the weighted average is $25.62—but there would have been problems with either choice. In the first place, both numbers represented wages that were paid to no individuals, and therefore were about as far from conforming to the definition of prevailing as they could be. Second, if DOL had chosen either to be the prevailing rate, it would have had no union contract to use for updating the rates in the future, as is the established practice.

The alternative, however, is equally troublesome. For the union rate to have prevailed, the five different union rates had to be considered "identical to the penny" ($21.08 counted to be no different from $21.11, $28.90, $28.96, or $29.55). This is a long stretch, but it is what DOL did here (and in many other rate settings I have witnessed). The rate selected by the wage specialist might possibly have been linked to 7, 12, or 19 survey rates in the $21-range, but it clearly could not have been linked to the 23 other, higher, survey rates that averaged $29.50. So even compounding for small differences that could be time-related, the rate chosen is not the majority rate within the union portion of the data set.

The prevailing rate rules say it is the rate to the penny that is paid to over 50 percent of the survey, or it is the weighted average of all rates in the survey if there is no majority. Had those rules had been followed in this case, and had all 72 of the survey rates been accepted (that is, had none been eliminated because of data inadequacy or error in submission), the prevailing rate for each county or group of should have been set at the not-union rate of $17.75 per hour, and because it would have been a not-union rate it would have remained at $17.75 per hour until a new survey was performed for the area. The difference is substantial between $17.75 and the current union rate, $35.66, the rate that would have been in effect for all six counties were they still covered by a single determination.

This should have been the end of the analysis of the drywall finishers' rates, but their story became more complicated. In January 2004, Allegheny County was split off from the other counties and given its own determination, although the purpose for doing it or the process by which it was done are both unclear.[12] After this occurred,

[12]The split-off of Allegheny County was possibly in retaliation for pressures by a nonunion trade association to correct alleged survey errors, omissions, and irregularities in accepting certain union survey data and rejecting certain nonunion data for Allegheny County. No new survey was performed, however, and the 6-county determinations continued to reflect in the 5-

the rate for drywall finishers in Allegheny County disappeared and for that county no rate was issued for drywall finishers (although, as just discussed, there were adequate survey data to support issuing a not-union weighted average rate of $18.48). For the other five counties the, determined rate remained the same as it had been ($22.44), even though the weighted average of the remaining five-county-combined survey rates would have yielded a higher prevailing rate of $25.65.

The issuance pattern of wage determinations changed again after the Allegheny County split-off. From clues found in current determinations this might have happened around the start of 2010. Greene County was added to the building determinations, then, but not to the residential ones. The residential determinations were repackaged so that there became four for the six-county area: one each for Allegheny, Butler, and Westmoreland counties, and a fourth for Beaver, Fayette, and Washington, together.

An interesting question arises with respect to these new determinations, all of which were presumably based on the same initial survey data. What would the rate have been if it had been calculated independently by ordinary prevailing rate administrative rules for these new county groupings? The answer is shown in Exhibit A5-4, whose contents I will now discuss.

In the table, the current (2011) union contract rate is the one that appears in the determination for Butler County. If all the other counties were still being covered by a single six-county determination and all the drywall finisher rates were still being set by reference to the union contract, then the $35.66 rate would apply to all—a rate about twice as high as it had been 9 years previously. However, the residential determination for the six-county area had undergone two transformations of its own in the intervening period.[13]

---

county one without substantive change until the determination publishing structure was again modified in about 2010, again without benefit of a new survey.

[13]Rate transformations after determinations are established, and changing geographic application within determinations without additional surveys

Exhibit A5-4

Original Rates That Would Have Been Calculated by Ordinary Rules for Counties Split to Reflect Current (2011) Wage Determination Issuances, Compared With Current Published Rates
Drywall Finishers, Residential Construction

County or Grouping	By Ordinary Rules, Alternative One[1]	By Ordinary Rules, Alternative Two[1]	Per Current Determination	Probable Rate That Would Have to Be Paid[2]
Allegheny	$17.80	$17.80	$18.48	$18.48
Beaver, Fayette, and Washington	$21.11	$21.11	$16.74	$16.74
Butler	$29.55	no rate	$35.66	$35.66
Westmoreland	$14.48	no rate	no rate	$30.15

Notes: [1]Alternative One uses original (2002) survey data and conforms to the ordinary rule of "rates as found," not consolidated if union. Alternative Two also uses original survey data and conforms both to "rates as found" and also to "data disregarded if fewer than 3 rates from at least 2 projects."

[2]This would be the closest related prevailing rate, if none specified for job title, here, that for painter (if established), or carpenter.

In the first, Allegheny County was given its own, separate determination, and the other five counties shared a second one. In the second, the residential determination was split into four parts: Allegheny; Beaver, Fayette, and Washington; Butler; and Westmoreland. (The building determinations were split internally for some trades into various county groupings, and Greene County was added to the others.) What would the prevailing residential rates have been for these county groupings if they were independently calculated from the

being performed, are not uncommon. But they seldom give rise to new determinations.

original survey data? Exhibit A5-4 illustrates the answer. Allegheny County would have been calculated alone, based on 30 nonunion rate submissions and 10 union ones. Assuming that because the union rates were not a majority these amounts would not have been consolidated, the prevailing determination based on the weighted average of all rates ($17.80) would have been used instead.[14]

For the current determination, the Allegheny County drywall finisher rate is a nonunion rate of $18.48, indicating it was calculated by weighted average of union and nonunion wages somewhat differently construed, but I have been unable to make that rate drop out from the existing survey submissions regardless of how arranged. Having been established, however, it will remain until superseded by a new one based on some new survey (or possibly some additional DOL recalculation).

For the combination of Beaver, Fayette, and Washington counties, the original survey showed only 12 union rates on one project in Washington (at $21.11) and 4 union rates on one project in Beaver (at $28.90). If accepted and not consolidated (alternative one), this would have produced a union determination of $21.11, if selected by majority, or $23.06, if selected by weighted average. DOL would probably have picked $21.11, as this is a rate that could be updated from later union contracts, so this is the rate I have listed in the table. Since such a rate would have been based on at least three rates from two projects, it would have also been the rate specified in alternative two.

The current determination rate for these three counties is a nonunion rate of $16.74. Since there was not a single nonunion rate in the original survey, the origin of this rate is a mystery, but it is the rate for the present time. (In contrast, had one of the union rates been initially

[14]Note that in this case, although nonunion rates clearly prevailed (30 nonunion rates to 10 union ones), union rates were not disregarded in setting the prevailing rate minimums at a not-union rate. As a result, if the same nonunion personnel were employed again on a public works job governed by this determination, 27 of the 30 would have to be paid higher wages or fringe benefits than before because of the large influence of the 10 union rates, and especially of their much larger fringe benefits. The not-union average was $1.87 more per hour (12 percent) than the nonunion average.

selected, the current prevailing wage requirement would probably be about the same as that in Butler, that is, about $35 an hour.)

Butler County now has its own determination. Had its rate been based on the original data, it would have been based on 16 union rates from one project, at $29.55 for alternative one. Alternative two would have yielded no rate, since all the rates derived from a single project. The current determination pegs it at the union rate of $35.66. Whether derived from alternative one or alternative two, this is the rate that would currently be required (the union painter's rate being the same, had no rate been issued for drywall finishers).

Finally, Westmoreland County also now has its own residential determination. Original data for it showed two individual nonunion rates averaging $14.48, which would have been determined by alternative one. Alternative two would not have seen a rate issued. In the current determination, no rate is issued, but the rate that would probably have to be paid is the painters' rate of $30.15.[15]

Reviewing these tables, it is not hard to miss the significance of the highly disparate prevailing rates that arose from the original survey submissions and the way they were assembled, consolidated, issued for 6 counties, or 5-plus-1 counties, or 3-plus-3 individual counties. From data that were alleged to identify the wage rate that

[15]If no rate is issued, a contractor needing to use the job title must pay workers on the job at some prevailing rate, or possibly get a rate added to the determination. Adding positions or rates to a determination after it is issued is technically possible, but is a cumbersome process and one that may also expose certain contractors to unnecessary risk. The regulation cited on every federal determination, 29 CFR 5.5(a)(1)(ii), requires specific application for each addition, contemplates approval times of any questionable rate of 60 days or more, and nevertheless requires some prevailing rate to be paid from the first day of employment. One of the three conditions for approval [at 29 CFR 5.5(a)(1)(ii)(A)(3)] is that "any proposed rate must bear a reasonable relationship to the wage rates contained in the determination," which mitigates in favor of union rates in any determination where union rates outnumber not-union ones. Contractors also know they assume great risk in paying a not-union rate, even if justified, because of possible challenges raised by "compliance investigators" sponsored by the unions.

actually prevailed in the area at the time the survey was conducted, at least 6 alternatives sets of rates have been derived in different proportions of union, nonunion, and no-rate alternatives. The current "prevailing rate" for drywall finishers doing residential work in the region of the survey range from no rate to $16.74 and up to $35.66—for the same work in the same area and derived from the same data. It has gone from a union rate in all counties to a union rate in five counties but no rate in the sixth, to a nonunion rate in the one that previously had no rate, three counties with a nonunion rate, and one with a union rate. The DOL apparently nudged or violated several of its own administrative procedures in arriving at these rates, and there is some (external) evidence that it caved to political pressures to carve out a (justified) nonunion rate for the Allegheny County practitioners of this trade. Perhaps supporters of the nonunion side should be grateful that their protests eventually relieved several of the counties of having to have a union rate, but the whole process illustrates only too well how the sausage of prevailing rates is made, why the end results in determinations are illogical and arbitrary, and why the entire system should be junked.

Appendix Six:

A Few Anomalies from Current Pennsylvania Determinations

Here are some examples of determination anomalies from current residential and building determinations in Pennsylvania in 2011:

- A Butler County determination setting electricians' wage rates only for Fayette and Washington counties.
- In one determination, 3 different rates for the same electrician job differing by $13.54 in different sub-areas covered by the determination. (PA 16)
- In another, electricians having five different rates differing by as much as $24.25 ($51.46 to $75.71) per hour in the same determination in the same county. (PA 31)
- In another, electrical line construction groundhands (a union category of helpers) having rates differing by $15.56 and ironworkers differing by $17.27 in different areas covered by the same determination. (PA 1)
- A plasterer tender (a union helper) having a rate set at $35.30 but no rate set for the plasterers they would be helping. (PA 21).
- A plasterer tender's rate, along with a brick mason tender's rate and an unskilled laborer's rate, set for Lackawanna, Wayne, Susquehanna, and the Northern part of Wyoming counties, despite the fact that the determination is issued for Susquehanna, Wayne, and three other counties not including Lackawanna or Wyoming. (No laborer rates identified for the southern part of Wyoming County.) (PA 21)
- Four pages of description (actually two pages of description mostly but not completely repeated twice) for six groups of laborers' rates in "(COUNTY OF LUZERNE: NORTHERN PART)" and for the same six groups though at slightly different wage rates for "COLUMBIA AND LUZERNE Southern part (Hazleton Township) COUNTIES)." Neither Luzerne nor Columbia counties are covered by the determination issued. (PA 21)

- Within the repeated descriptions one finds "Walk Along Lifts & similar machines" twice at a group 1 rate, "walk-behind forklifts" twice as a group 3 rate, "walk-behind forklifts" as a group 6 rate, and "FORKLIFT LABORER" twice as having its own group, group 4, at unique rates, which gives such employees a total of 7 slightly different "prevailing" wage rates in 14 different amounts in the same determination in the same two counties, neither of which happens to be within the area covered by the determination. (PA 21)
- In the same listings in this determination one finds laborers' rates for skid-steering loaders and for welders in several different wage categories, and for asbestos worker work, mason tender work, and operating Bobcats and several identified brands of cranes—all of which are usually within the province of competing unions. (PA 21)
- Power equipment operators in the Berks County building determination having a nonunion wage of $10.37 for bulldozers, a not-union wage of $24.55 for backhoes, a union wage of $63.14 for loaders, and no rate for scrapers or compactors, skid-steers, oilers, cranes, or other common machines. (A footnote to the "power equipment operators" section of the determination specifies that there are six paid holidays, but neglects to add a requirement to honor them as additional fringe benefits.) (PA 31)
- One determination has these rates for oilers (helpers) of power equipment: "OILERS/ On Tr.Cr. 100-ton and over.$ 23.65On Tr.Cr. 50-ton up to bu/ On Tr.Cr. 50-ton up to/ but not including 100-ton. .$ 22.90 13.91 [*sic*]" and this note: "Oilers on Truck Cranes: les than 50 ton shall receive $.10 over the Oiler's base rate; 50 ton up to 100 ton rated capacity shall be paid an additional $.25 per hour over the Class III base rate; 100 ton and over shall be paid on additional $1.00 per hour over the Class III base rate [all *sic*]." [Unfortunately, neither an oiler's base rate, a Class III base rate, or a defined Class III exists in the determination.] (PA 38)
- From the same determination, forklift operators are at the union rate of $40.785, whereas bulldozer, pavers, graders,

loaders, and roller operators and PEO mechanics are at mixed rates about half as much, between $22.86 and $25.79, although theirs is substantially more impressive and difficult equipment to master. (PA 38)

- The same local of the asbestos workers' union has two different rates in two different parts of "Carbon, Columbia, Lackawanna, Luzerne, Montour, Pike, and Wyoming Counties vs. Clinton, Lycoming, and Union," but the determination this appear in is issued for Carbon and Pike counties, alone. (PA 7)
- In this same determination, carpet layers in Carbon and Pike except for five named townships have a rate of $42.17, whereas carpet layers in five named townships have a rate of $39.18 and carpet layers in Pike County have a conflicting rate of $38.51. (PA 7)
- Ironworkers in Carbon County have two different rates depending on whether the project they are working is under or over $25 million, a type of wage differentiation not sanctioned by Davis-Bacon rules. (PA 7)
- Sometime between 2004 and 2011, a union rate for steamfitters (an adjunct of plumbers) was added to a determination covering 6 named townships in Carbon County. There is no equivalent rate for the rest of the county or for the other county (Pike) covered by the determination; there is a rate for "Plumbers and Pipefitters (Including HVAC pipe work") for both counties except for the named townships; and there is a plumbers' rate for the six named townships. There is a not-union rate for pipelayers (also related to plumbers) in all townships and counties in the determination that is approximately one-quarter the amount of any of the others. (PA 7)
- Fringe benefits for elevator mechanics, for example in Chester County but pretty universally throughout Pennsylvania, are footnoted with a requirement to pay additional fringes that cannot be cashed out by a nonunion employer: "PAID VACATION: Employer contributes 8% of basic hourly wage rate for 5 years or more of service of 6% for 6 months to 5 years of service./ Eight Paid Holidays (provided employee has worked 5 consecutive days before and

the working day after the holiday)." [The holidays are named.] (PA 26)

- In 37 named townships in Chester County, structural, reinforcing, and ornamental ironworkers working on "$200 million plus jobs" are to receive $.50 more per hour than others, but still less than ironworkers outside of those 37 townships. (PA 26)
- Laborers in Chester are divided into 11 classes with different rates, one whole class of which is for wagon drill operator (single), another for caisson bottom man, one for yard workers, and another for landscape laborers. (PA 26)
- Roofers in Chester County have different rates for composition roofing ($52.70), shingles ($37.02), and slate and tile [the one undoubtedly requiring the greatest skill] ($40.20). All of these rates are listed as "+A." "A" is defined in a footnote as "PAID HOLIDAY: Election Day," but is contradictorily restricted to composition roofers only. (PA 26)
- Two counties, Columbia and Luzerne, have the same 8 groups of power equipment operators paid different rates. Within each are "machines doing hook work" in two different groups, and "machines handling machinery"; also in at least two different groups are "cranes" and "all types of cranes," tractors, spreaders, rollers, and skid-steers. There are rates for "directional drill machines 8 [inches] and up" and "hydraulic pipe pusher 8 [inches] and up" and also for "directional drill machines 7 [inches] or less" and "hydraulic pipe pusher 7 [inches] or less," but no rates for those machines between 7 and 8 inches. There are conflicting rates for crane operators between operating engineers and laborers, and conflicting rates for laborers associated with forklifts, concrete pumps, swing scaffolds, slings, and bosun chairs, all being assigned to different categories at different rates. (PA 26)
- Truck drivers in Delaware, Montgomery, and Philadelphia counties have three different rates for "BUILDING CONSTRUCTION" and three more for "SITE PREPARATION, PAVING, AND UTILITIES ON BUILDING CONSTRUCTION." Both groups have paid

holidays on Memorial Day, Independence Day, Labor Day and Thanksgiving Day [Christmas and New Years' are not mentioned] and 5 personal holidays, but only the latter group is entitled to additional "PAID VACATION: Employee will earn one vacation day for every two months, provided employee has worked twenty-six days in each consecutive two month period, up to a maximum of five vacation days per calendar year. After 130 workdays the employee is entitled to all five days of vacation. Employees with 5 years of seniority, earn an additional week of vacation, accrued in the same way." (PA 5)

- Four categories of laborers in the determination for "Monroe County Except Tobyhanna, Including Tobyhanna Army Depot" covering about 160 named tasks, e.g., "Stocking scaffolds with masonry materials including brick, block, mortar, teera [*sic*] cotta, architectural pre-cast concrete, natural stone, insulation & mastic, flashing, anchors & ties, grout," which must have seemed important to someone to list.[1] The building determination for laborers in Chester County has seven grades of laborers, plus two additional grades of "landscape laborer," separately.

  (The survey data from which these building determinations were drawn are not available—the last known building survey in Chester County occurred in summer 1988, 23-1/2 years before the current determination. But it probably contained no survey submissions for "powdermen" or "wagon drill operators (single)" or many of the other named categories within the multiple grades of laborers; clearly, these were all added by copying them from various union contracts.)

- Etc., but these should be enough to get the true flavor of these things.

[1] Such specificity as often adds to confusion as relieves it. The stocking of scaffolds with other materials than those listed, for example, may or may not be covered by the same category of laborer or at the same rate.

Appendix Seven

Excerpts from the Statements of Jeff Lester, Deputy Commissioner, Oklahoma Department of Labor

This statement was first voiced before the Joint Hearing on Davis-Bacon Fraud and Abuse, Committee on Economic and Educational Opportunities, U.S. House of Representatives, One Hundred and Fourth Congress, Second Session, January 18, 1996. (It has been lightly edited, here.)

I am Jeff Lester, Deputy Commissioner of Labor for the State of Oklahoma. I was lead investigator in the Oklahoma Department of Labor investigation into the Federal Davis-Bacon wage survey process.

Today, I will show you documented examples of bogus survey data submitted to the Federal Government during the Federal Davis-Bacon wage survey process – bogus information submitted by individuals who apparently had no direct knowledge of the projects for which they submitted data.

I will show you U.S. Department of Labor documents which confirm that phantom projects and ghost workers were the basis of actual wage rates issued by the Federal Government. I will show you U.S. Department of Labor findings that confirm that bogus data was submitted by officials from within the hierarchy of organized labor.

I will show you examples from a growing pool of evidence – evidence that illustrates the depth of this serious problem and showcases the U.S. Department of Labor's apparent mismanagement of the survey process.

Sadly, I will show you that the Federal Government knew about the poor quality of data prior to the time that the fraudulently inflated wage rates were forced upon the taxpayers of Oklahoma. And finally, I will show you the actual financial impact on Oklahoma's taxpayers – a documented impact of up to 30 percent of the total cost of construction on a multimillion dollar project.

The first slide I am going to show you is a representation of the 12-step process used by the U.S. Department of Labor to determine Federal wage rates. The regional office for us is in Dallas, Texas. They conduct the survey. They plan an annual survey activity and the regional administrator told us with these words, "The squeaky wheel gets the grease." So that means that not all regions get surveyed in a timely fashion. In fact, some Federal Government documents indicate that the average wage survey occurs every seven years.

The survey instrument is one side of one 8 by 11 page, something similar to the IRS 1040-EZ form – basic questions such as the name of the contractor who performed the work, a description and address for the project. Among other things, a list of the types of construction workers used, whether or not they were paid according to a union contract. And then at the bottom of the form is the signature of the individual who submitted the data. This has been a particular bone of contention between us and Secretary Reich, who has made public a number of these documents in his own verification process. However, he maintains to us that the statistical information on the forms is apparently a public record, but the signature of those who submitted the information is protected by the Federal Trade Secret Act. We do not buy that argument.

Once the survey instrument has been distributed and collected, they conduct a follow-up if they feel that there are open spots on the survey, or blanks that were not filled in. If they cannot read the handwriting or they cannot interpret the information, they call the individual who submitted it. Of course, that may or may not, according to our findings, be someone who knew anything about the actual project. Then through these steps they determine the adequacy of the data. Can they read it, can they understand it well enough to type it into their computer database.

If so, based on those wage summary sheets, they compute the Federal prevailing wage rates and transmit them to the public for use to pay for public construction projects.

In our direct communications with the regional office in Dallas, they told us directly and specifically there has never, historically, been any practice or attempt to verify the accuracy or the authenticity of any of the information submitted.

Now I would like to move into some actual evidence. First, I want to point to the fax indicia at the very top of this page. This was faxed on May 9 of 1995 from a 202 area code, which indicates that it came from the U.S. Department of Labor Wage and Hour Division in Washington, DC. It was faxed to a local contractor, the Concho Company. And in a telephone conversation, they asked the Concho Company to confirm or to verify the accuracy of this information. It indicates that the Concho Company worked on a high lift pump station at Oklahoma City's Lake Hefner Water Treatment Plant. It indicates that 16 specific categories of workers worked on the project, were paid according to a union collective bargaining agreement, and you can see listed out on the right-hand side, the wage rates and the fringe benefits.

This document was date-stamped in at the U.S. Department of Labor March 18 of 1993. That is a critical fact for you to remember, and we will come back to this slide.

The Concho Company, citing two of these forms that they were faxed – Lake Hefner Treatment Plant high lift and Lake Treatment Plant chemical building – they told us in late May, "The above-referenced attached jobs were not projects awarded to the Concho Company." In other words, they did not work on those projects.

We wanted to find out more about the nature of their dialogue with the U.S. Department of Labor. The bottom line is a Concho Company employee told us the U.S. Department of Labor refused to tell that company who signed the information and falsely attributed it to their company.

We wanted to make sure that we were not misunderstanding anything about the nature of the facts, so we went to the City of Oklahoma City and asked whether the Concho Company had done any work at Lake Hefner at the treatment plant. And the city indicated to us that sure, Concho is a contractor who does a lot of work for the city, and although the project in and around that time was not at the high lift, it was actually at some site grading at a location adjacent to the Lake Hefner water treatment plant, as it indicates in the upper left-hand portion of this exhibit. The city engineer told us this was not to be confused with the high lift pump station.

We asked the city who actually constructed the high lift pump station. You can see in this letter from the city's engineering manager with regard to that facility that Flintco, another local contractor, constructed it. Further, the city says their records indicate that Concho was not used, even as a subcontractor on the project. They also indicated that they do not know of any other high lift pump stations that were constructed in and around that time.

We asked the city to tell us more about the high lift pump station, the project that was apparently falsely reported on that form. So they gave us a copy of the letter that they sent to Flintco, the real contractor, to initiate the work. Note that the letter is dated May 14 of 1993. Attached was a copy of the contract. The contract, signed by the city on this $27 million high lift pump station, was signed April 6 of 1993; the contract was signed to initiate that project.

The apparently false wage form indicates that Concho did the work in July of 1992. Here's the peak week of activity for these employees. And you will note that again, it was date-stamped in at the U.S. Department of Labor, March 18 of 1993, nearly a month before the contract was even signed.

We knew at this point that there was something to this alleged problem. I indicated to you that Concho had received another fax. This one is regarding a chemical building at the Lake Hefner water treatment plant. You can see again, it is from the same address in Washington, DC, USDOL Wage and Hour. Chemical building – interestingly, the same exact categories of workers, paid exactly the same wage rates, and as the city indicated to us in this correspondence in June, no chemical building was constructed at the Lake Hefner water treatment plant. And in fact, Congressmen, you can drive to the Lake Hefner water treatment plant today where this alleged chemical building might have been built, you will find snow and dirt and grass and barbed wire.

Now I want to show you an example of another bogus project. This one actually verifiably resulted in Federal wage rates. This is a U.S. Department of Labor general wage decision. You can see the number up here, General Decision 950033. It is for heavy construction for the six counties in the Oklahoma City metropolitan area. This is for heavy construction that does not include water and sewer lines or treatment plant projects.

On page 2 of that wage decision, you see a category for plumbers and pipefitters, the wage rate being $17 per hour, the fringe benefits being $4.05 per hour for a total compensation of $21.05.

Through the Freedom of Information Act, we received from the U.S. Department of Labor their Federal document. This is a summary sheet, the top half of one of the summary sheets that Lists all of the wages and how they were determined. You can see the two categories here of plumber and pipefitter, the two that were listed on that form; $17 and $4.05, which is consistent. And out to the right we find out how did the U.S. Department of Labor arrive at that specific wage rate. As we have been told by the regional administrator, by the folks at USDOL, all it takes from the accumulation of all the forms submitted in a survey is a total accumulated amount of six employees listed under any specific job classification in order to have the minimum threshold to establish a prevailing wage rate. This means, based on the two methods for establishing it, either a weighted average or by majority, that a simple majority of four workers making the same wage rate is the minimum threshold required to establish Federal prevailing wage rates for an entire area.

In this instance, we see that like most of the work categories here, the rates were not an average, but were arrived at through the majority rule, which is the first rule of thumb in the Federal process. In the case of the plumbers, they say that of the 14 total plumbers identified on all the forms, 12 of them were making exactly the same wage and fringe benefit package. In the case of pipefitters, 10 of 12 making exactly the same wage and fringe benefit package, that being the basis.

We looked further to find out where those 10 pipefitters and 12 plumbers were located. And in fact, we found the majority, all 10 pipefitters and 10 of the 12 majority plumbers on one project, an underground storage tank in Mustang, Oklahoma.

Through numerous and exhaustive investigation, we are certain there is no $2 million underground storage tank in Mustang, Oklahoma. Therefore, these specific employees identified on this project, ghost employees on a phantom project, prevailed. This indicates to us that there is no accountability and no integrity in the U.S. Department of Labor wage survey process.

Further, the U.S. Department of Labor, in one of its own documents in attempting to verify our findings, verified that on that project, data was from the plumbers' union and per their call to the contractor, the contractor said they did not do the work. Folks, that is pretty much in black and white. This is the U.S. Department of Labor's own words, their own finding from their own document. As a result of this and other evidence, they withdrew that entire wage decision at the end of May.

Mr. Marshall. Mr. Chairman, had the Oklahoma Department of Labor not stepped in with its investigation, those wage rates that had been established would be in existence today and the citizens of Oklahoma would be paying that inflated amount based upon the submission of false information.

Mr. Lester. Let me show you now some more documents from the U.S. Department of Labor, a few wage summary sheets with the U.S. Department of Labor's own confirmed findings after they began their own investigation.

- **Here, we have a Lake Hefner golf course, $28 million project. USDOL confirmed per call to the contractor, the contractor did not work on this project.**

- **Water wells at Tinker Air Force Base, a Federal military facility. The information came directly from Operating Engineers local union, per call to the contractor, the contractor did not work on this project.**

- **Sanitary sewer project in Oklahoma City, data submitted as union scale, listed contractor is not a union contractor. Data omitted after review.**

- **Wastewater treatment plant, Langston, Oklahoma. Data submitted by plumbers' and pipefitters' union. Per call to the contractor, the contractor was only a consultant and did not use plumbers.**

- **Lake Overholser treatment plant. Data submitted by plumbers' and pipefitters' local union. Per call to the contractor, they did not employ plumbers.**

- **Wastewater treatment plant El Reno. Data submitted by plumbers. Per call to the contractor – did not work on this project.** [Emphasis added.]

This goes on and on and on. And if you were to look at all of the U.S. Department of Labor's verifications and not just take their word for it, I think you would probably find many, many, many more examples of this same confirmed finding from the Federal Government.

We of course became interested in who might benefit in this. Obviously the innocent workers working to make a living to put food on their tables, they would obviously be unknowing beneficiaries of this. We also found evidence that there might be others who would benefit.

We looked at several collective bargaining agreements. In this particular instance, which comes from the plumbers' and pipefitters' local union, there is a specific portion of their contract, money to be withheld from employees' gross wages, a working assessment checkoff, which is a percentage of the gross wages – not a dollar amount, not so many cents per hour to go to a benefit, but a percentage. The obvious conclusion is that if you double the wage rate, you double the amount collected, based on a percentage. I want it to be very clear today that because I am using this particular contract as an example, I am not accusing this specific union hall of any wrongdoing, I am simply using this as an illustration of what we have found as other possible beneficiaries, beyond the obvious.

Once we concluded our initial investigation into the heavy construction survey, we became concerned that the building construction survey, a much larger survey instrument, might be even more ripe for this type abuse because it covers a much wider category of employee classifications and amounts to a much more significant appropriation of tax dollars.

With the cooperation of a couple of local contractors, we received copies of many more faxes that were sent from the U.S. Department of Labor in Washington to local contractors in an apparent attempt to confirm the accuracy of that wage data. This form shows Connelly Paving Company worked on the Internal Revenue Service office building in Oklahoma City, ostensibly to pave a parking lot. You will notice on this form it indicates that among other things, there were seven asphalt laydown machine operators, seven roller finishers, seven backend men who would work in conjunction with that equipment. The wage rate here for asphalt laydown machine is $14.65 per hour, that is what is listed. Mr. Connelly indicated to us that that seemed awfully high. You will note that it is paid according to a union contract, according to whoever submitted this form, and it was also submitted in December of 1992. If only this form itself was submitted and received by the U.S. Department of Labor, those three classifications would be enough to establish a prevailing wage rate.

In a prevailing wage project, the workers would be paid the higher of two rates: they would either be paid the higher of the union rate, as indicated here, or the federally mandated rate. We wanted to know what was the prevailing wage rate required by the government at that time. We found out that in the case of the asphalt laydown machine operator, the rate was $8 per hour with no fringe benefits, so we assumed the prevailing rate must have been based on a union contract rate.

So we assumed that the union contract must call for $14.65 per hour. We received a copy of that collective bargaining agreement. We went to the page with the wage rates, found the asphalt laydown machine operator – lo and behold, $10.50 per hour. Then we became concerned about the fringe benefits listed. You will note that of that $3.73 that is listed, $2.30 was earmarked for health and welfare, $1.25 per hour to the pension fund. Again, we looked at the union contract and we found $1.80 per hour for health and welfare, 25 cents per hour for pension. If the union actually collected $1.25 per hour for pension, we would like to know what they did with that extra dollar.

And by the way, they indicated seven asphalt laydown machine operators, working simultaneously in a parking lot had spaces for 30 automobiles and it is a concrete parking lot. There is no asphalt.

Here is one for a Circuit City Superstore at Penn Square. Penn Square is a mall located on Pennsylvania Avenue in Oklahoma City. You will note that it again is a union contract that claims Connelly Paving used, among other things, seven asphalt laydown machines to pave the parking lot. There is no Circuit City store at Penn Square Mall. [Emphasis added.]

All in all, Mr. Connelly provided us with nearly 40 forms that had bad information, 40 forms falsely attributed to him. He is the victim in this. Altogether on those forms, they indicated he worked on 21 projects just during the month of June, 1992. And during the course of that time used a cumulative 658 union employees. In reality, Mr. Connelly used seven union employees. And to confirm that to us, he provided us with a copy of his employer monthly remittance report which he turned in for the month of June, 1992, turned in to his union, the Operating Engineers, Local 627. You will note here that we have blocked out the name and social security numbers. But of those seven employees, none of them worked more than a 50 or 60-hour week. Hard to imagine that they could have spread themselves out and done the work of nearly 700 people on 21 projects.

To add to that, we will show you another example from the stack provided by Mr. Connelly, University of Oklahoma football stadium. This claims a $20 million stadium renovation project. University officials in both their architectural and engineering services office that handled their bids and in the athletic department confirmed to me that during the summer of 1991, the summer of 1992 and the summer of 1993, there was no major construction of any sort at the football stadium.

This one claims the use of seven asphalt lay down machines. All the parking lots around the football stadium are concrete that was poured in the mid-1980s. [Emphasis added.]

This is a U.S. Department of Labor wage summary report on that project, which indicates that the U.S. Department of Labor identified the project, accepted the data and calculated it into the Federal wage rates.

Mr. Marshall. Mr. Chairman, there is more than one victim. The taxpayers of Oklahoma, they have been victimized by this process; Mr. Connelly has been victimized by this process, and the good name of Connelly has been victimized by this process.

Mr. Lester. Now I want to show you the really sad part of all this, sad because we believe it is information that indicates this could have all been prevented. Here is a June 2, 1995 memo from Maria Echaveste, the Administrator of the Federal Wage and Hour Division in Washington, DC. I want to point to the first couple of sentences. "Incorrect information submitted by third parties has been found in several surveys. Therefore, strategies to deal with the verification of data submitted by other than someone in actual possession of project payrolls is being considered." Congressmen, it is about time.

What is really troubling about this is the General Accounting Office information that was presented to Congress in February of 1994, on page 6 of that report, a discussion of data quality, which says the U.S. Department of Labor does not perform a response bias analysis to determine whether there are a disproportionate number of responses from certain types of employers, such as employers with a unionized work force, or data from much larger employers. The response bias analysis, we are told, would prevent a single local contractor of substantial size or a single local union hall of substantial size from being able to dominate the process. Additionally, they say that without the response bias it could result in survey results that differ significantly from the actual wage prevailing in the area. Again, this is a Federal General Accounting Office document. It goes on to say the U.S. Department of Labor does not verify the accuracy of the data received. We think that has become painfully apparent.

And now I would like to discuss with you on my final couple of slides, how bad is this; specifically, how bad is this for Oklahoma's taxpayers.

I am pointing here to an October 26 article which appeared in the "Tulsa World" in the subhead, it is talking about the construction of a major treatment plant in Tulsa and it says, "The bids are about $10 million under the city's cost estimate. The death of the State prevailing wage law may be the cause." There is a line in here that says the savings may actually eliminate the need for future utility rate increases in Tulsa. It indicates that the city's engineers had estimated the project prior to the overturning of the State Davis-Bacon law, they had estimated the cost at $40.2 million. The bids went out shortly after the State's little Davis-Bacon Act was thrown out. Based on free market rates, the bids came in ranging from $28.8 million to $31.1 million, which would seem to indicate that based on Davis-Bacon, the original estimates were inflated by approximately 30 percent, or $10 million on what otherwise would have been a $30 million project.

You might ask yourself how could wage rates have that much of an impact on a single project. The evidence is clear in a side-by-side comparison comparing the wage rates for heavy construction not including water, sewer or treatment plants – heavy construction – in Oklahoma City, rates in effect in July of 1994 versus the new inflated rates which were issued in November of 1994. An asphalt laydown machine operator went from $8.30 per hour to $20.25 per hour, an increase of 144 percent. And as you can see, of the several examples we included, they range up to 162 percent on a particular category of crane operator.

It is very clear that this has negatively impacted the taxpayers of Oklahoma, all of whom contribute to the cost of public construction projects, and most of whom are the work force that makes the wheels of Oklahoma's economy turn every day.

Selected Bibliography

Northrup, Herbert R., Armand J. Thieblot, and Maurice Baskin, (2008) *Construction Union Tactics to Regain Jobs and Public Policy* (Olin Institute, George Mason University)

Thieblot, A.J., Jr., (1975) *The Davis-Bacon Act* (IRU, University of Pennsylvania)

________, (1986) *Prevailing Wage Legislation: The Davis-Bacon Act, State "Little Davis-Bacon" Acts, the Walsh-Healey Act, and the Service Contract Act* (IRU, University of Pennsylvania)

________, (1995) "The Failure of Arguments Supporting Prevailing Wage Laws and a New Evaluation of the Benefits of Repeal," *Govt. Union Review,* Vol. 16, No 4

________, (1995) "State Prevailing Wage Laws, An Assessment at the Start of 1995" (for Associated Builders and Contractors, Inc.)

________, (1997) "Fraud Prevalent in Prevailing Wage Surveys," *Govt. Union Review,* Vol. 18, No. 1

________, (1999) *Union Violence: A Study of the Record and the Response By Courts, Legislatures, and the NLRB (Rev.)* (Olin Institute, George Mason University) (With T. Haggard and H. Northrup)

________, (1999) "Helper Regulations Should Not Be Rescinded." (Unpublished response to DOL opinion solicitation, May 1999. Copy available from the author.)

________, (2000) "Review of the Guidances for a Union-Only Project Labor Agreement for Construction of Wilson Bridge," for Maryland FREE

________, (2001) "Differences in Impact Between a Union-Only PLA (Such as Associated with Washington Convention Center) and a Labor-Stabilization PLA (Such as Associated with Baltimore Ravens' Stadium," for Maryland FREE

________, (2005) "The Twenty-Percent Majority: Pro-Union Bias in Prevailing Rage Determinations," *J. Labor Research* XXVI, No.1, Winter 2005

________, (2006) "Perspectives on Union Corruption: Lessons From the Databases," *J. Labor Research* XXVII, No. 4, Fall 2006

________, (2008) *Job Targeting and Market Recovery Practices of Construction Unions: Their Apparent and Hidden Costs* (Olin Institute, George Mason University)